AF305321

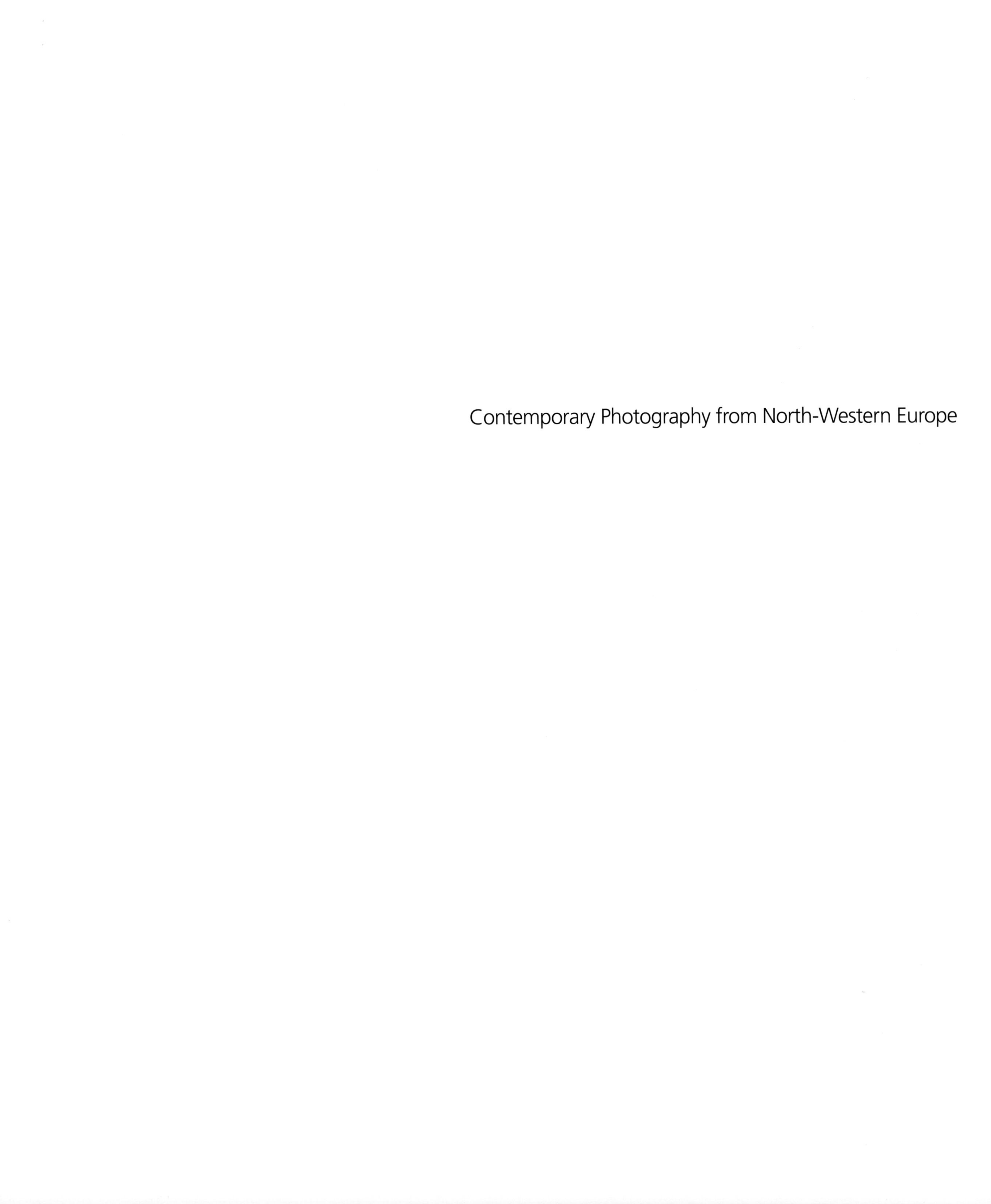

Contemporary Photography from North-Western Europe

Contemporary Photography from North-Western Europe

edited by
Filippo Maggia
Francesca Lazzarini

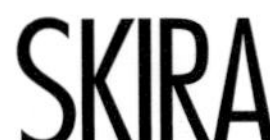
SKIRA

Cover
Wolfgang Tillmans, *Lux*,
2009 (detail)

Art director
Marcello Francone

Design
Luigi Fiore

Editorial coordination
Eva Vanzella

Copy editor
Emanuela Di Lallo

Layout
Sabina Brucoli

Translations
Gordon Fisher, *Liquid Translations*

First published in Italy in 2015 by
Skira editore S.p.A.
Palazzo Casati Stampa
via Torino 61
20123 Milano
Italy
www.skira.net

Printed and bound in Italy. First edition
ISBN: 978-88-572-2988-1

Distributed in USA, Canada, Central
& South America by Rizzoli International
Publications, Inc., 300 Park Avenue
South, New York, NY 10010, USA.
Distributed elsewhere in the world by
Thames and Hudson Ltd., 181A High
Holborn, London WC1V 7QX,
United Kingdom.

Established in 2007, the contemporary photography collection of the Fondazione Cassa di Risparmio di Modena has been enriched piece-by-piece over the years through various series of acquisitions concentrated on different geographical areas: from Africa to the Far East, from the US to South America, and from India to Eastern Europe. The collection currently includes more than 1200 works by almost 200 artists: an exceptionally wide-ranging cultural asset that the Fondazione Fotografia, as a special purpose vehicle, aims to make the most of through its painstaking commitment to cataloguing, conserving and displaying. From the outset, the collection was conceived as an homage to Modena – one that could succeed in encapsulating the city's cultural identity, which has traditionally been intertwined with photography – and as a heritage to be passed on to subsequent generations. Appropriately, *inheriting* is the theme of the festival*filosofia* 2015, with which the exhibition of the most recent photography purchases is associated; the purchases in question concern North-Western Europe, and they have not been displayed until now. We are showcasing them in this publication: around 70 works by 19 artists, from Wolfgang Tillmans to Tom Sandberg, which together are capable of evoking the vibrancy and the heterogeneous nature of the current trends of a geographical area that takes in Germany, the UK and Scandinavia.

As before, this exhibition will feature the same openness that has always been a feature of the contemporary photography collection of the Fondazione Cassa di Risparmio di Modena. The plurality and variety of the artists on show are, then, among the main strengths of this new set of works (to be followed in due course by a second set, concerned with South-Western Europe), encompassing everything from landscapes to portraits, staged photography to snapshots, and even incorporating reportage and installations. The artists deal with a multitude of themes, facing up to the most pressing matters that real life requires us to focus on, and investigating issues linked to the history of the medium of photography and the nature of contemporary images.

Andrea Landi
Chairman, Fondazione Cassa di Risparmio di Modena

Contents

Visions from the North-West

Six years on from the presentation of the works from Eastern Europe in the *History, Memory, Identity* exhibition, the new collection, displayed in the exhibition and organised in this book according to the customary alphabetical sequence, introduces now Western Europe. The research is divided into two sections, the first of which focuses on the North-Western countries. In contrast to other areas of the world that have been explored over previous years, the recent acquisitions intended for the international collection of the Fondazione Cassa di Risparmio di Modena are more concerned with the classical figurative tradition of the individual countries than with current, shared trends. The purchases in question highlight how the use of the language of images and the concomitant approach to the world conform to well-consolidated expressive and interpretative modes, with deep, extensive roots; the works differ markedly in terms of content, subject matter and tone, with the formal aspect being aligned in certain cases with contemporary mores and styles.

Far from wanting to paint a comprehensive picture of the art scene that can be discerned from the contemporary photography being produced in these countries, pledging to look in more detail at some of the countries over the coming years, the current anthology of artists (nineteen in all) and works encompasses, as it did for the previous selections, both established artists and young, emerging talents; this stands as a testament to the fact that, specifically over the past decade, photography has, on the one hand, become more refined while, on the other, it has allowed itself to be contaminated by other artistic disciplines and creative models. In a Europe that is struggling to define itself and to put itself forward as a continent regulated by a harmonious project-based strategy – compressed as it is between nationalistic claims and contingent necessities of a free market of ideas and cultures, even more so than one of material goods – the rigid and rigorous North seems to want to maintain a detached attitude towards the current ferocious and dramatic demands being made by the (economically weaker and by nature indolent) South, and especially by those living in the Mediterranean basin. The North is abdicating its responsibilities in a certain sense, preferring a quiet life that, at the same time, marks out the distances involved, and renders even more improbable the creation of a Europe united in terms of its people and its actions, rather than just in geopolitical terms; it is a distance that can also be felt in many Eastern European countries, still engaged on the reconstruction of a social and political identity with the capacity to enter into a dialogue with the West and at the same time able to rein in the push towards jingoism. But while the artists of the East feel that performing artistic research is their duty, their mission even, carrying out a conscious act of intellectual honesty by eviscerating and recomposing their own story, their own past, Northern Europe – which does not have these problems – looks at itself reflecting on those themes that have always characterised its artistic output. Photography is, then, the perfect means to analyse the real; it is an investigation that begins with the self, and takes in social relations, measuring itself against nature (and often coming away the loser), sometimes absorbing its primordial effluvia while making the most of its almost plastic beauty and aesthetics, until dissolving into cultured visions veiled with melancholy and existential nihilism, in which reality and fiction are intelligently amalgamated.

A Bergmanesque atmosphere pervades the

saturated whites and blacks of Tom Sandberg – images that appear to become entangled in themselves, demonstrating all the difficulty faced by the artist in his dealings with others, constrained, condemned almost, to a lucid isolation; an approach inherited by Morten Andenæs and rendered even more raw and spectacular in his colour photographs, a sort of conscious displacement that becomes the subject matter of the delicate yet ferocious works by Sarah Jones: whether the subjects are adolescents, flowers or horses, they all undergo a form of artistic exploration that aims to extend beyond the surface of the subject portrayed, excised as if with a scalpel, a psychoanalytical exercise that mutates into an experiential practice in the photographs and videos of Gillian Wearing, who – in contrast to Sandberg – enters directly into the scene, in an exploration of the social relationships that govern the way in which people interact. Trine Søndergaard looks at the history of art, and specifically at the noble and extremely complex art of portraiture, which in her hands becomes an osmotic exercise through which the photographer scrutinises herself in the portrayed subject; it is similar to what Olivier Richon – Swiss-born but a long-time British resident – does in his work, in a cross-referencing of allegories that induce the viewer to reflect on what he or she is seeing in order to 'solve' pictures that seem to be *bona fide* puzzles, making it possible to arrive at numerous viable solutions; as many solutions, in fact, as there are points of view offered by Barbara Probst in her compositions, which are assemblages of shots taken in the same instant but from different perspectives – a method borrowed from cinematography that leaves very much unresolved the question of which, out of the many, is the 'decisive' perspective.

Willie Doherty is preoccupied with the deceptive appearance of images, the lies they can tell, the uncertainties they can generate, the content that they communicate over and above what they represent. His photographs are encapsulations of the painful history of Northern Ireland, experienced first-hand and, for this reason, all the more authentic and unalloyed, rendered definitive by texts or captions that accurately affirm the truth. The images of Wolfgang Tillmans are fragments of life, recomposed 'as is' in the staging of his exhibitions. He is a full ten years younger than his celebrated compatriots of the so-called Düsseldorf Academy, but is relatively distant from them, a real anomaly in the German panorama that has dominated the international scene since the mid-1990s and still strides confidently across it. In contrast to them, Tillmans – recent winner of the Hasselblad Award – manipulates and mixes up styles and languages, experimenting with photography and turning it into the mirror of everyday suburbia, whether in Berlin or in Britain.
The young Nordic artists make reference to nature in their work: much more than a simple landscape where the eye searches out particular circumstances or extraordinary events, nature is like a placenta that protects and at the same time nurtures; it is sometimes awkward, occasionally disturbing, but also a place of shelter. Nature is a dreamlike journey in which to lose oneself, an unstable border – as photographs themselves become over time – between the real and the imaginary, in the works of Astrid Kruse Jensen; a metaphor for harsh, rough lived experience, lashed by the freezing wind that transfigures the edges of everything until the most basic perception of it is lost, in the images of the Icelandic artist

Hallgerður Hallgrímsdóttir; a partner in a symbiotic relationship in which the body becomes, as if by magic, the element through which communication takes form, becomes experience, primitive memory breaking through, in the performances of Melissa Moore; a theatre of mysterious, incomplete events that have their source in mankind, before remaining suspended and unresolved, in the compositions of Annabel Elgar; enigmatic in the high-tech bioarchitecture of Ilkka Halso; refined, delicate, fragile in the works of Sandra Kantanen; and soft and flexible in the hummingbirds captured in flight, like little divinities, by Sanna Kannisto.
Last but by no means least, through their mixed media works, collages and installations, Jonny Briggs, Lilly Lulay and Johann Arens lead us into the current scene in which photography searches out a (probably new) identity of its own, rendering it contemporary once again. It is a language that enters into a dialogue with other modes of expression, not necessarily derived from classical artistic disciplines; a language that more than others, perhaps more than any other, perceives the fatal responsibility of having to represent its own time.

Morten Andenæs
Johann Arens
Jonny Briggs
Willie Doherty
Annabel Elgar
Hallgerður Hallgrímsdóttir
Ilkka Halso
Sarah Jones
Sanna Kannisto
Sandra Kantanen
Astrid Kruse Jensen
Lilly Lulay
Melissa Moore
Barbara Probst
Olivier Richon
Tom Sandberg
Trine Søndergaard
Wolfgang Tillmans
Gillian Wearing

Morten Andenæs

After graduating in 2002 from the School of Visual Arts in New York, Morten Andenæs lives in Oslo, where he was born in 1979. In 2005 and 2006, he worked as an assistant to Tom Sandberg who, the following year, curated Andenæs's first solo show (together with Ola Rindal), at the Fotogalleriet in Oslo. An artist and a writer, Andenæs structures his research as an analysis of the verbal and visual languages and of the relationship that binds them together. His minimalist photographs are always accompanied by titles that are provocatively tautological or that, on the contrary, contradict what is apparently being said by the images. It is, then, representation itself that is thrown into question, and with it the possibility of photography to contribute to the construction of the identity. For example, as the artist explains in his statement, '*Third Party* (2010) is a photograph of a photograph of my parents embracing. The original embrace is staged by me, and the title refers to the third person actively intruding into the scene: the photographer'.

Despite the absence of emotions – even in the case of personal subject matter such as this – and the neutral arrangement, Andenæs's works expose the very fact that any attempt to reproduce reality is anything but objective: every representation implies an inevitable disconnect between appearance and reality. His works also flag up the fact that all of those involved, viewers included, participate in moulding that residual space. *View* (2012) portrays a child turning to watch something. While the title is undoubtedly descriptive – the photograph shows us someone engaged in the act of looking – the gaze to which it refers is not that of the viewer, who in fact cannot see the object being observed. *Tiger* (2006) is defined by Andenæs as 'a photograph of what was once a tiger. Despite our calling it a tiger, it has lost its essence, lost its "tigerness". A photograph seems able to show this, to account for this loss of essence'. And it is thanks to the deliberate disconnect between title and object, and to the anthropocentric reading on the part of the viewer, that the perception of this loss becomes possible. With the diptych *Seat 23F, OSL–WAW* (2012), Andenæs triggers a different type of mechanism: whereas from a formal perspective the images can immediately be traced back to the aesthetics of war, similar to those generated by drones or bombers, the title of the work clearly refers to the seats assigned to passengers on civil aircraft. As such, the semantic shift overturns the overall reading of the image: they are not shots taken by a pilot searching out his next military target; rather, they depict the landscape below as seen out of the window by a passenger flying from Oslo to Warsaw. Through just a few, essential elements, Andenæs lays bare all of the ambiguity implicit in the act of representing, bringing into question the role of photography as a witness to the events of the world.

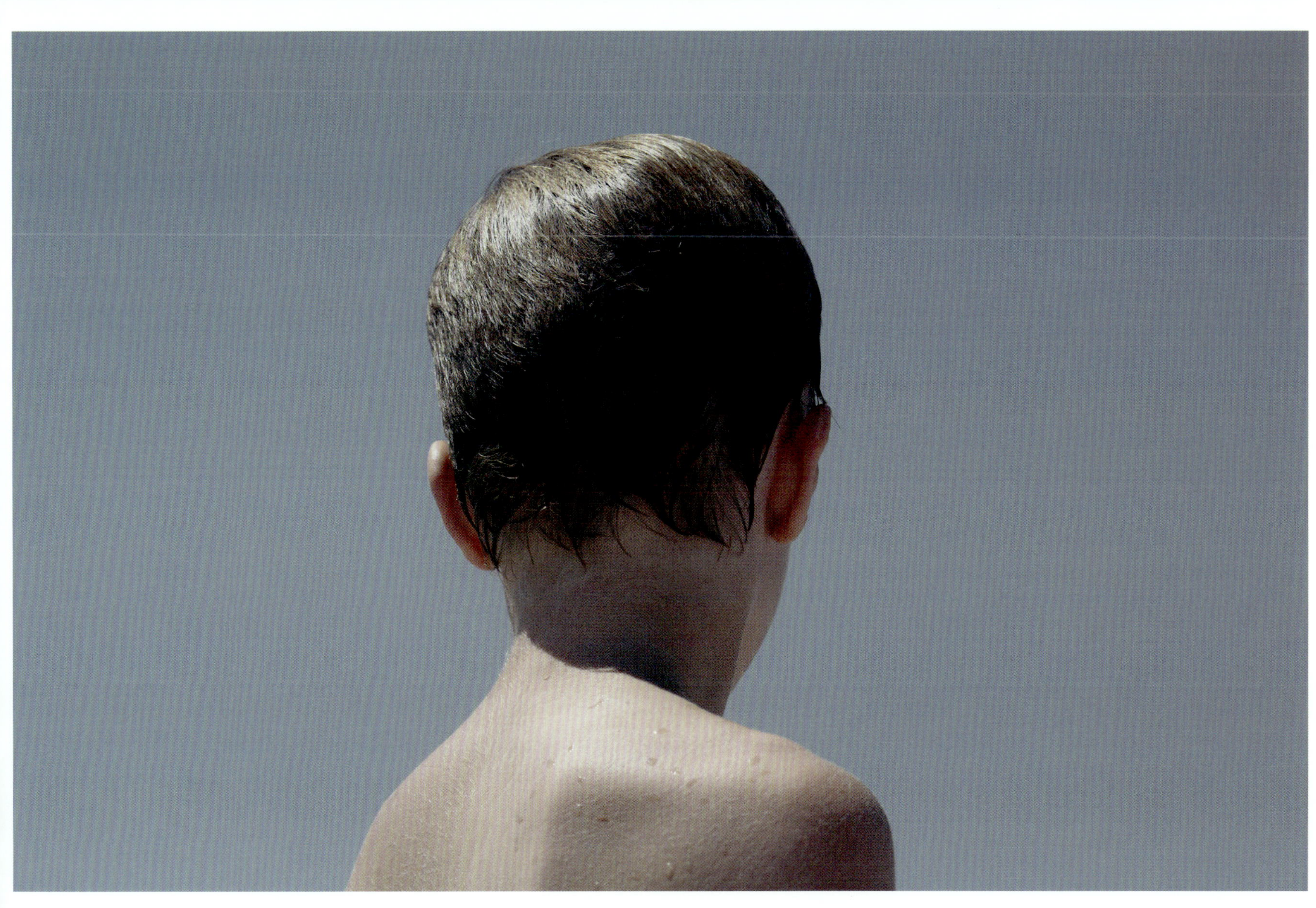

View, 2012
Giclée inkjet print
56 x 84 cm

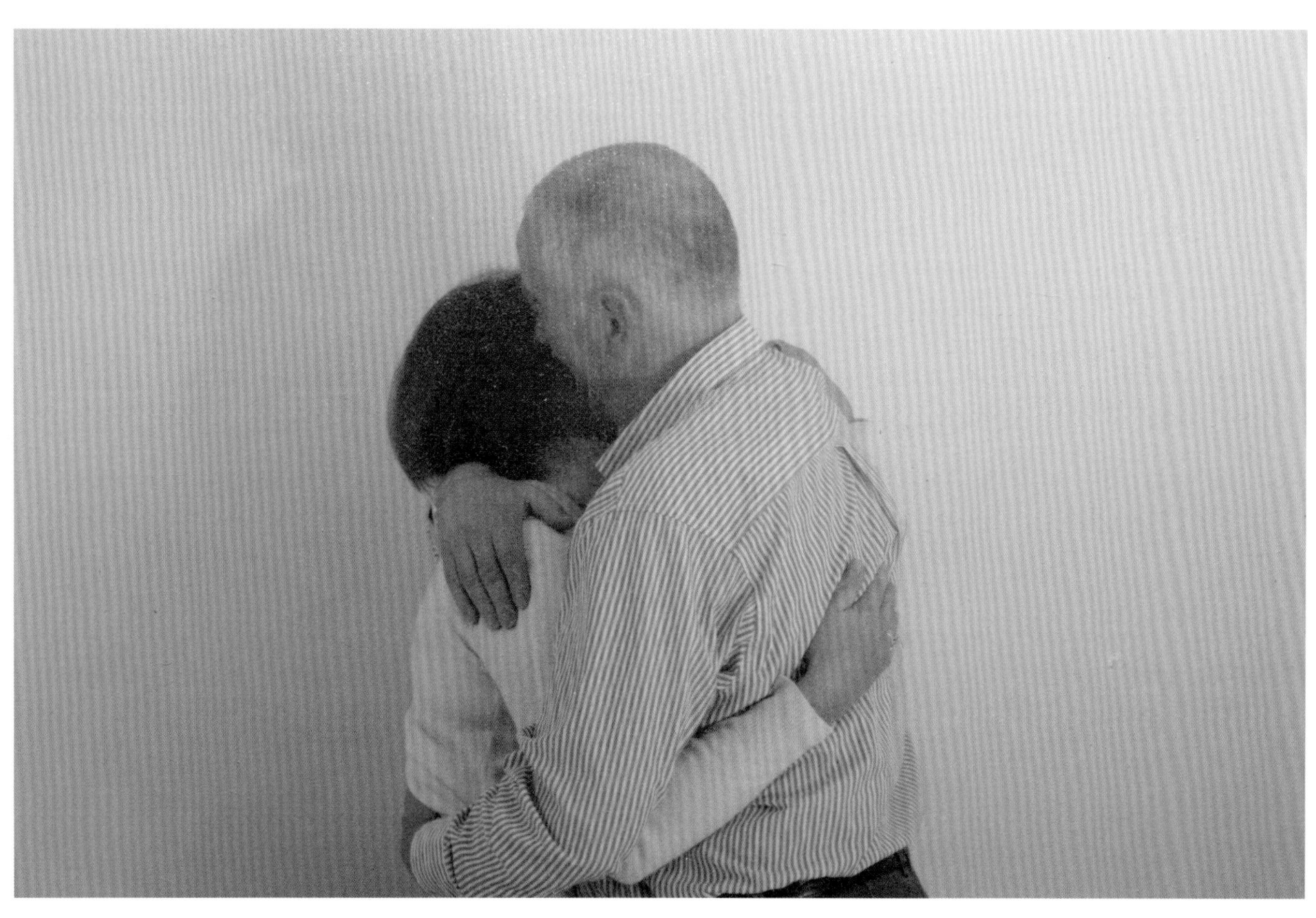

Third Party, 2010
Giclée inkjet print
47.5 x 71 cm

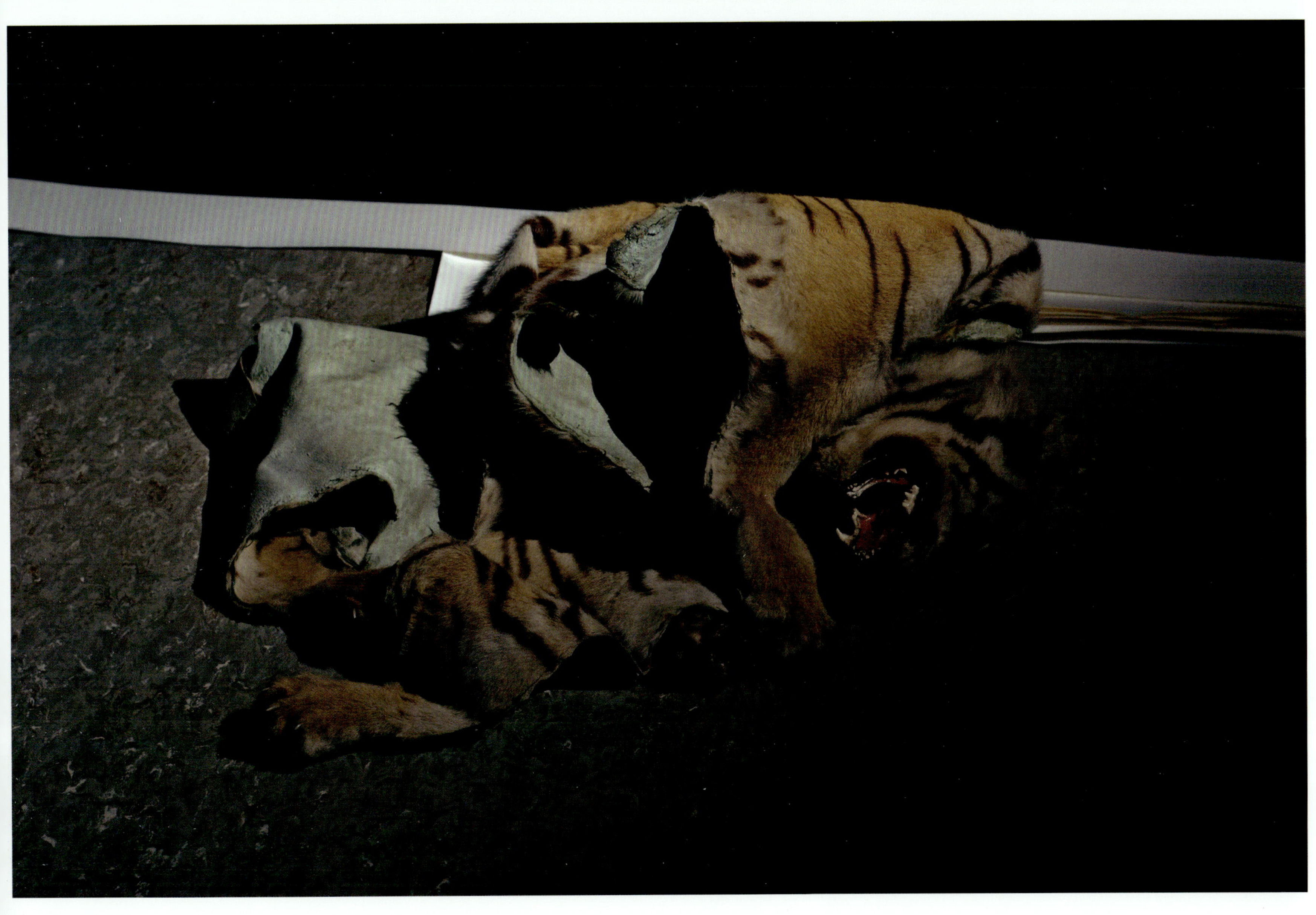

Tiger, 2006
Giclée inkjet print
60 x 89.5 cm

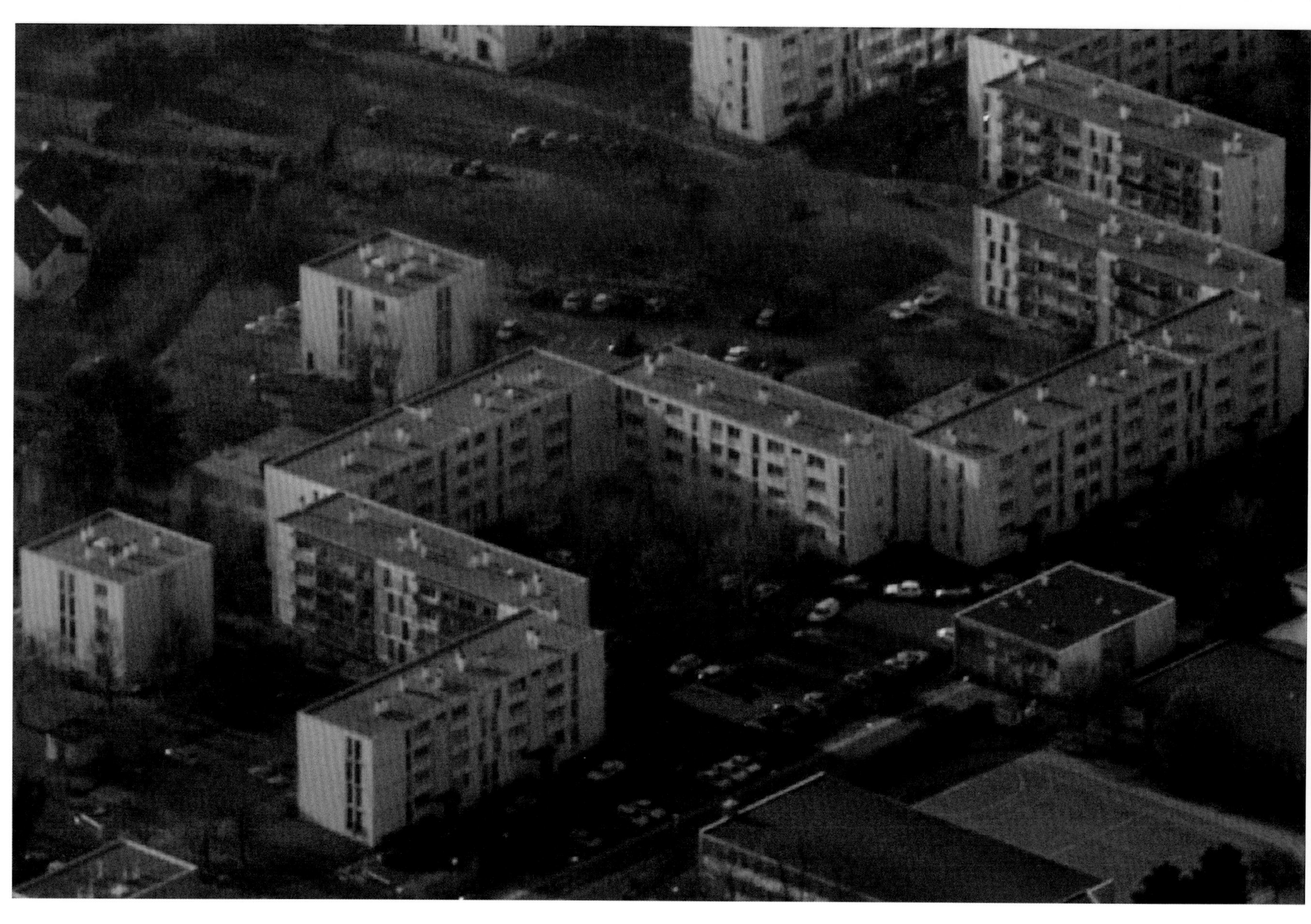

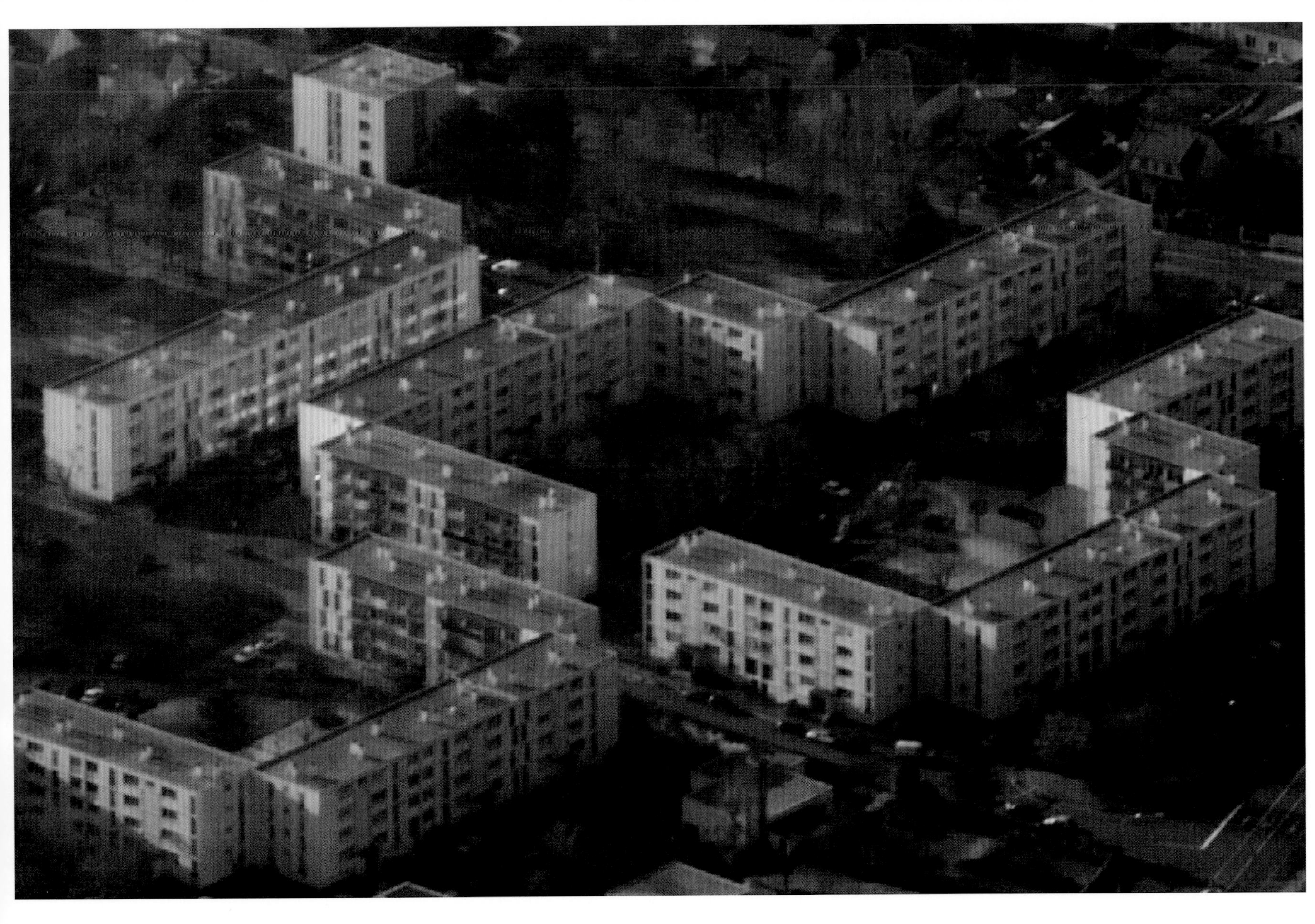

Seat 23F, OSL–WAW, 2012
Giclée inkjet print, diptych
27 x 80 cm

Johann Arens

Born in 1981 in Aachen, Johann Arens studied at the Gerrit Rietveld Academie in Amsterdam before embarking – thanks to a scholarship from the Netherlands Foundation for Visual Arts, Design and Architecture – on a Master of Fine Arts at Goldsmiths College, London, which he completed in 2011. His residences at the British School in Rome, the Fondazione Ratti in Como and the Rijksakademie in Amsterdam (begun in 2014 and set to last two years) are the most recent stages of his training, and are indicative of the mobility of which young European artists can benefit these days. The relationship between visual culture and real social spaces is the focal point in the work of Johann Arens, whose preferred means of expression are video, sculpture and large-scale installations. Mixing found and fabricated elements, display furniture and custom-made devices, Arens creates what he calls 'landscapes of objects'. Those installations recall cinematographic language into which the viewers can immerse themselves, undergoing direct perceptive experiences. As in the filmmaking process, a great deal of attention is lavished on the construction of the scene, in which every detail is painstakingly positioned to create a set that is at once convincing yet fictitious, since it is the outcome of the creative action of the director. The tension between the reclaimed and the artificial material is the key that allows Arens to channel the viewers' attention onto the meaning of places, leading them to ask questions about the nature of what they are looking at and its function. An emblematic example taken from the artist's oeuvre is the 2013 *Internet Centre & Habesha Grocery* installation, which is the reconstruction in an artistic context of an internet centre, which actually existed in the London borough of Tottenham until 2013. This work, which has become part of the collection, is the upshot of a syncretism between furniture, equipment and objects salvaged by the artist when the shop was closed down, and the exhibition modalities of art spaces. And so we see, alongside computer workstations (where the PCs have screensavers displaying Biblical quotes), packets of coffee as once sold in the grocery and now displayed in Perspex, and flyers advertising IT services beside tangles of cables and monitors on show atop white pedestals. The semantic shift implemented by Arens forces us, then, to analyse the subject of the installation in a different light: while on the one hand, the museumification of the internet centre seems to make us reflect on the obsolescence of technology and to highlight how, with the advent of mobile devices, these places are losing their original function, on the other hand, walking around the traces left by the habitués of the centre reminds us that the phenomenon is far from extinct and that, due to the technology gap, these IT centres still constitute the only way for a large section of the planet's population to access telecommunications.

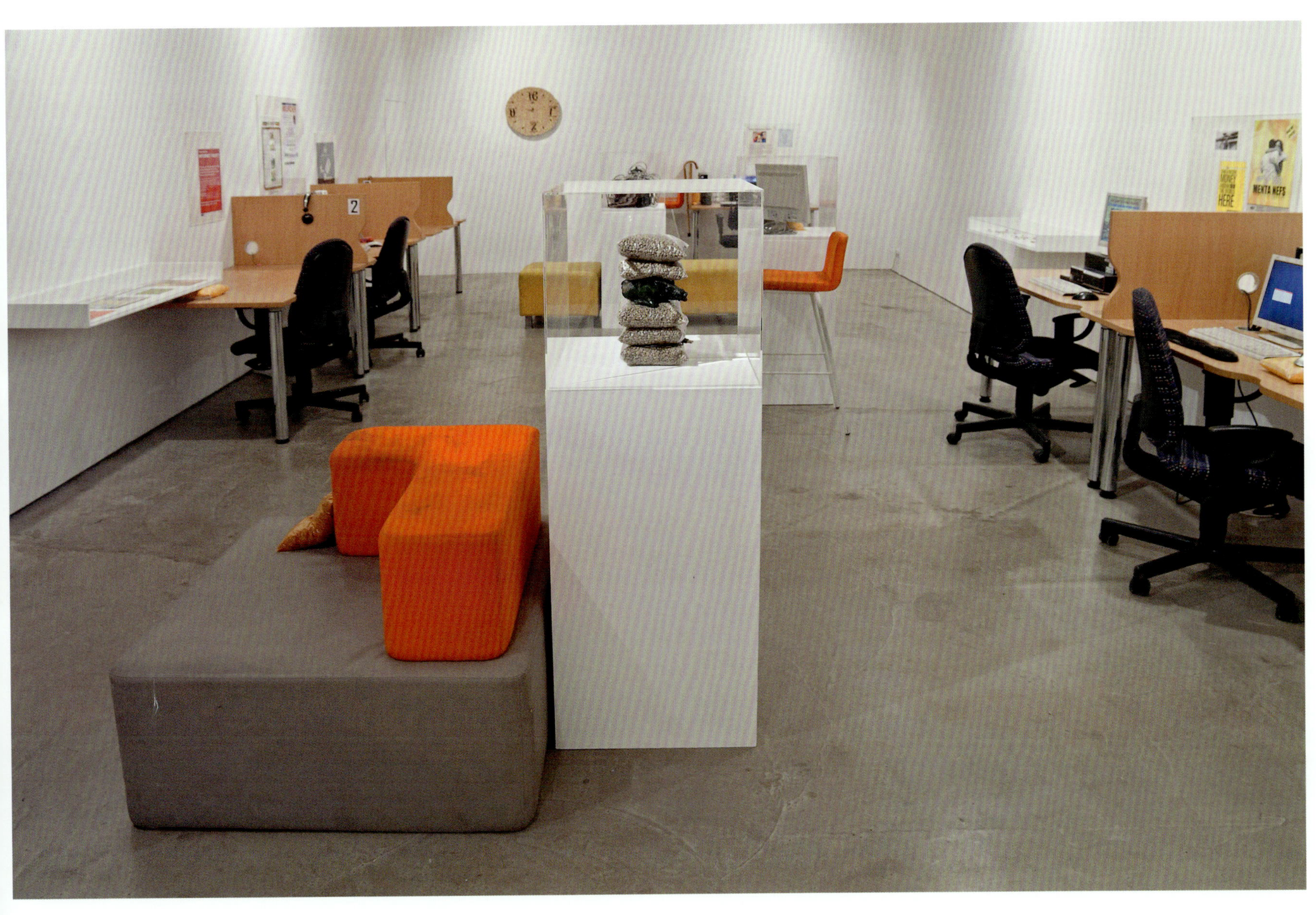

Internet Centre & Habesha Grocery, 2013
installation, various materials
variable dimensions

FREE BASIC COMPUTER TRAINING

Ms Word

- How to open a file
- Typing your 1st letter
- Spelling & grammar check
- Copy, cut & paste techniques
- How to insert a text & an image
- Tables in word

Ms Excel

- A first look at MS Excel
- MS Excel Rows & Columns
- How to create text & numbers
- How to save your work
- The sum function in Excel

Ms PowerPoint

- A first look at PowerPoint
- How to open a file in PowerPoint
- Inserting a new slide
- Bulleted list in PowerPoint
- Adding an image in PowerPoint

How to use the Internet

- Opening your email account
- Sending your 1st email
- Attaching a file in your email
- How to search on-line
- How to use Facebook

ARE YOU INTERESTED?
CONTACT US TO REGISTER

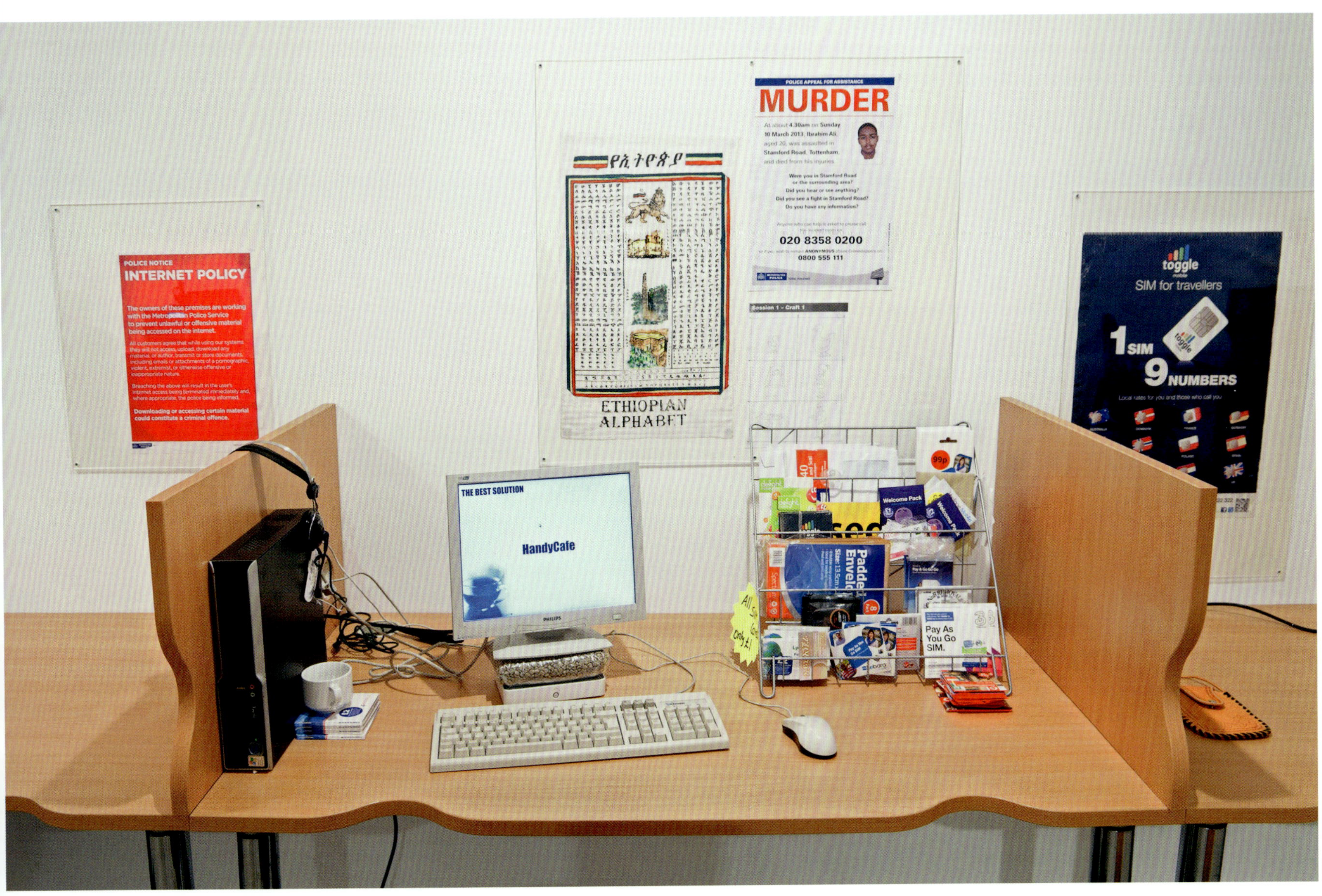
POLICE NOTICE
INTERNET POLICY
የኢትዮጵያ
ETHIOPIAN
ALPHABET
POLICE APPEAL FOR ASSISTANCE
MURDER
020 8358 0200
0800 555 111
THE BEST SOLUTION
HandyCafe
toggle
SIM for travellers
1 SIM
9 NUMBERS
Pay As You Go SIM.

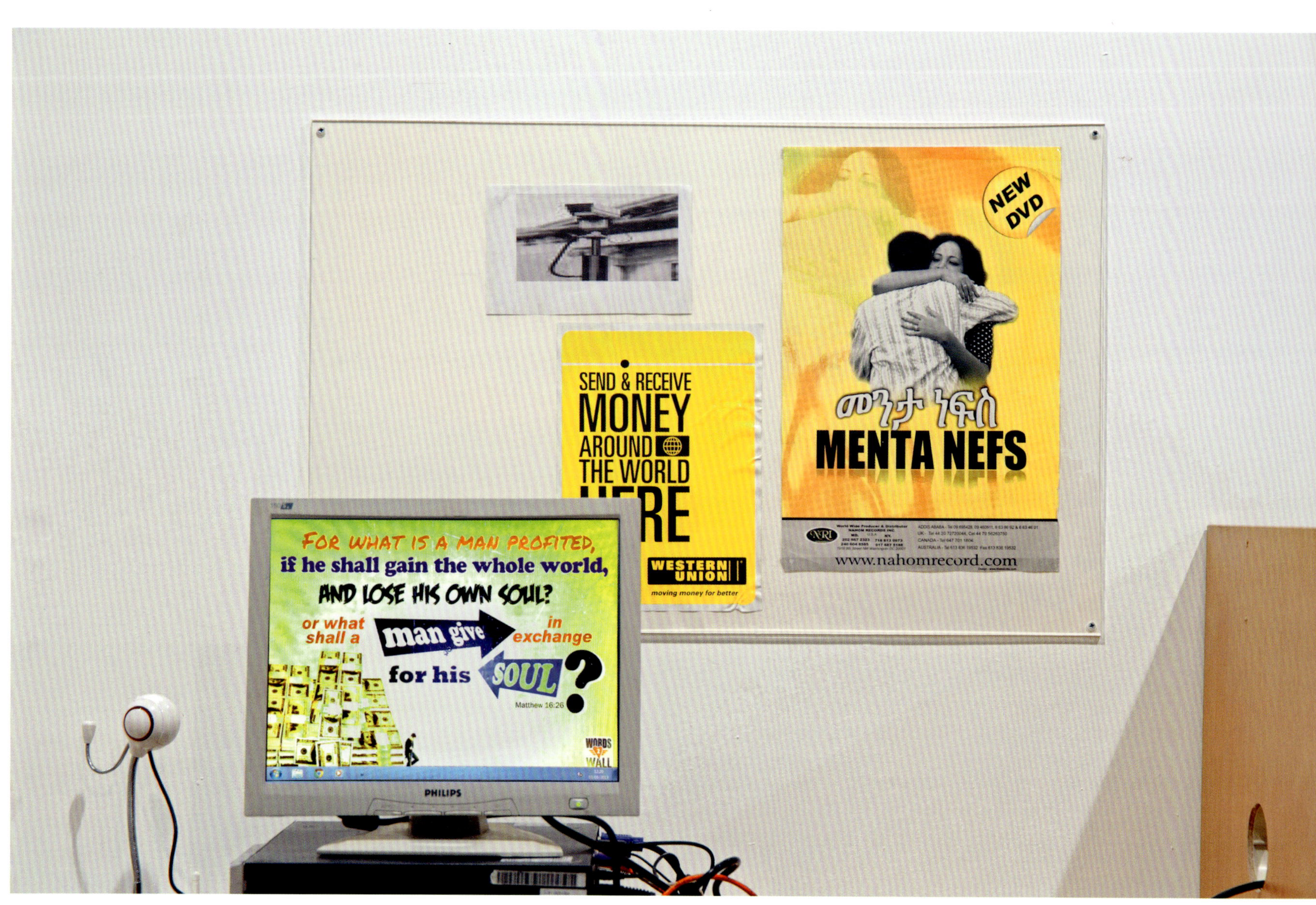
SEND & RECEIVE
MONEY
AROUND
THE WORLD
HERE
WESTERN UNION
moving money for better
NEW DVD
መንታ ነፍስ
MENTA NEFS
www.nahomrecord.com
FOR WHAT IS A MAN PROFITED,
if he shall gain the whole world,
AND LOSE HIS OWN SOUL?
or what
shall a
man give
in
exchange
for his
SOUL?
Matthew 16:26
WORDS
ON THE
WALL
PHILIPS

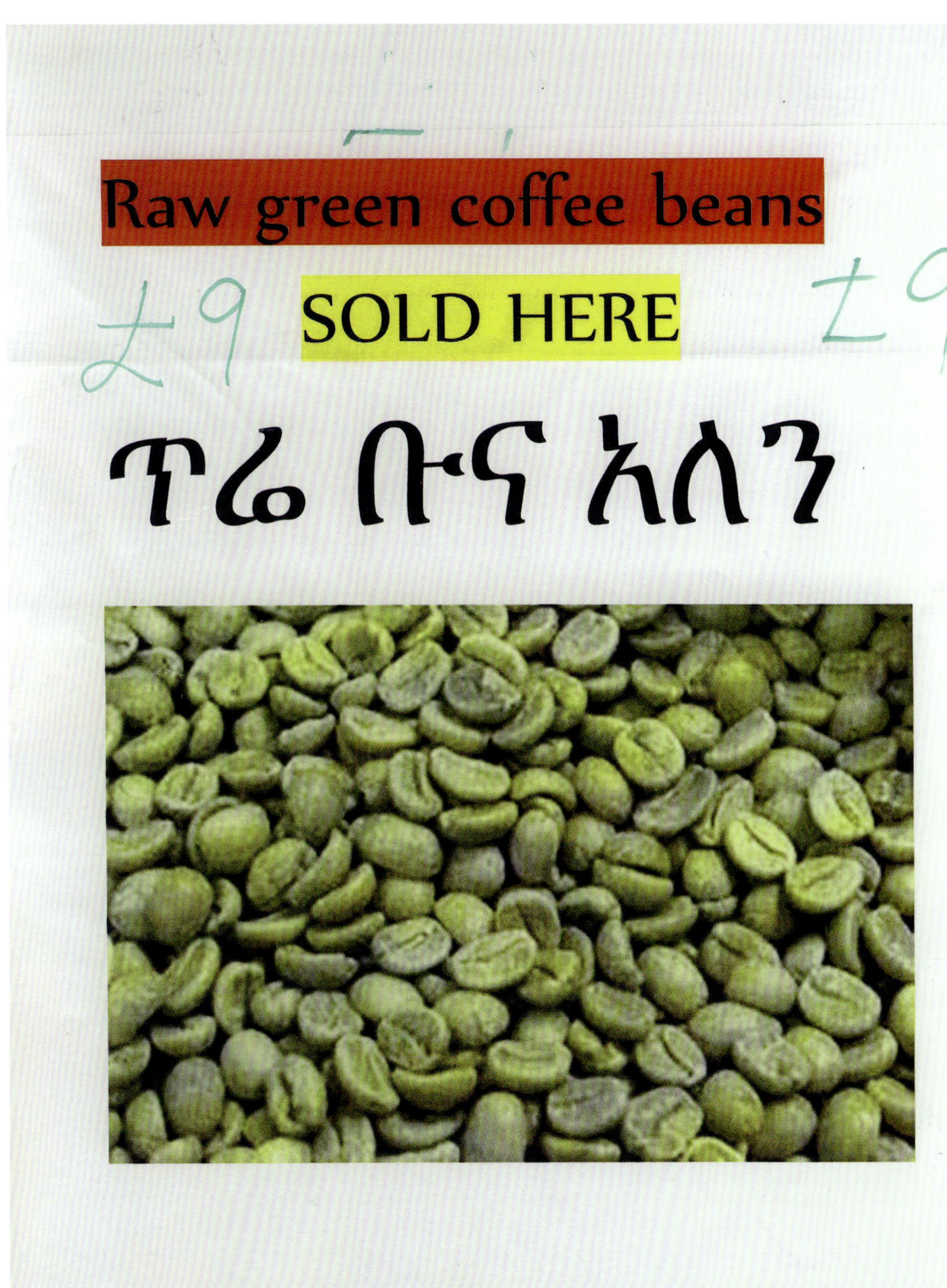

Raw green coffee beans
SOLD HERE
ጥሬ ቡና አለን

STICK YOUR CHEWING GUM HERE PLEASE!

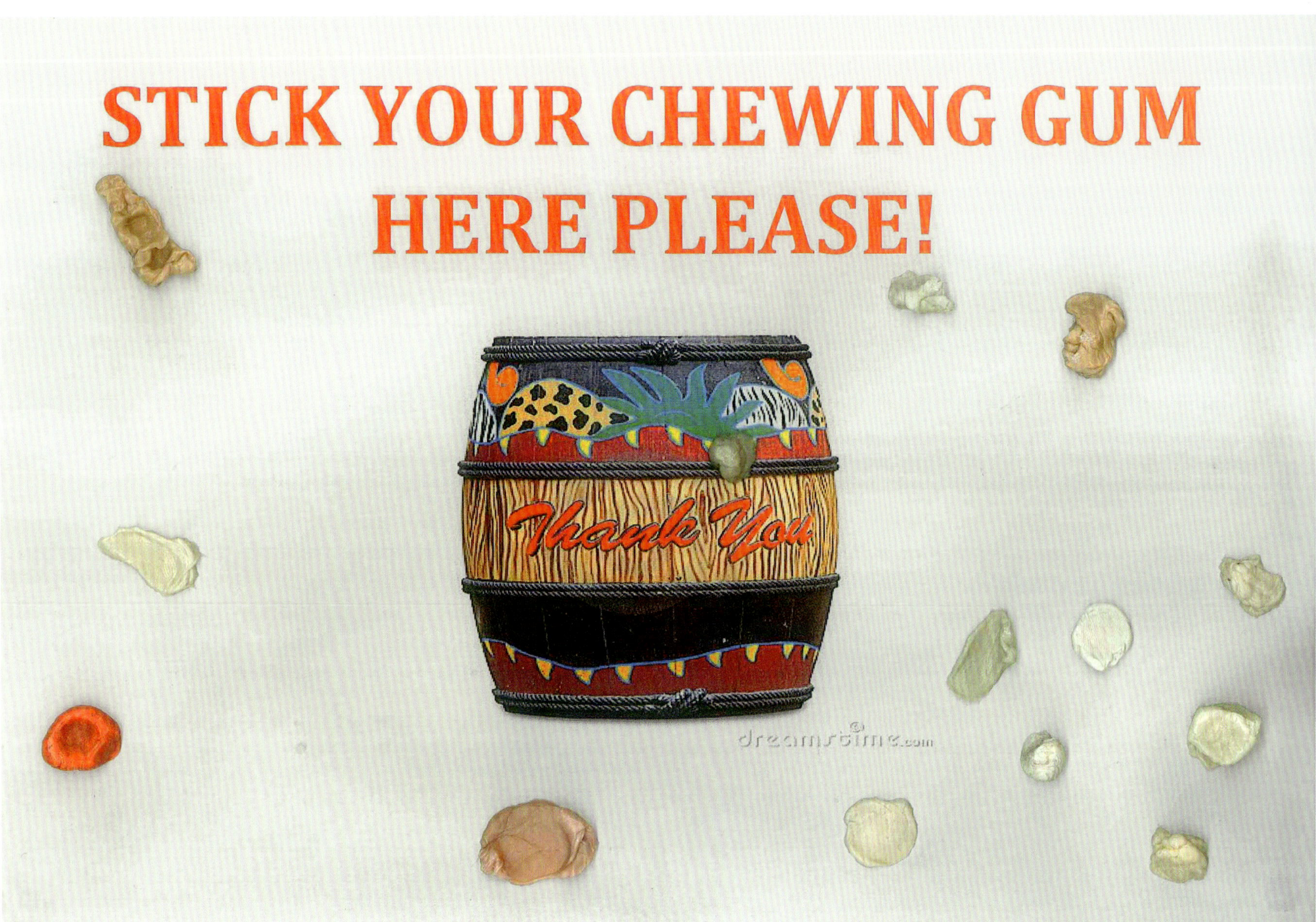

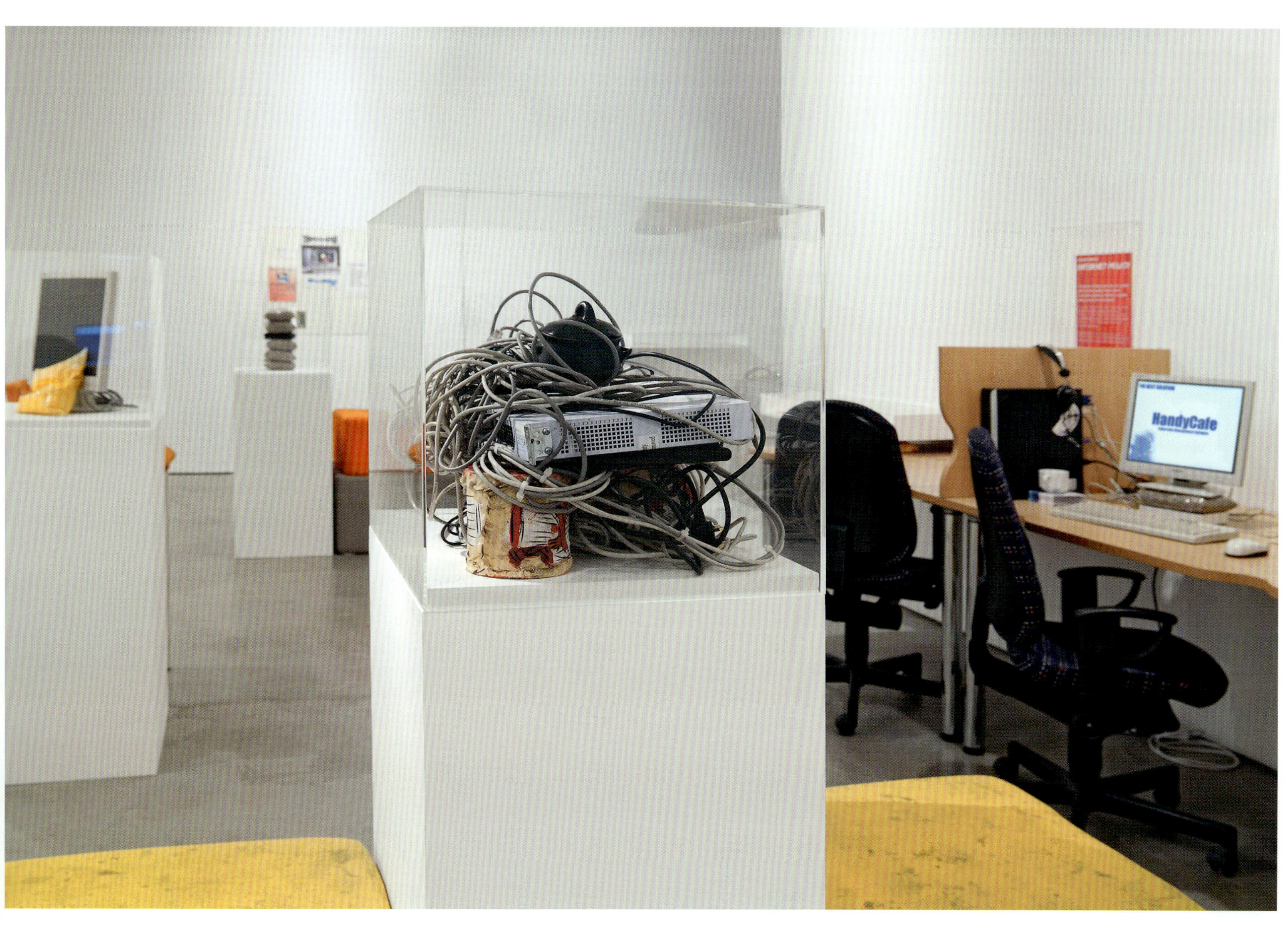

Jonny Briggs

Born in 1985, Jonny Briggs is one of the most interesting artists to have emerged recently from the British art scene. Grown up in the woodlands of Berkshire with his parents and four older sisters, he moved to London to study at the Chelsea College of Art and Design, before completing a Master's at the Royal College of Art, where he was taught by, amongst others, Olivier Richon and Sarah Jones. His photography – which over the years he has complemented with sculptures, objects, fabric pieces and videos – won him the 2011 Saatchi New Sensations Prize and saw him named as a finalist at the 2012 Catlin Art Prize – all achievements that have been an important drive for his work. Although he lives in London for career purposes, Briggs has maintained strong links with his native county, to which he returns regularly to draw inspiration from its natural environment in order to develop new ideas. His family not only provides another source of creative inspiration but also serves as the raw material for his works, in which his parents and relatives often appear, alongside domestic materials such as family photographs and objects. As he himself puts it: 'I use photography to explore my relationship with deception, the constructed reality of the family, and question the boundaries between my parents and I, between child/adult, self/other, nature/culture, real/fake in an attempt to revive my unconditioned self, beyond the family bubble'.

Briggs's entire oeuvre takes its cue from the world of childhood, not yet contaminated by social conditioning and norms, and invites us to adopt the wide-eyed perspective of the child who does not distinguish the real from the imaginary, the normal from the absurd, and for whom everything is still possible. Many of his photographs seem initially to have been digitally altered but, when looked at up-close, they betray their material nature: the surreal effects of his works are, in actual fact, produced three-dimensionally, within the physical reality of the things that are then photographed. And so, for example, *The Empathetic vs. The Mimic* (2011) is the result of a painstaking symmetrical staging of objects he found in his parents' house, and not a digital mirroring of the image. With the left part arranged instinctively and the right recomposing the left, the entire scene alludes to the contrast between intuition and practical thinking – the characteristics that, for the artist, distinguish him from his father, whose face is depicted by the wooden mask split down the middle. The image of his father is also central in *Comfort Object* (2012), a work made of five photographs mounted in a single composition that explicitly evokes Michelangelo's *Pietà*. The title borrows the term coined by the psychoanalyst Donald Winnicott, who explains childhood attachment to an object used as a surrogate for the parental figure. Wearing his father's clothes and displaying his features, the artist holds his father's head in his lap, creating a sort of confusion of identity that forces the viewer to question the relationship that links parents and children and their respective roles.

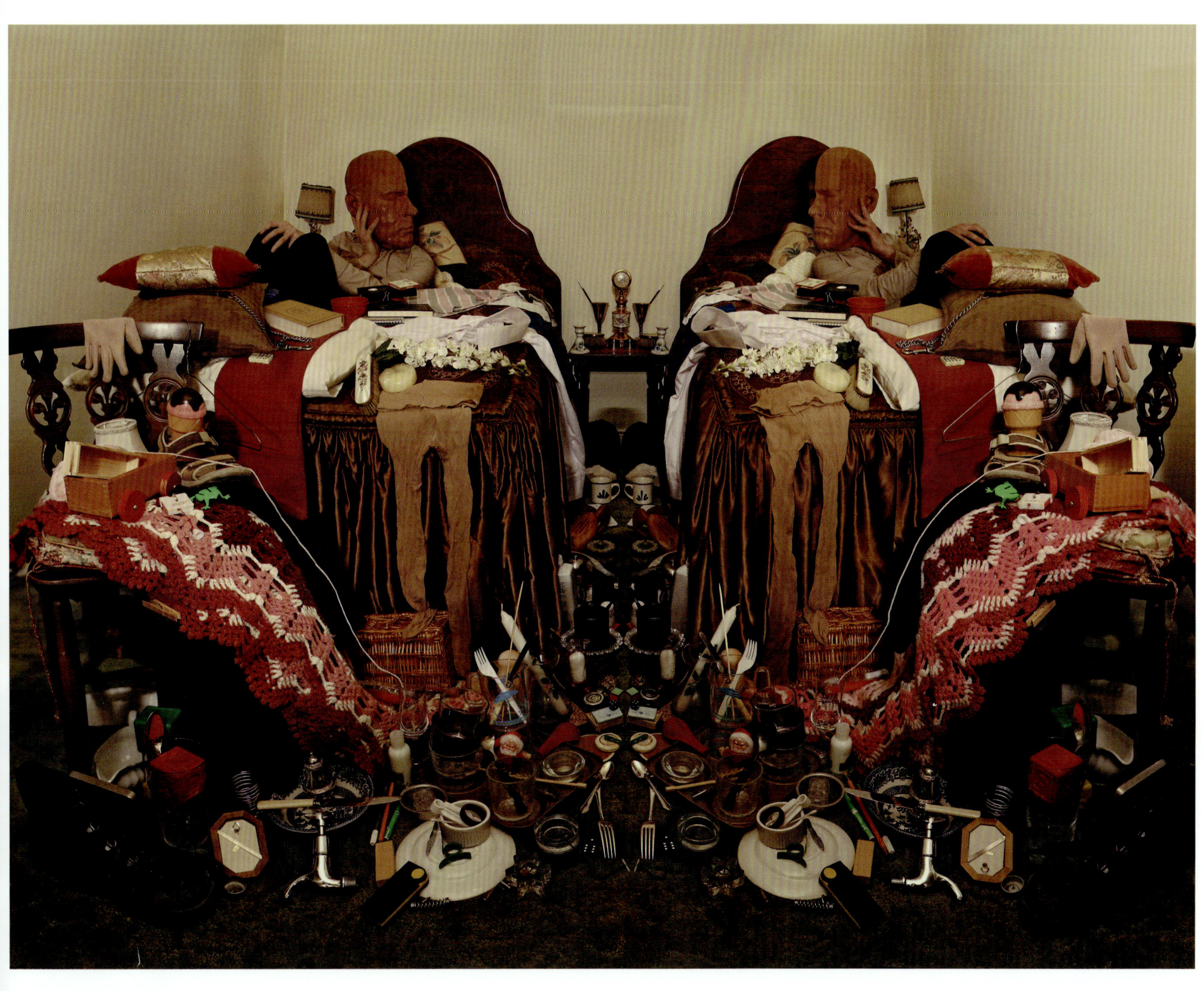

The Empathetic vs. The Mimic, 2011
Lambda c-print
101.5 x 127 cm

Comfort Object, 2012
5 Lambda c-prints
96 x 96 cm

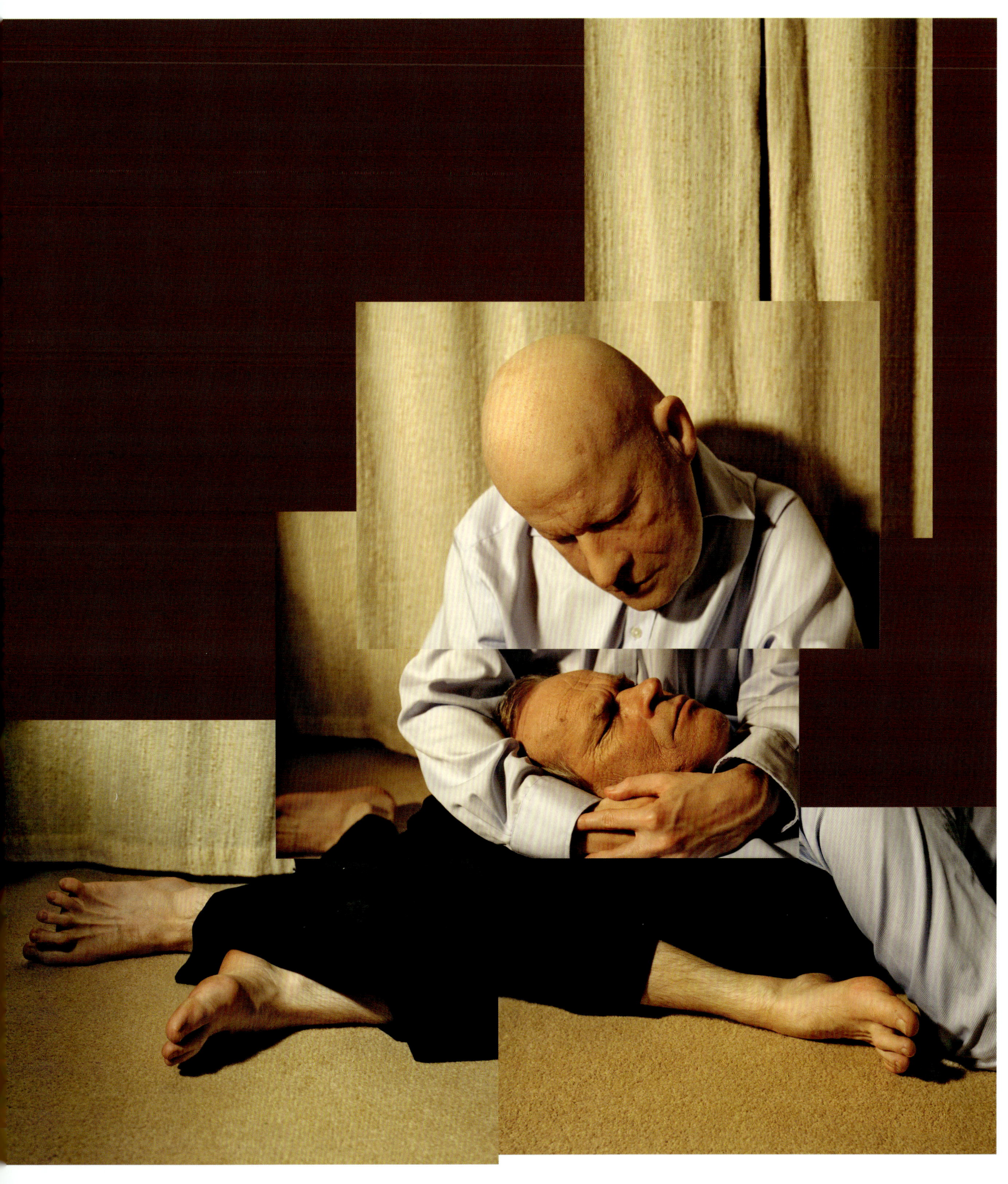

Willie Doherty

Positioning his documentary-style work from the very outset in the contemporary art world, Willie Doherty has contributed, over the course of his decades-long career, to the definition of what has since been called 'the documentary turn'. Taking the form of photographs, films and video installations, his work has focused since the 1980s on the themes of representation, the overcodification of the landscape and the rhetoric of identity. Doherty has concentrated above all on his homeland, Northern Ireland, and on the effects that its turbulent past – the 'Troubles' between Republicans and Loyalists – still exerts to this day. Born in Derry in 1959, he returned there after studying at Ulster Polytechnic in Belfast (1978–81) with the intention of making a contribution, from the privileged position of an insider, to the representation of an area that was being widely photographed and was considered a laboratory for every kind of surveillance method. Having witnessed Bloody Sunday first-hand, and having seen the media deny that any massacre had in fact taken place in Derry on 30 January 1972, the whole event was for Doherty an illuminating experience on the untrustworthiness of communication. Perhaps for this reason, his work has always been directed towards undermining any unequivocal, pre-packaged interpretation of reality and towards inviting the viewer to evaluate independently the position to adopt with respect to what is being shown.
Willie Doherty has dedicated a large part of his work to his hometown, challenging from a critical standpoint the theme of stereotypical representation through an analytical reading of the landscape. In *Derry* (1985), the artist portrayed an uneasy evening image of an industrial estate within the city, where – swathed in a fog of uncertain origin – there appear a small group of human figures and clear political slogans. His black-and-white photographs of the 1980s and 1990s, presented to the public for the first time in 2012 within the *Lapse* exhibition in Dublin, oscillate between present and past, showing contemporary viewers a reality on which time and history have inevitably left their mark. In his photographic work, the artist has always granted texts a central role, sometimes superimposing them on the images, on other occasions, such as this, using them in titles. *Against the Wall, Alleyway Used for Cover on January 30th, 1972* (1992) makes direct reference to Bloody Sunday, alluding perhaps to the routes taken by those protesting against the policy of internment as they ran away from British soldiers, or perhaps to the cover that the soldiers found in the alley to put the protesters up against the wall. The distance in time does not allow for an unambiguous interpretation. What is certain is that with this image, as with *Headlights Border Road at Dusk* (1993), Doherty uses the streets of Derry to investigate the overcodification of a landscape in which echoes of violence and conflict linger on to this day.

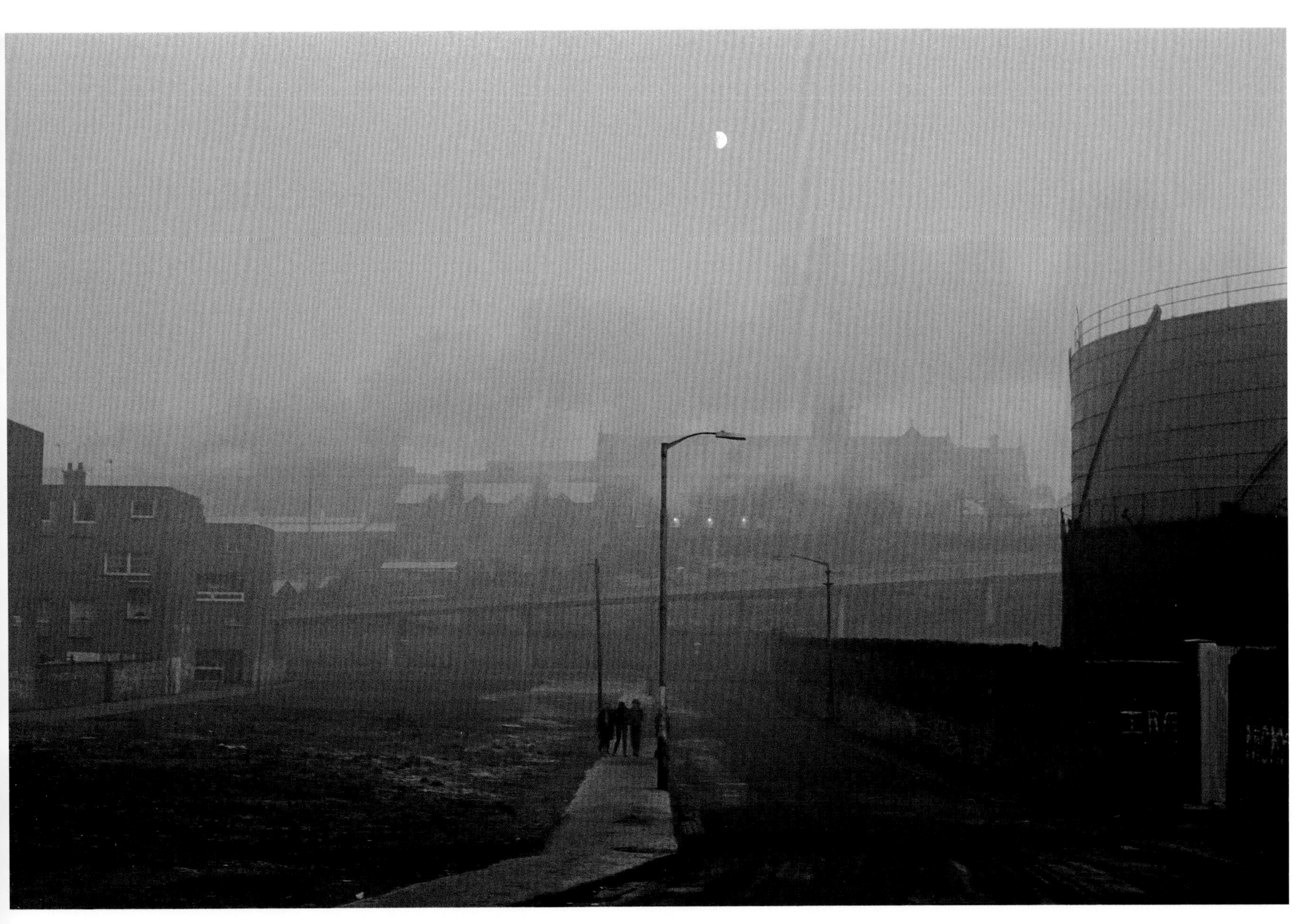

Derry, 1985
pigment inkjet print
40 x 54 cm

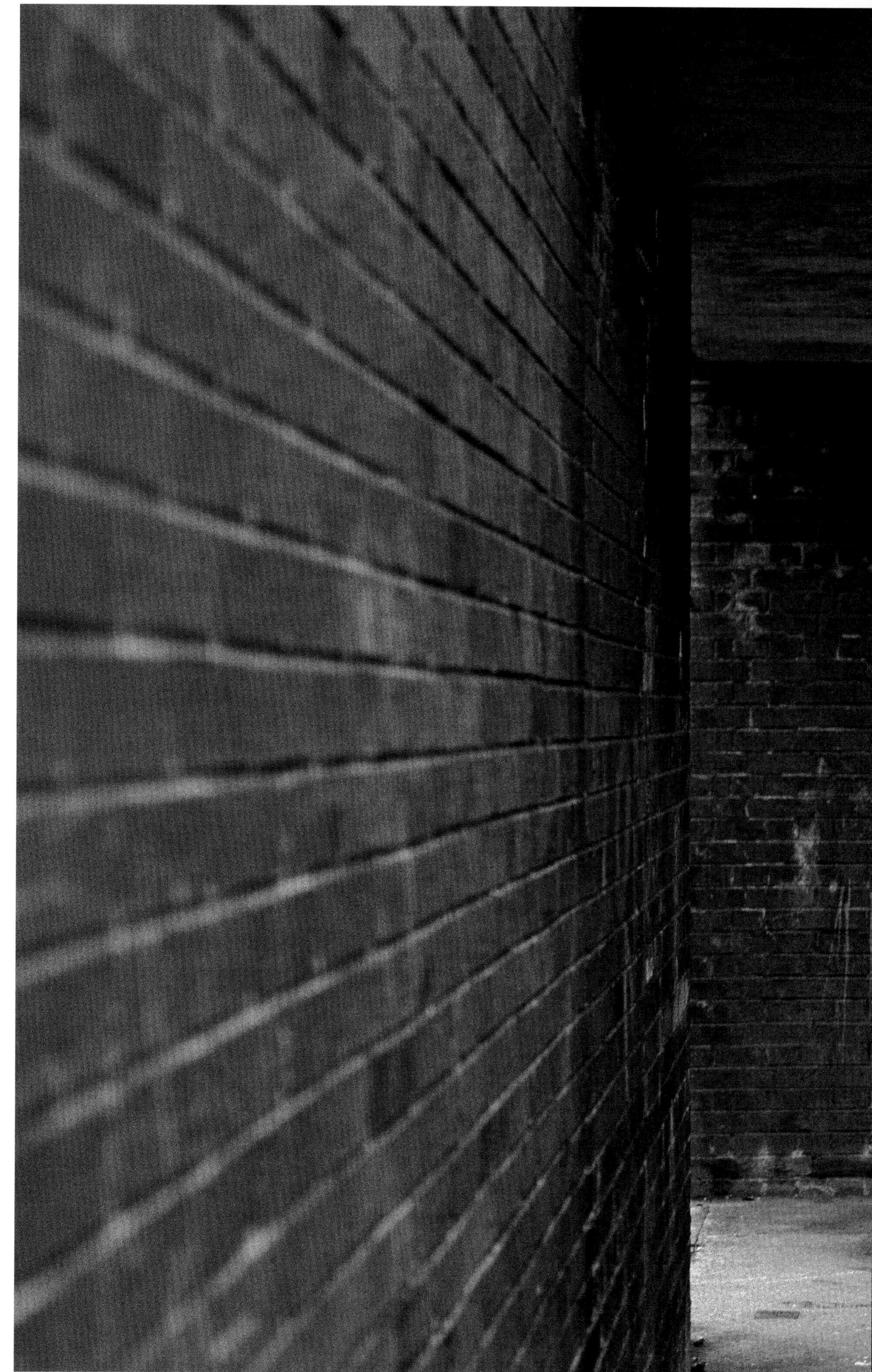

*Against the Wall, Alleyway Used
For Cover on January 30th, 1972*, 1992
Lambda print on gelatin silver paper
122 x 183 cm

34

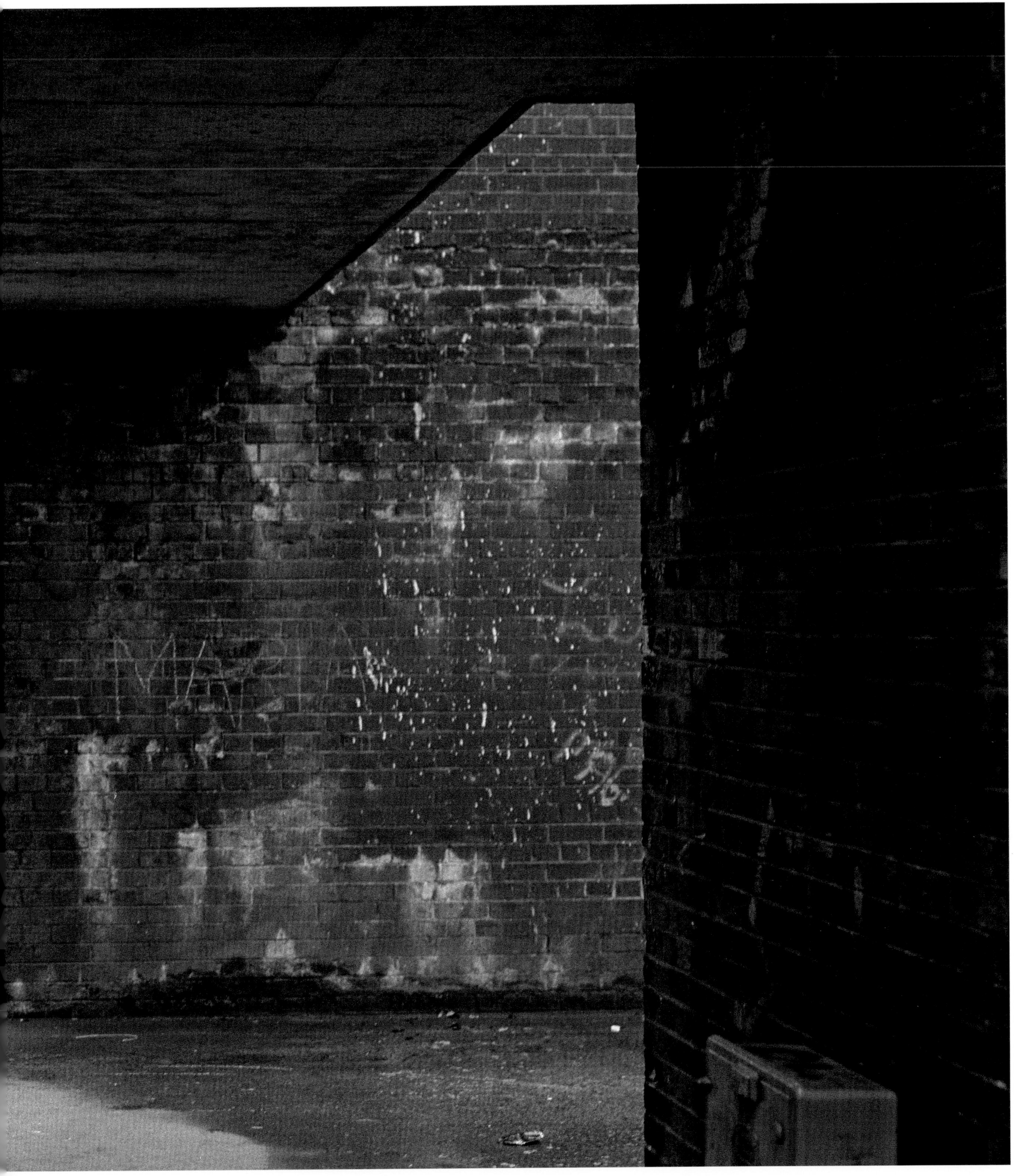

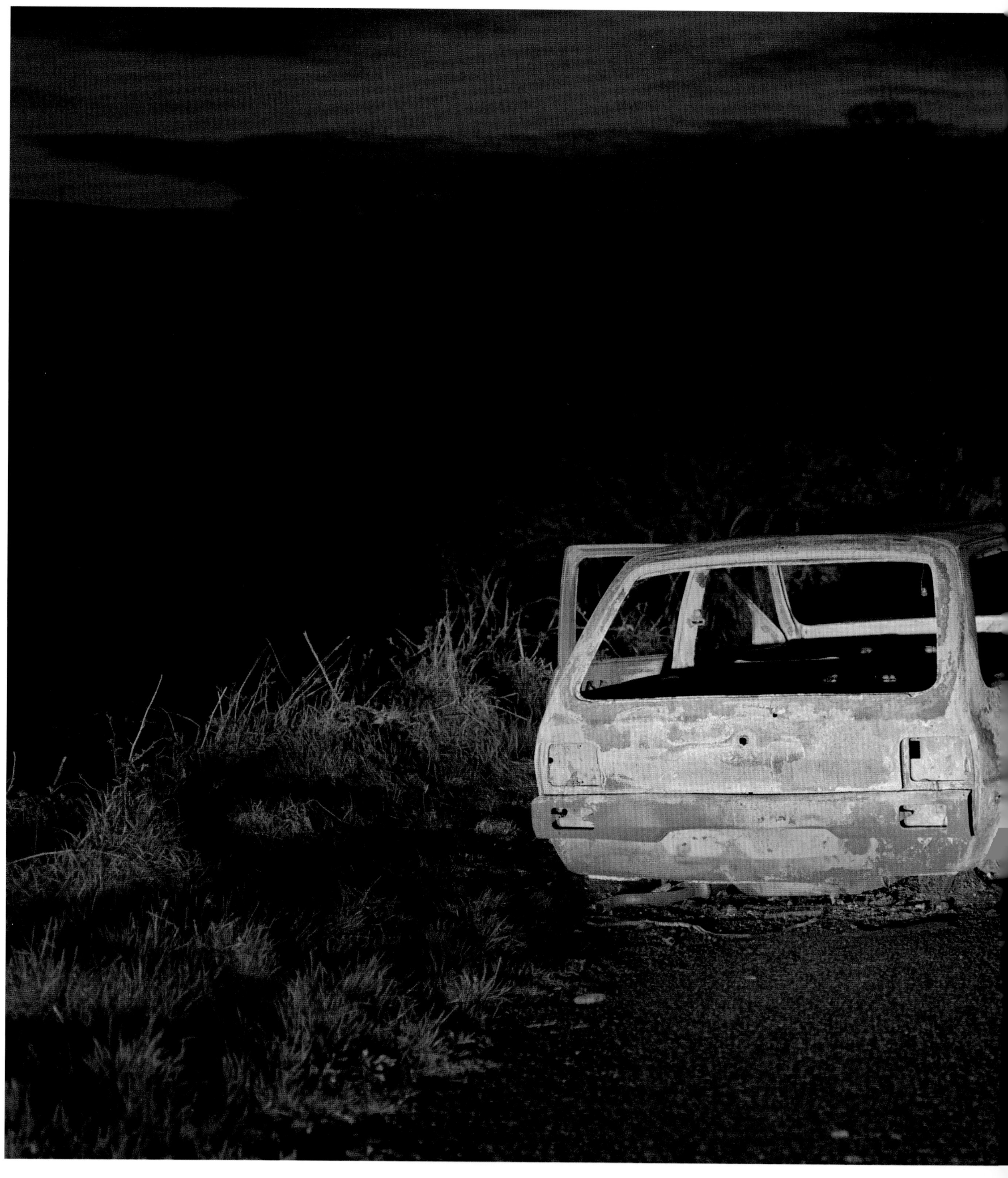

Headlights Border Road at Dusk, 1993
Lambda print on gelatin silver paper
122 x 183 cm

Annabel Elgar

A native of Hampshire – she was born in Aldershot in 1971 – Annabel Elgar has lived for many years in London, where she trained initially at the Polytechnic of Central London (1990–94) and then at the Royal College of Art, where she completed a Master's degree in Photography in 2001. Her work, which can be related to the 'staged photography' genre, dissolves the dividing line between reality and fiction, creating settings that draw their inspiration as much from popular culture and the news as they do from mythology, literature and art history. Like unsolved puzzles, these photographs hint at stories that are never fully defined, presenting a multiplicity of details that serve as narrative clues, which the viewers can then develop with their imagination. The two series *Refuge* (2006–13) and *Companion* (2007–13), to which the works in the collection belong, include visions located somewhere between the routine and the extraordinary, or – as the artist herself puts it – 'a fantasy labyrinth of oddball activity, conjuring up the fall-out of human interaction'.

The characters populating these places are never directly revealed in the photographs, but their presence emerges through the evidence left behind by their actions. Examples of this include: *The Method* (2013), where the remains of a plum cake and the routes marked out on the unreal maps that cover the walls make us think of weird plans being drawn up in the secret refuge of a bunker; *Companion (3)* (2011), in which a unicorn sculpted from a block of soap appears blind and vulnerable, like a new-born animal, alluding perhaps to the fragility of its creator; and *Companion (5)* (2012), in which a central role is played by a mythical horse – Pegasus this time, strangely made from woven horsehair. While seeming incomplete, the winged horse of Greek mythology is very much on display: standing on its hind legs, it looks ready to leap off the interior windowsill against which it is pictured. The artist has stated that she drew the inspiration for this image from a news story about the leader of a breakaway Amish group in Ohio who was found guilty of fomenting his followers to cut off the beards of other members of the community. The reference point for *Companion (4)* (2012) is a famous film: positioned on a table within a 1970s-style interior, a King Kong figure rises from a handful of earth. As Elgar explained, 'in contrast to the dusty serenity of the backdrop, the ape's emergence seems heroically misplaced, offering up a metaphor of social embarrassment'. Balancing the line between the fairy-tale and the documentation of bizarre realities, the artist's settings immerse the viewer in an enigmatic psychological space characterised by contrasting tensions to which it is possible to find solutions only through one's own imagination.

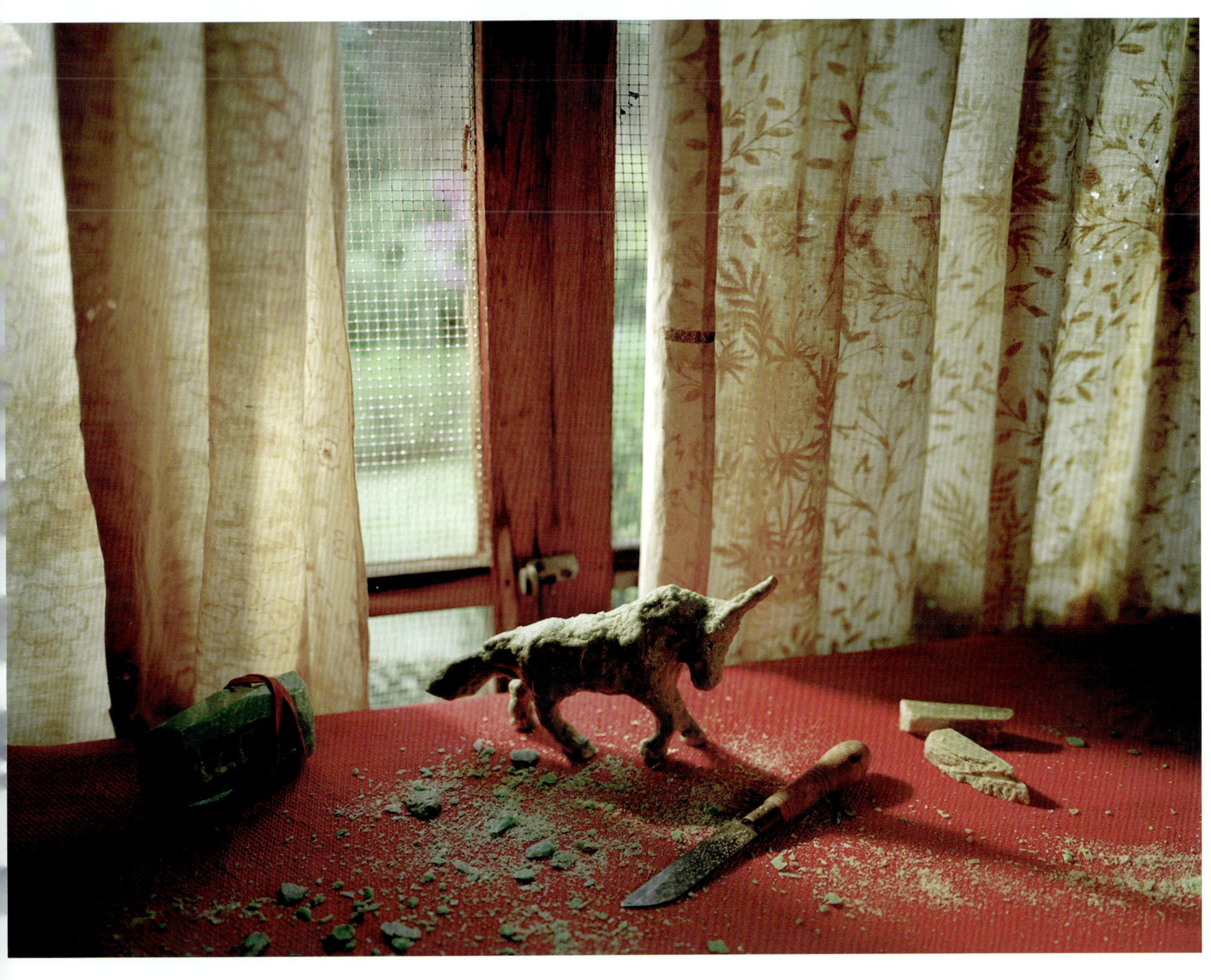

Companion (3), 2011
from the *Companion* series
c-print
40.5 x 50.5 cm

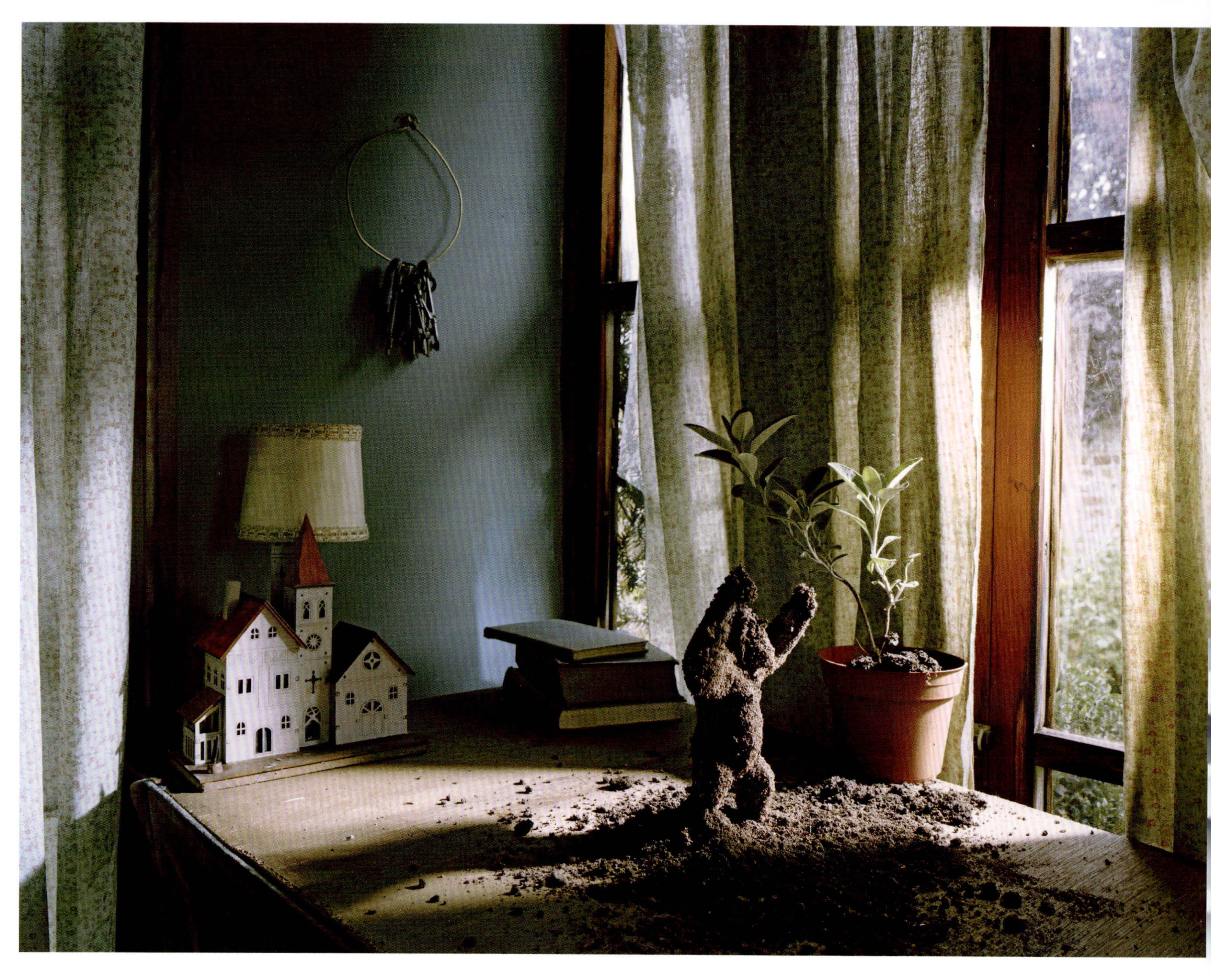

Companion (4), 2012
from the *Companion* series
c-print
40.5 x 50.5 cm

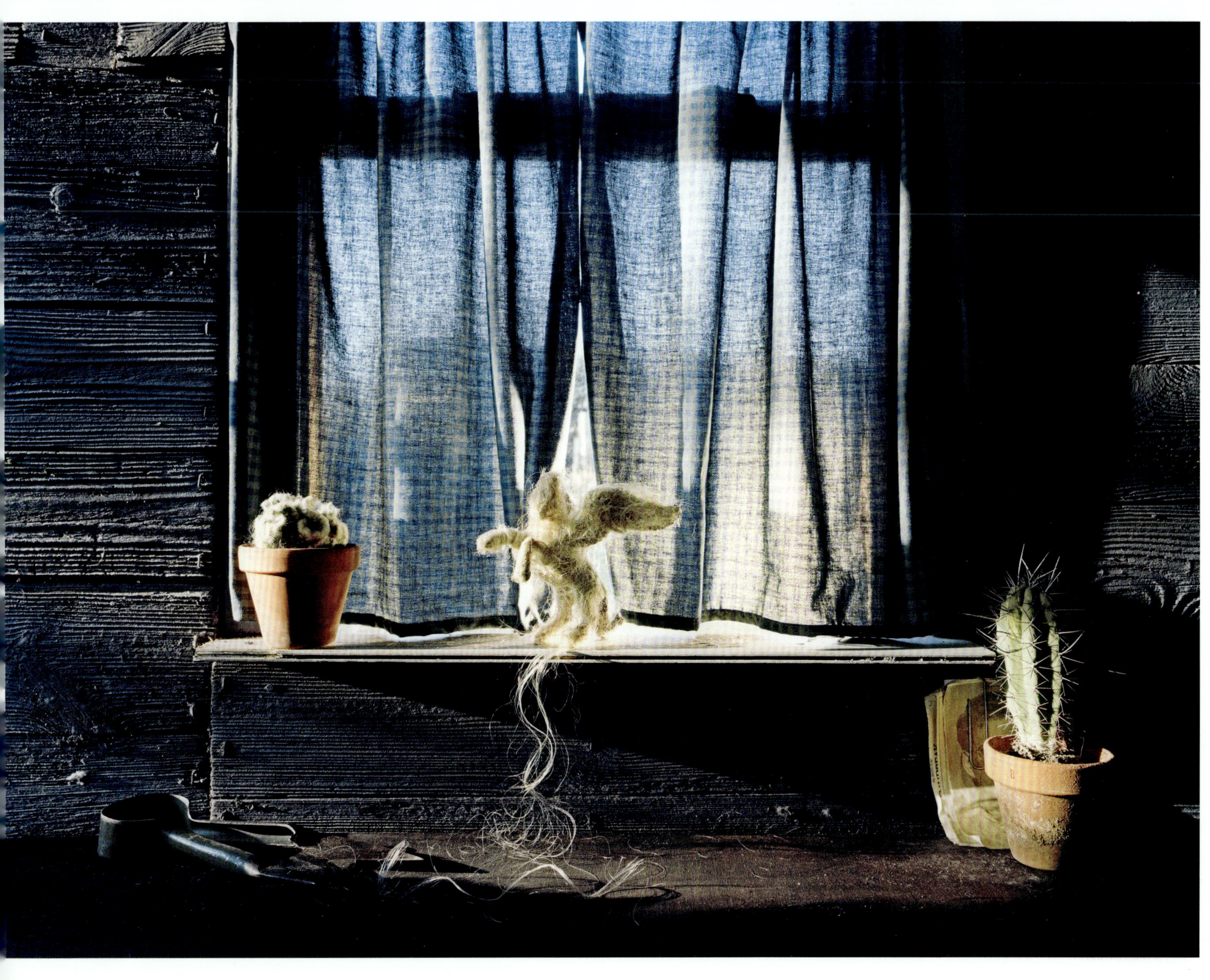

Companion (5), 2012
from the *Companion* series
c-print
40.5 x 50.5 cm

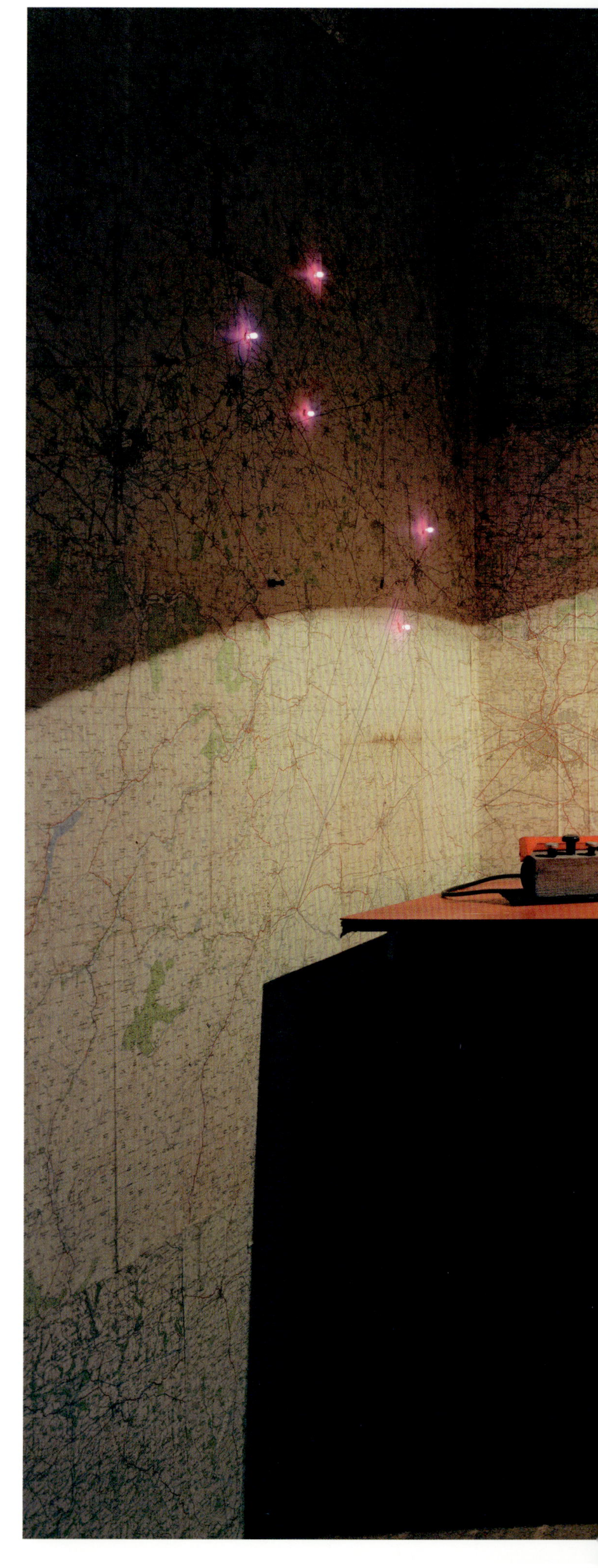

The Method, 2013
from the *Refuge* series
c-print
102 x 127 cm

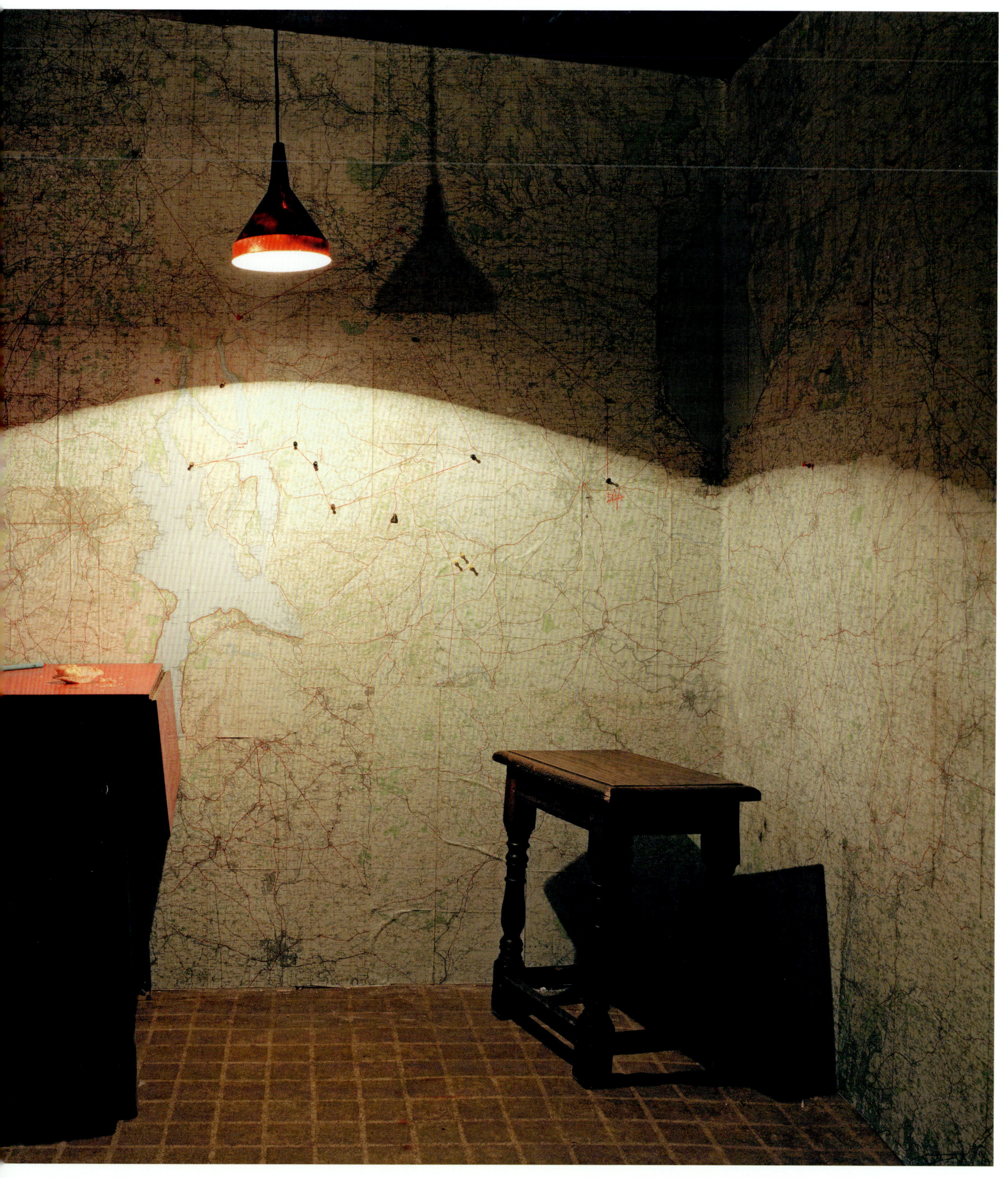

Hallgerður Hallgrímsdóttir

Hallgerður Hallgrímsdóttir began to take an interest in photography while studying Fashion Design at the Iceland Academy of the Arts, from which she graduated in 2007. Fascinated by the medium, she left Reykjavík (where she was born in 1984) to take a degree in Fine Art Photography at the Glasgow School of Art. In Scotland, she produced the series entitled *A Few Thoughts on Photography* (2010) – a conceptually-driven meditation on the limits and possibilities of photography.

Having completed her studies, in 2011 she returned to live in the Icelandic capital, where she continued to investigate the theme of photography while orienting her research towards the exploration of the landscape. As she explains in her biography: 'Making art in Iceland, nature is hard to escape. It seeps into your everyday, your rhythm, aesthetics; here, there is so much more nature than people, more mountains than skyscrapers, more cloud formations than opinions'. Yet the landscape that Hallgrímsdóttir chooses to deal with is not the one iconified by the great Icelandic photographers through dramatised representations of nature. As the artist herself states: 'To me Iceland is a wonderful mixture of great beauty and mundane ugliness, mostly utterly devoid of human life'. And so it appears in the photographs of the *Fog Patches* series (2014), a collection of images of different shapes and sizes that depict the fascination of life on the island through little tastes of the commonplace, images of non-events, silent fragments of immutability shrouded in fog. As in all of Hallgrímsdóttir's recent output, a great deal of attention is focused on the selection and combination of the photographs, with a view to building up a fragmentary, non-linear narration in which the missing images have the same weight as those that are there. As she herself put it, 'The photograph is not an answer, but a proposal. *Fog Patches* is a collection of proposals'.

The same approach underpins the *Untitled (2012)* series, produced as part of the trans-European 'Visual Narratives: European Borderlines' project, which in 2011 and 2012 saw the involvement of twelve photographers from Latvia, Iceland, Turkey and Portugal on the theme of borders. Each artist was invited to work on his or her own country and on another country, chosen at will out of those involved. The images in *Untitled (2012)* were taken by Hallgrímsdóttir in unidentified locations in Iceland and Turkey. Adopting a range of different techniques and shooting styles, which relate as much to amateur as to professional photography, the artist documented her trip by trying to look at both places with a pure perspective, taking on the untainted point of view of a foreigner. Hallgrímsdóttir explains: 'What remains is a collection of moments accumulated on the way. The space in between is there for the imagination to colour in'.

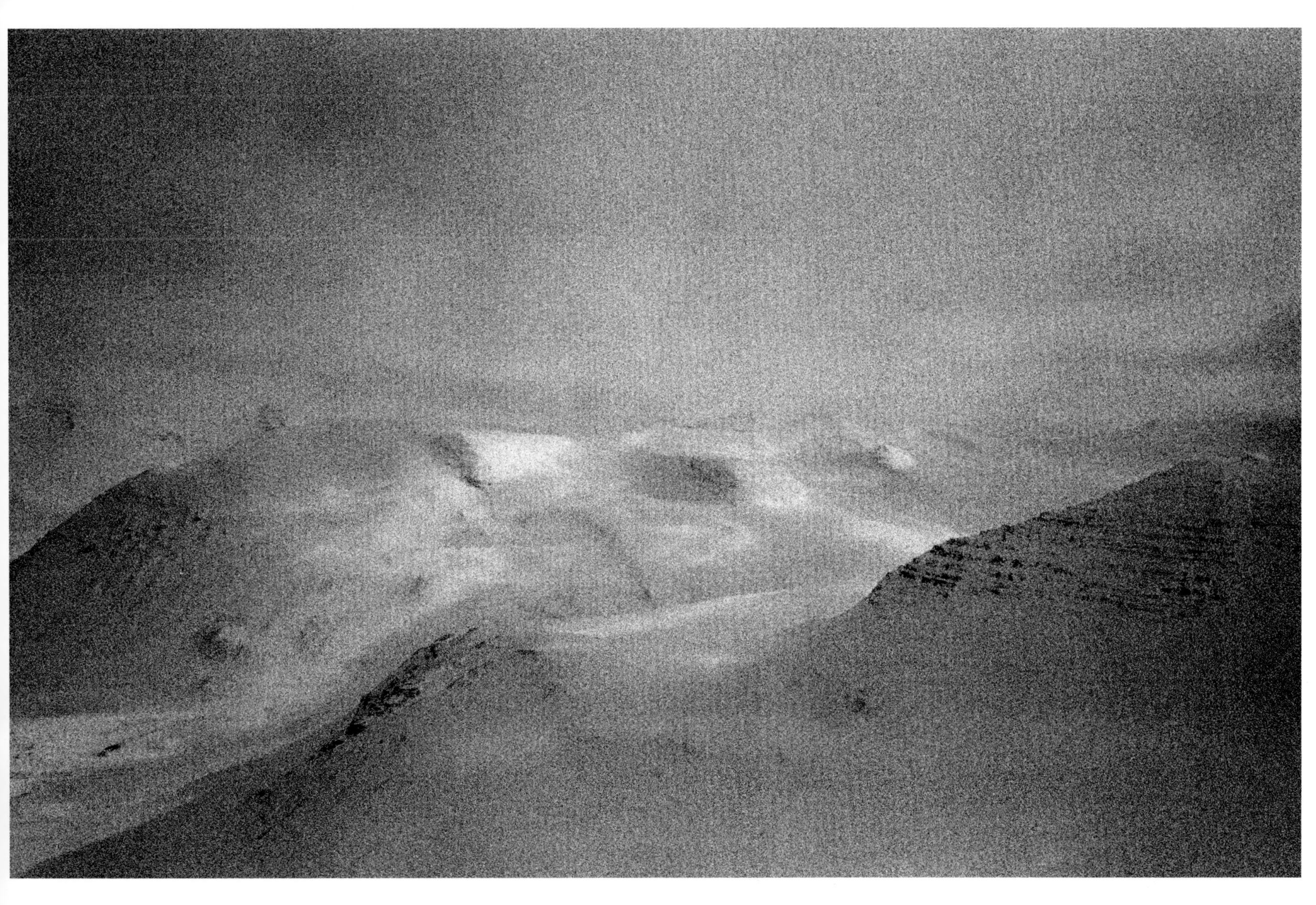

Snow, 2014
from the *Fog Patches* series
inkjet print
63 x 95.5 cm

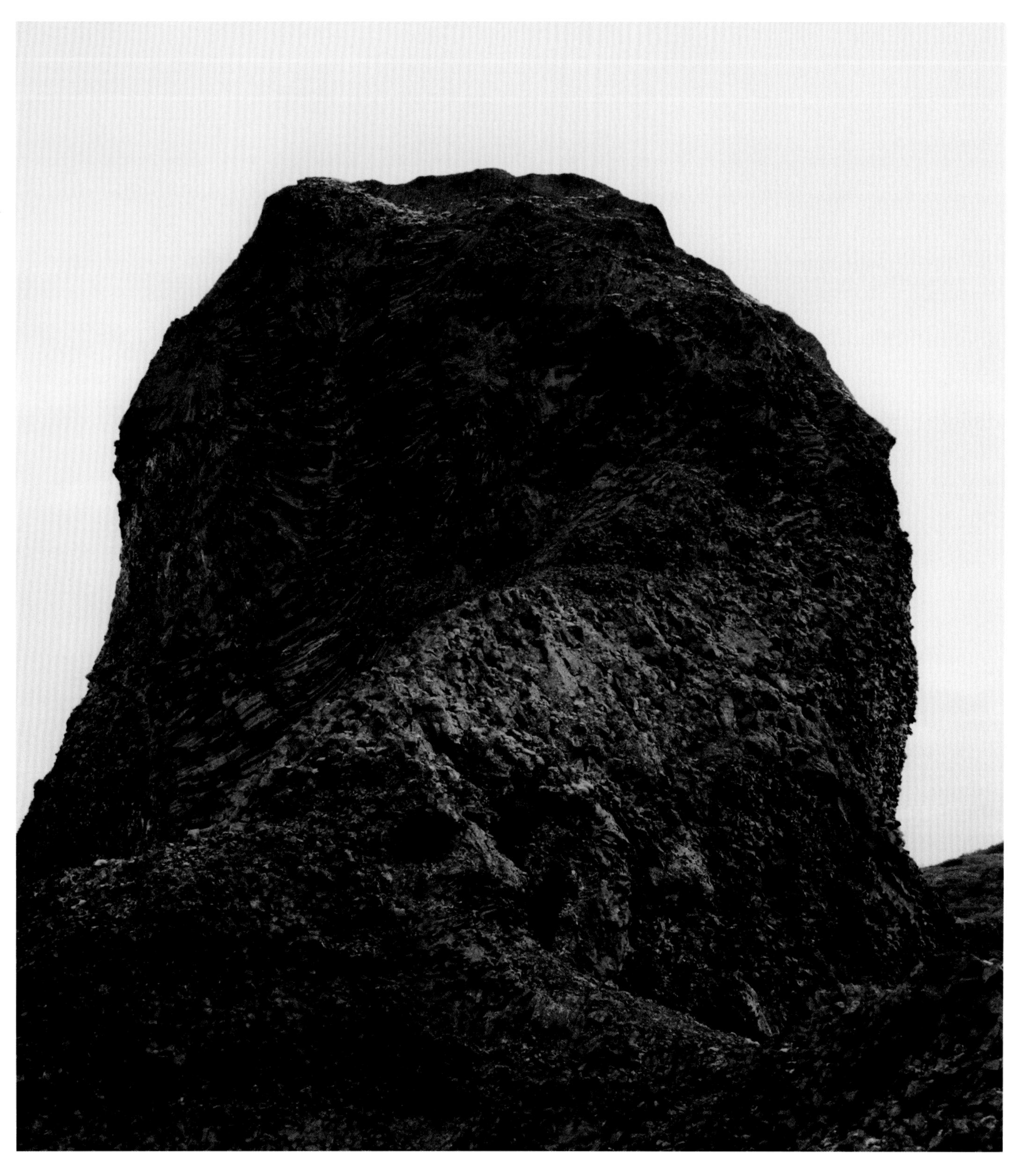

Hljóðaklettar, 2014
from the *Fog Patches* series
inkjet print
37.5 x 33 cm

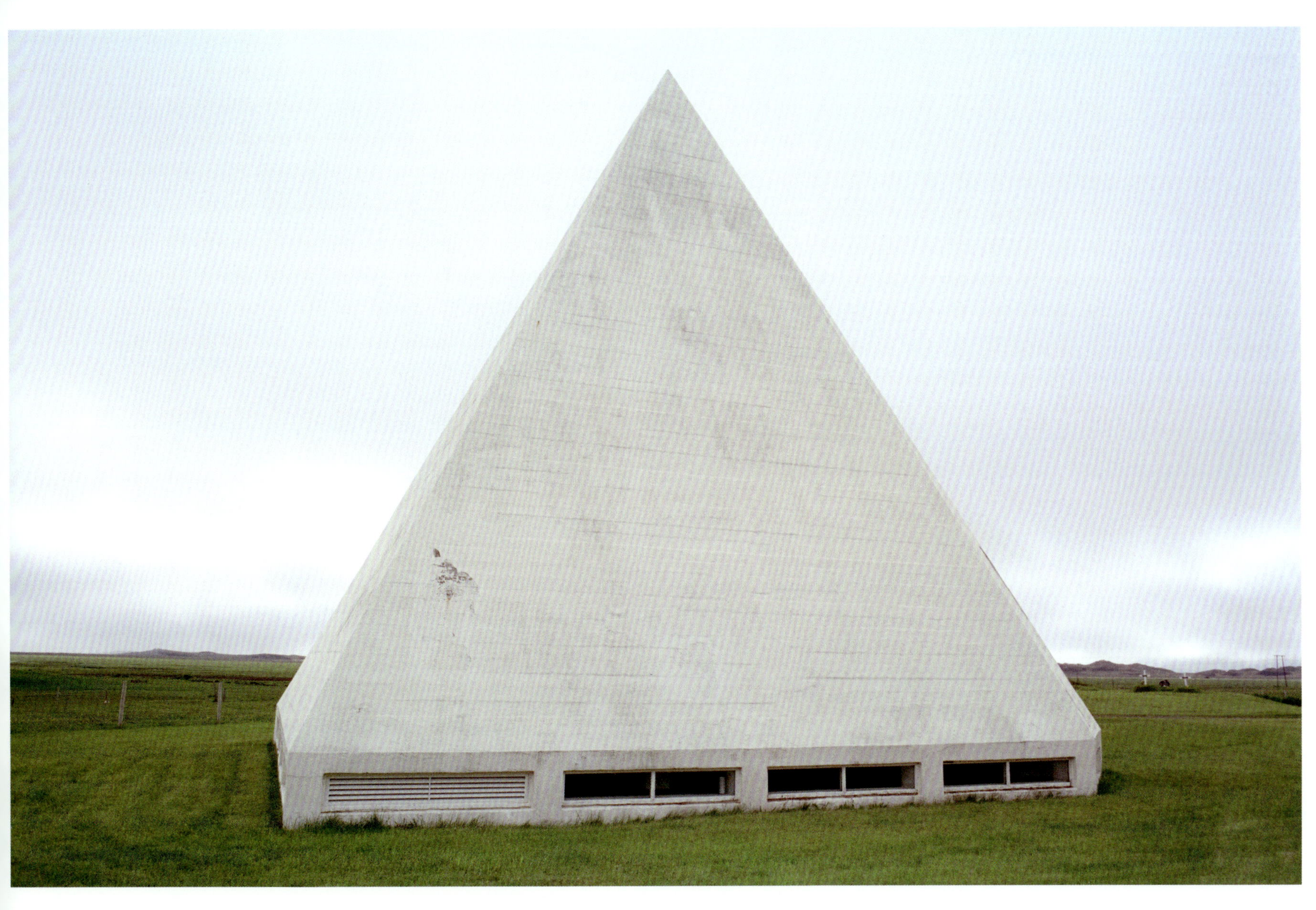

Pyramid, 2014
from the *Fog Patches* series
inkjet print
32 x 48.5 cm

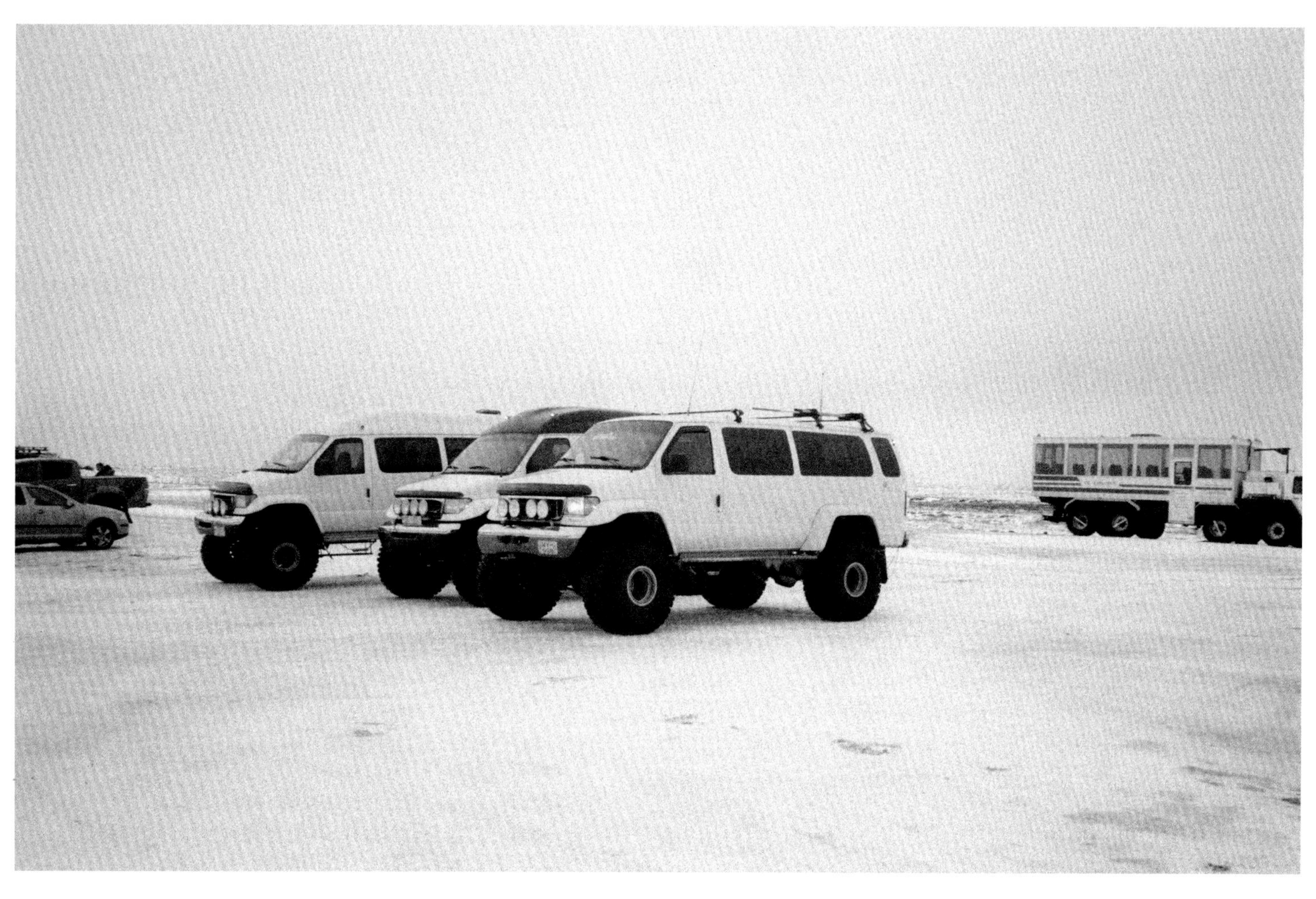

Cars, 2014
from the *Fog Patches* series
inkjet print
15 x 23 cm

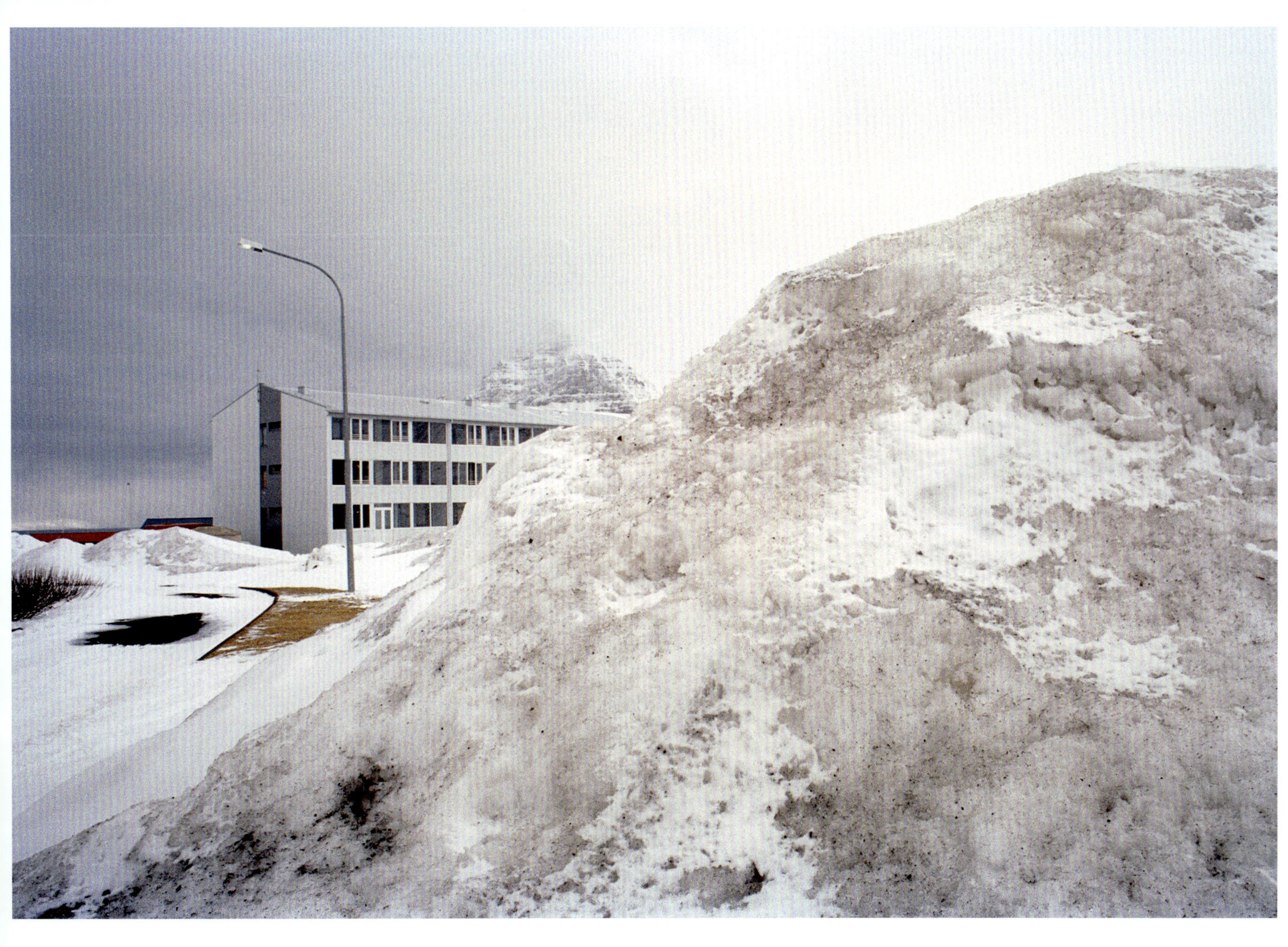

Snow Mountain, 2014
from the *Fog Patches* series
inkjet print
20 x 31.5 cm

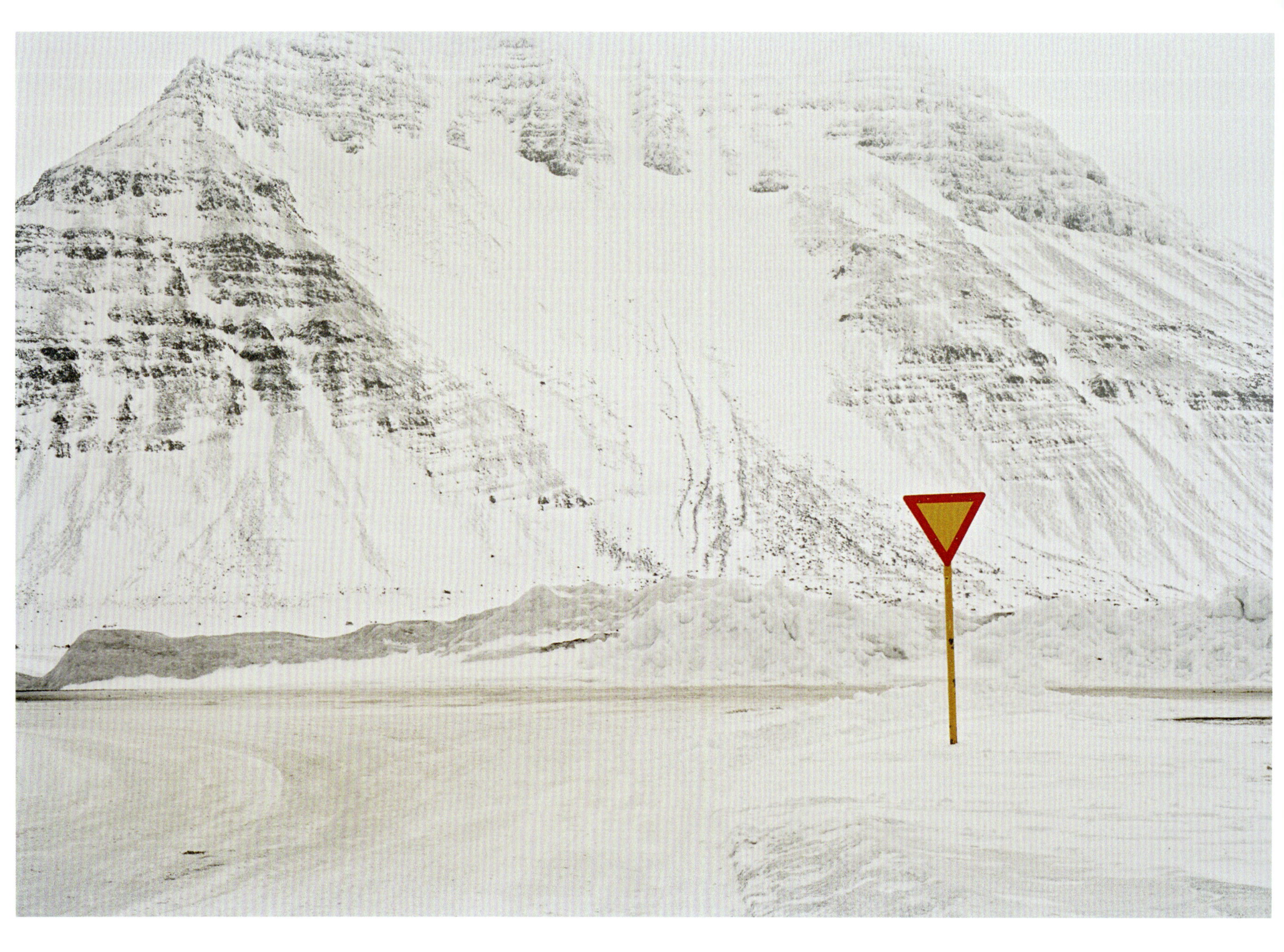

Yeld, 2014
from the *Fog Patches* series
inkjet print
33 x 47 cm

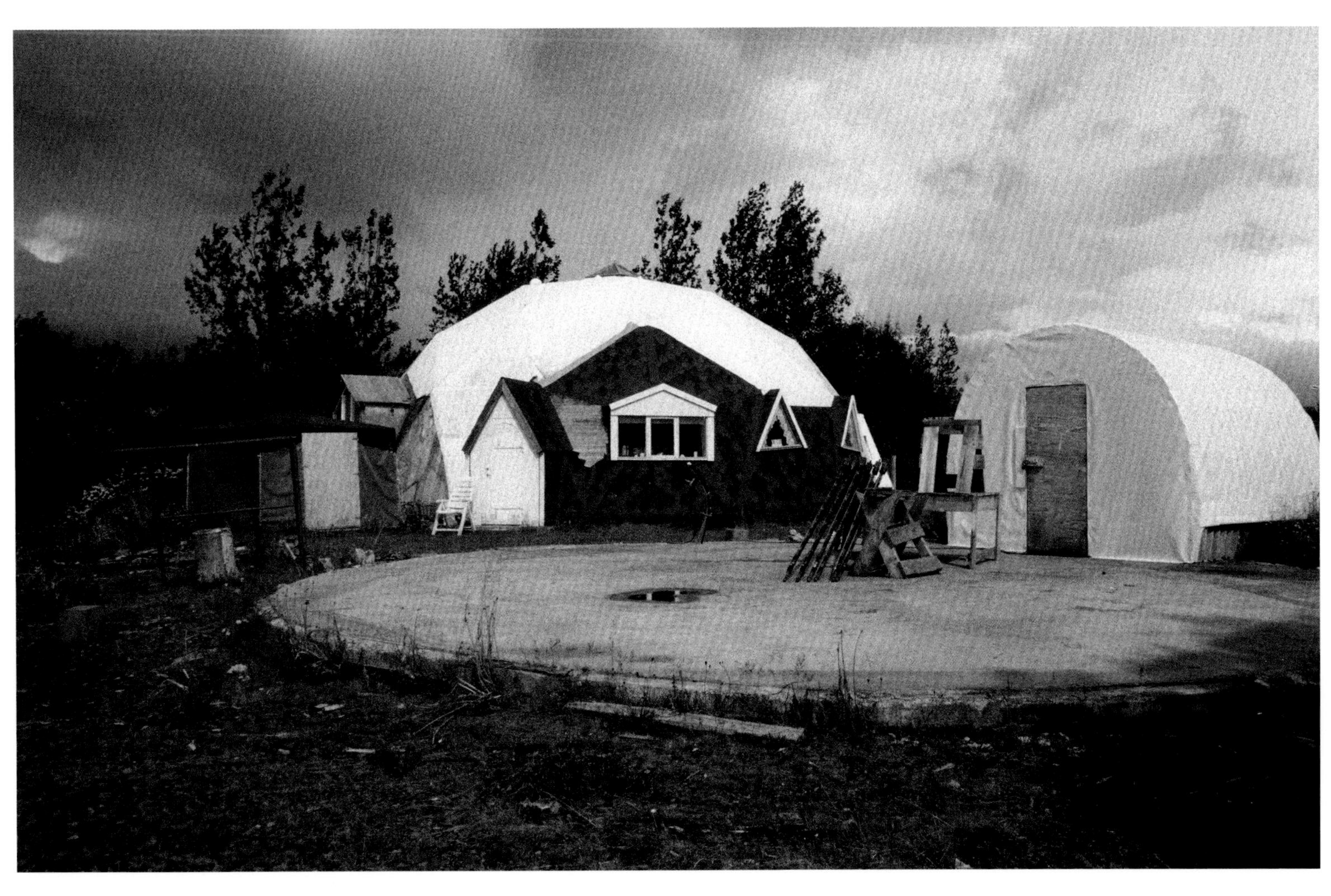

Dome House, 2014
from the *Fog Patches* series
inkjet print
15 x 23 cm

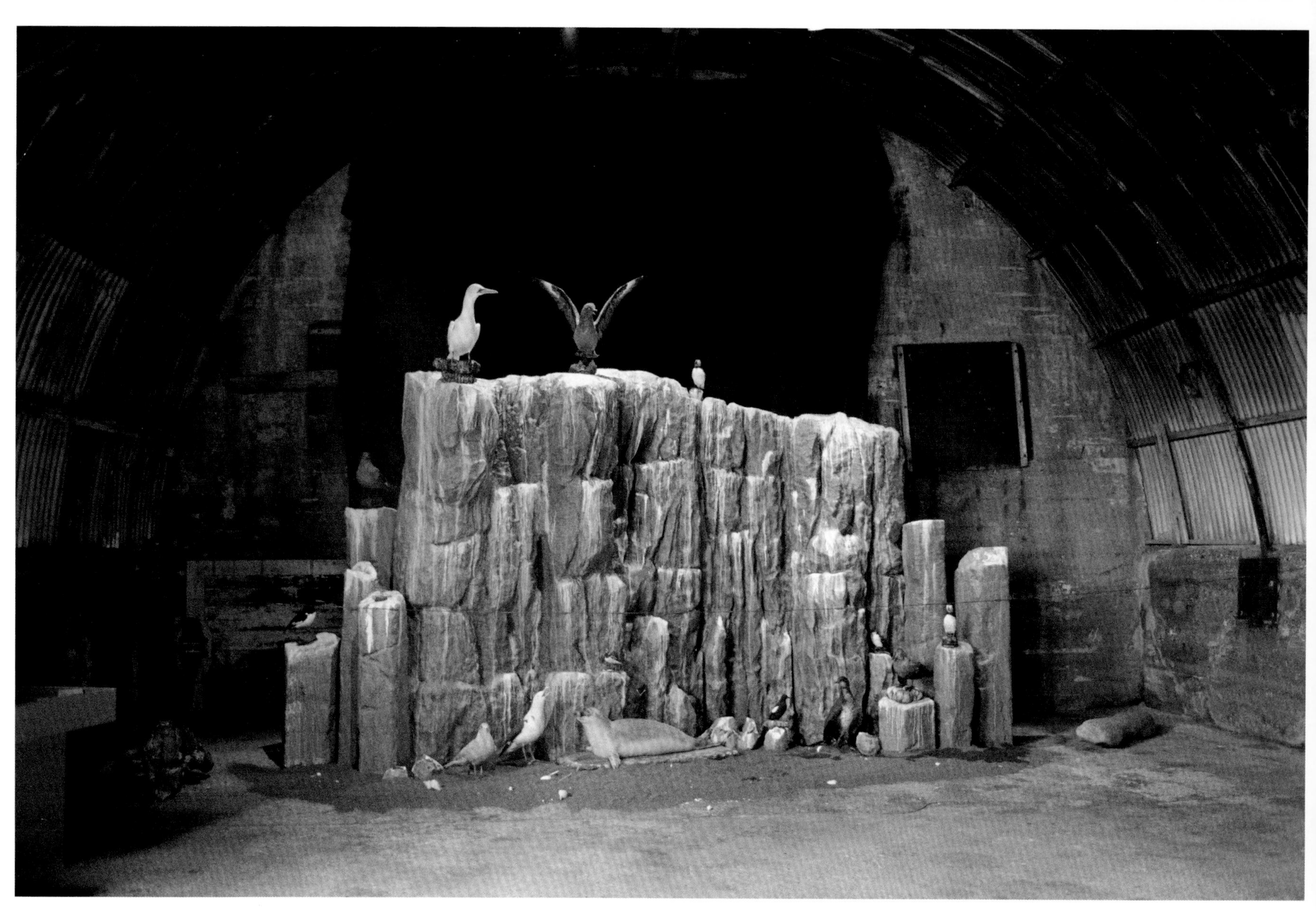

Taxidermy, 2014
from the *Fog Patches* series
inkjet print
33 x 49.5 cm

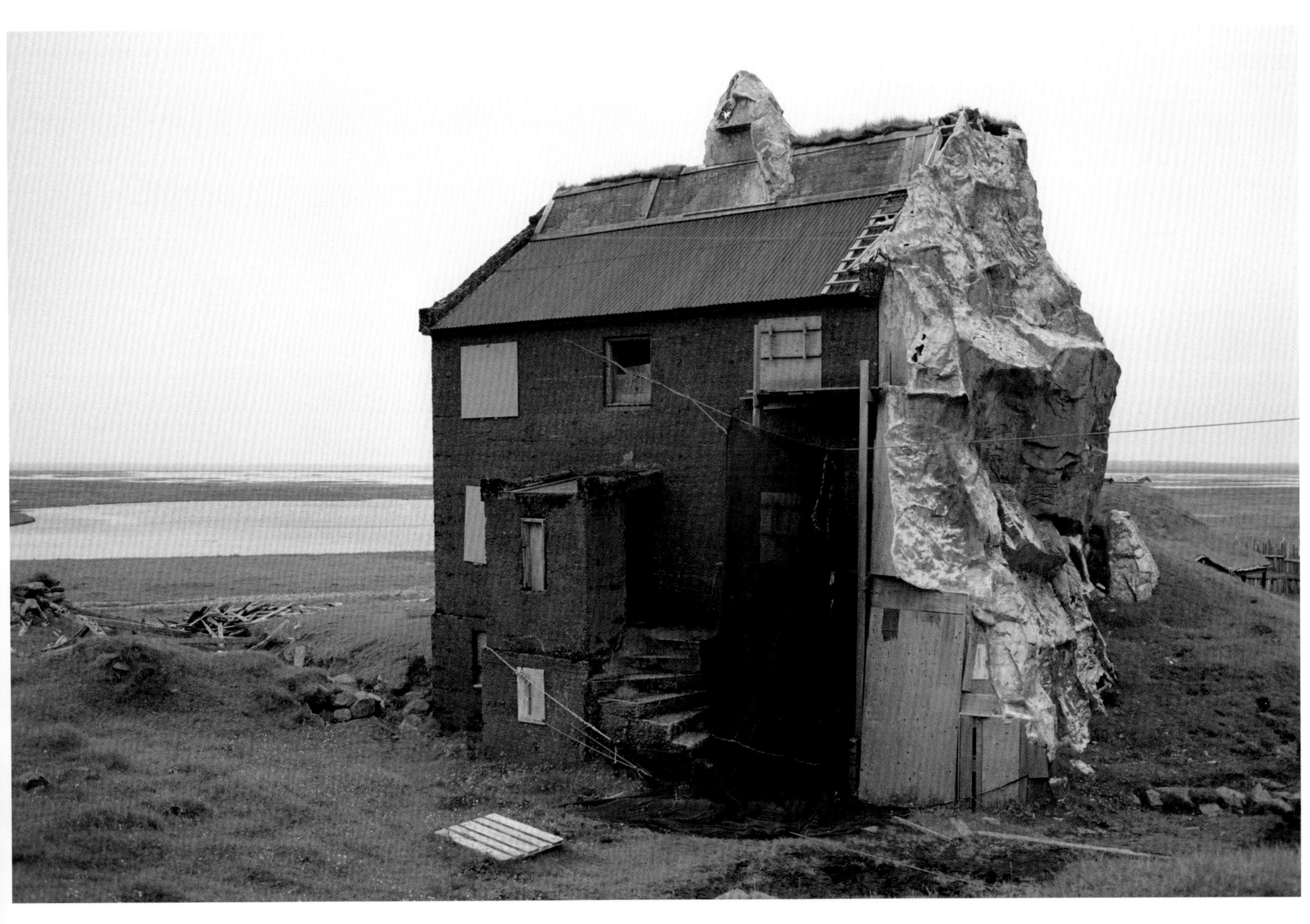

Rock House, 2014
from the *Fog Patches* series
inkjet print
33.5 x 48.5 cm

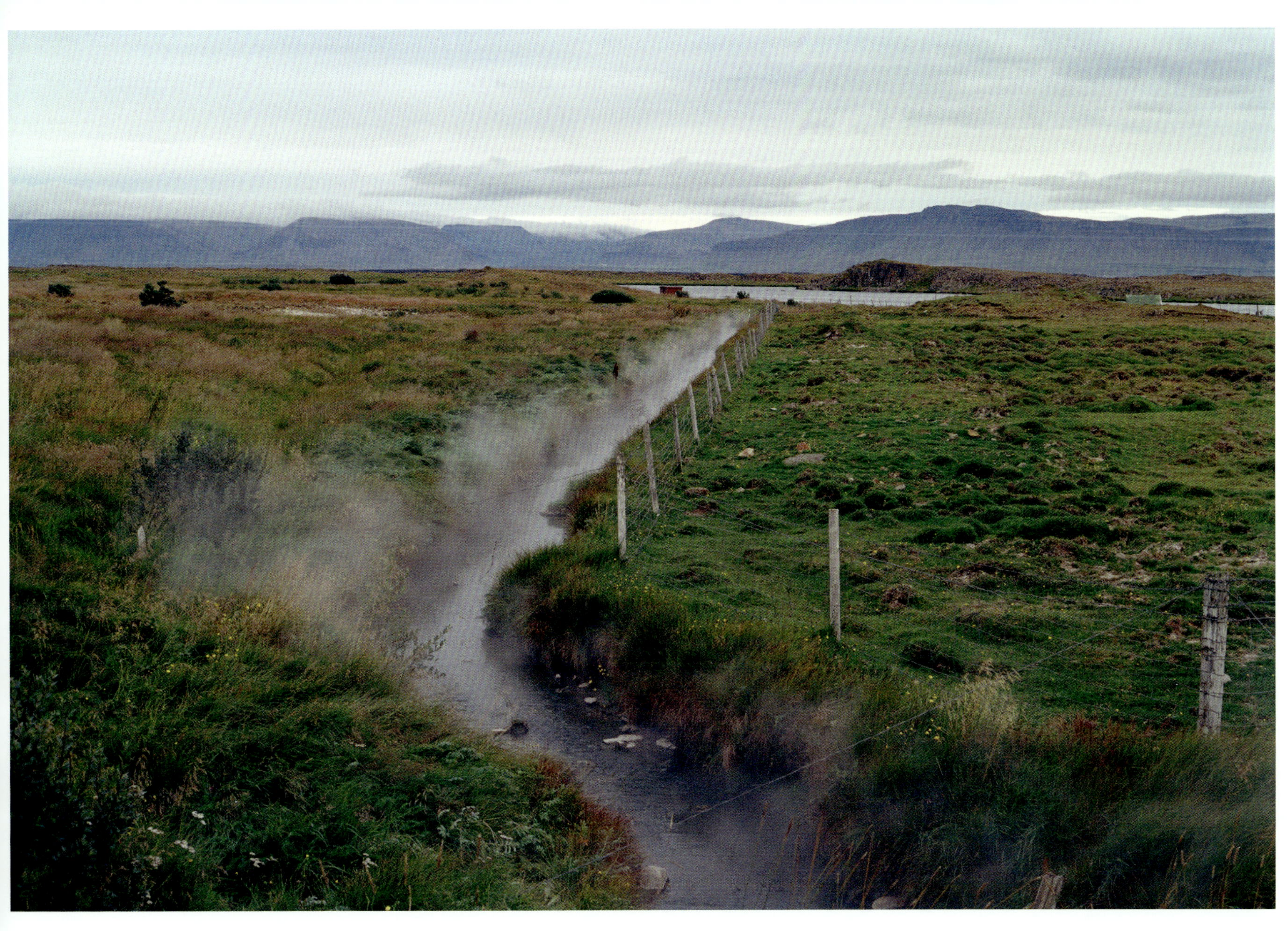

Untitled, 2012
from the *Untitled (2012)* series
inkjet print
42 x 60 cm

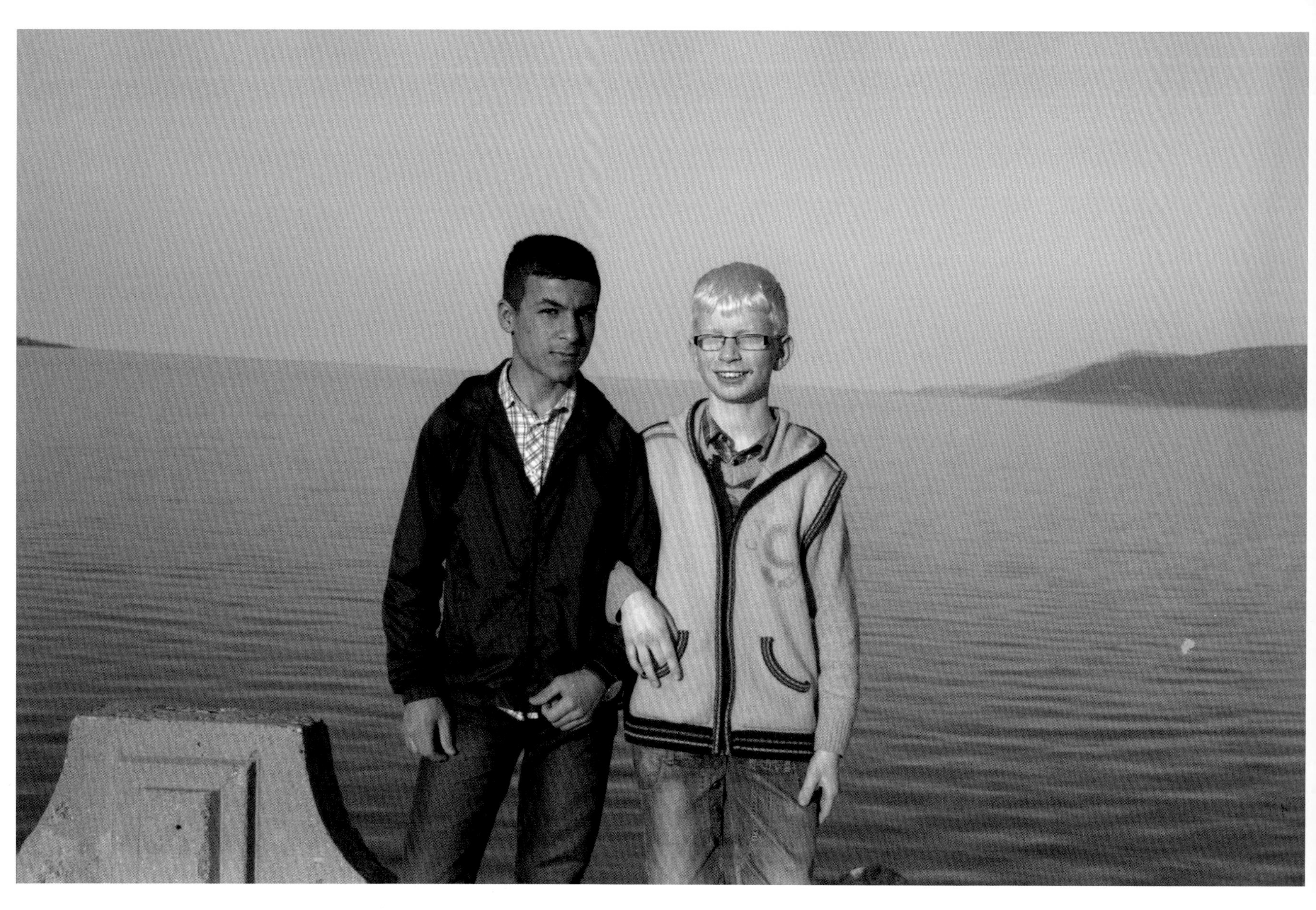

Untitled, 2012
from the *Untitled (2012)* series
inkjet print
67 x 100 cm

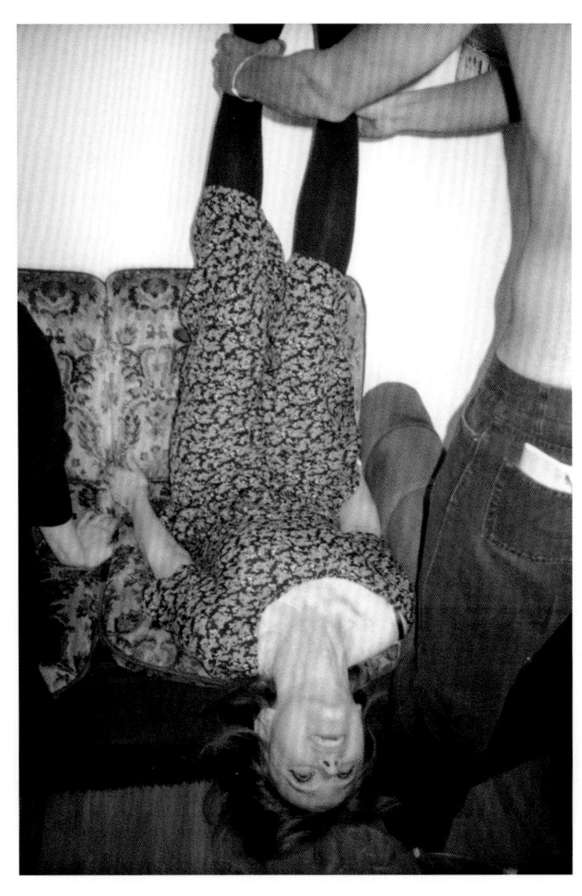

Untitled, 2012
from the *Untitled (2012)* series
inkjet print
20 x 13 cm

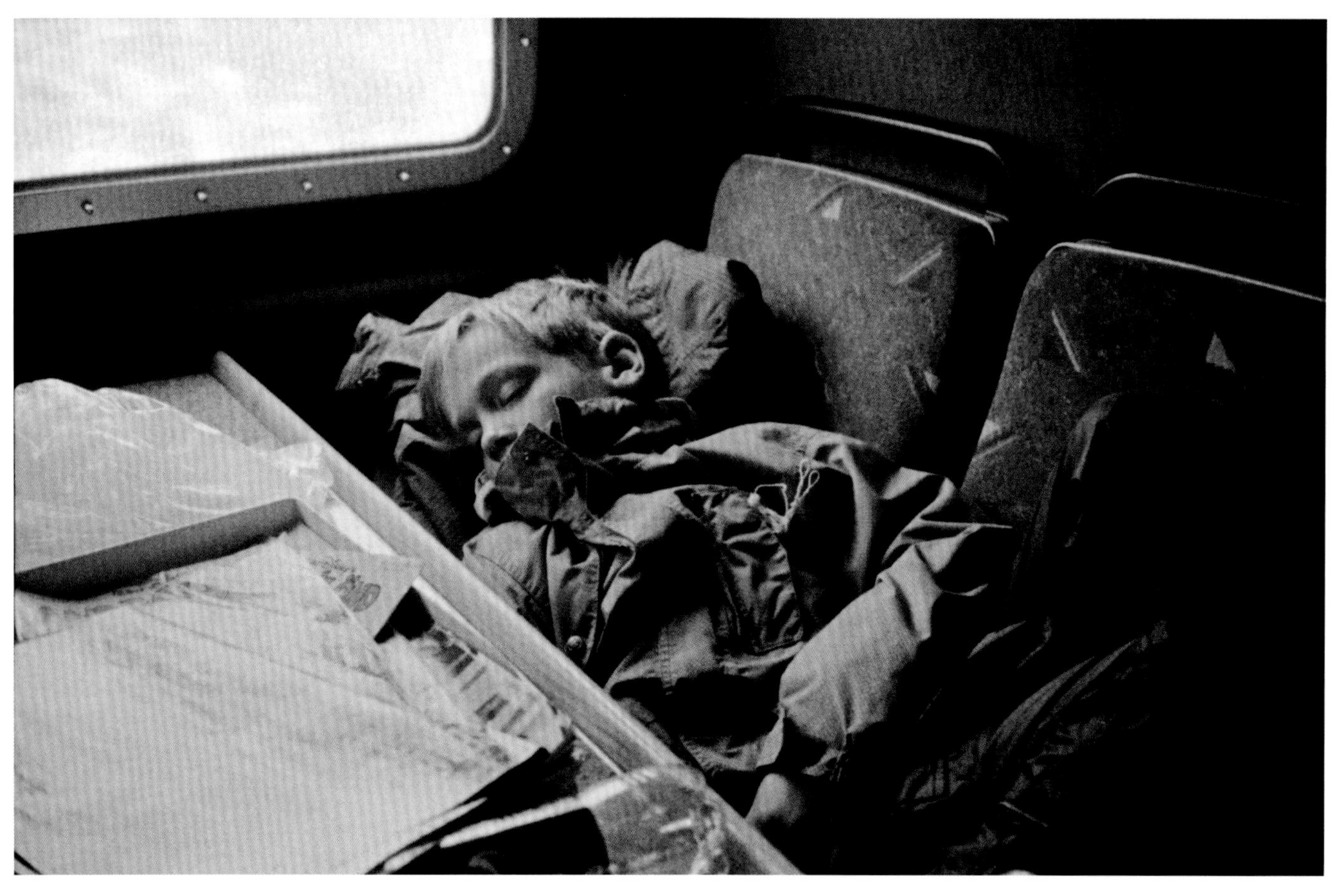

Untitled, 2012
from the *Untitled (2012)* series
inkjet print
13 x 20 cm

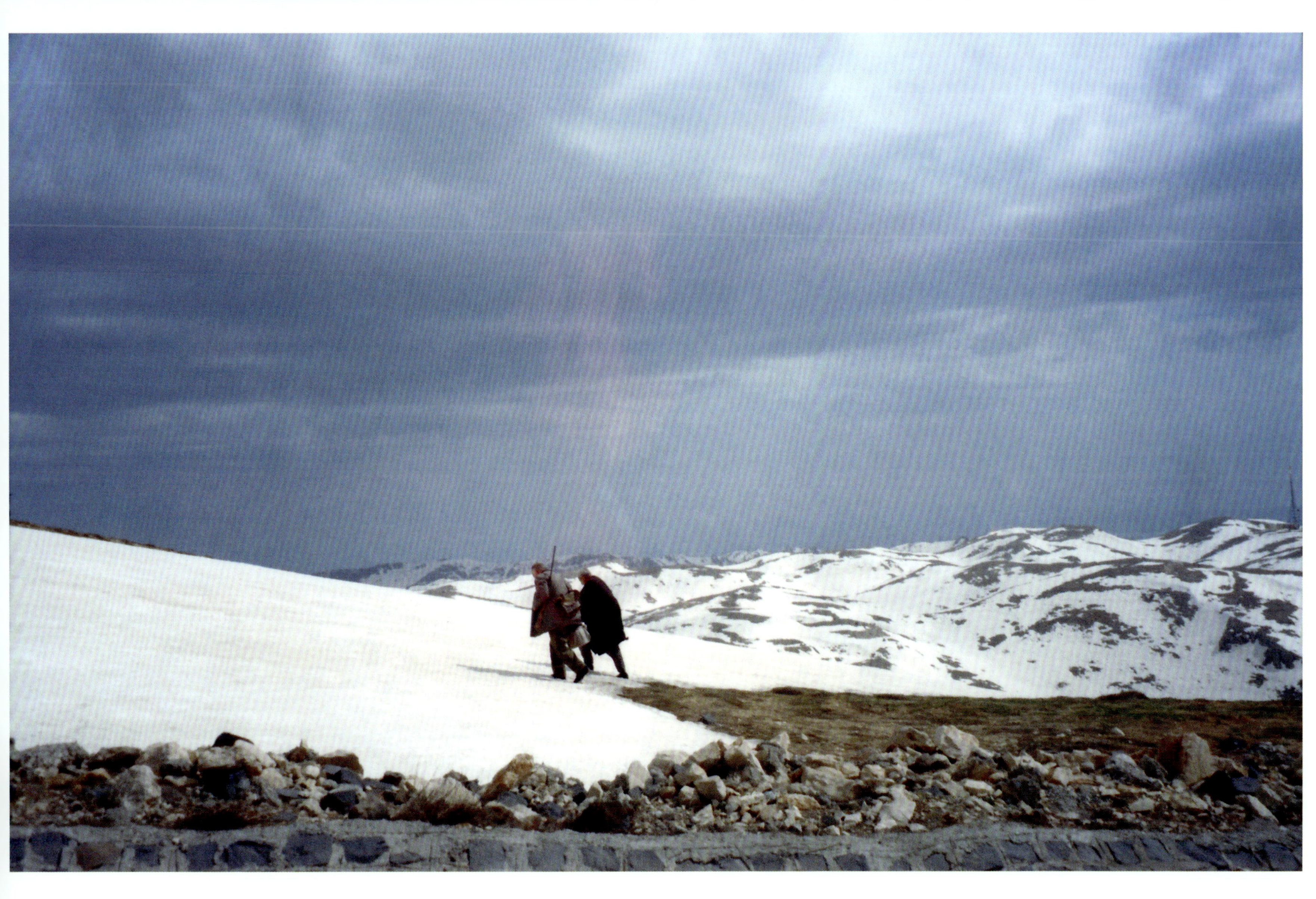

Untitled, 2012
from the *Untitled (2012)* series
inkjet print
46 x 70.5 cm

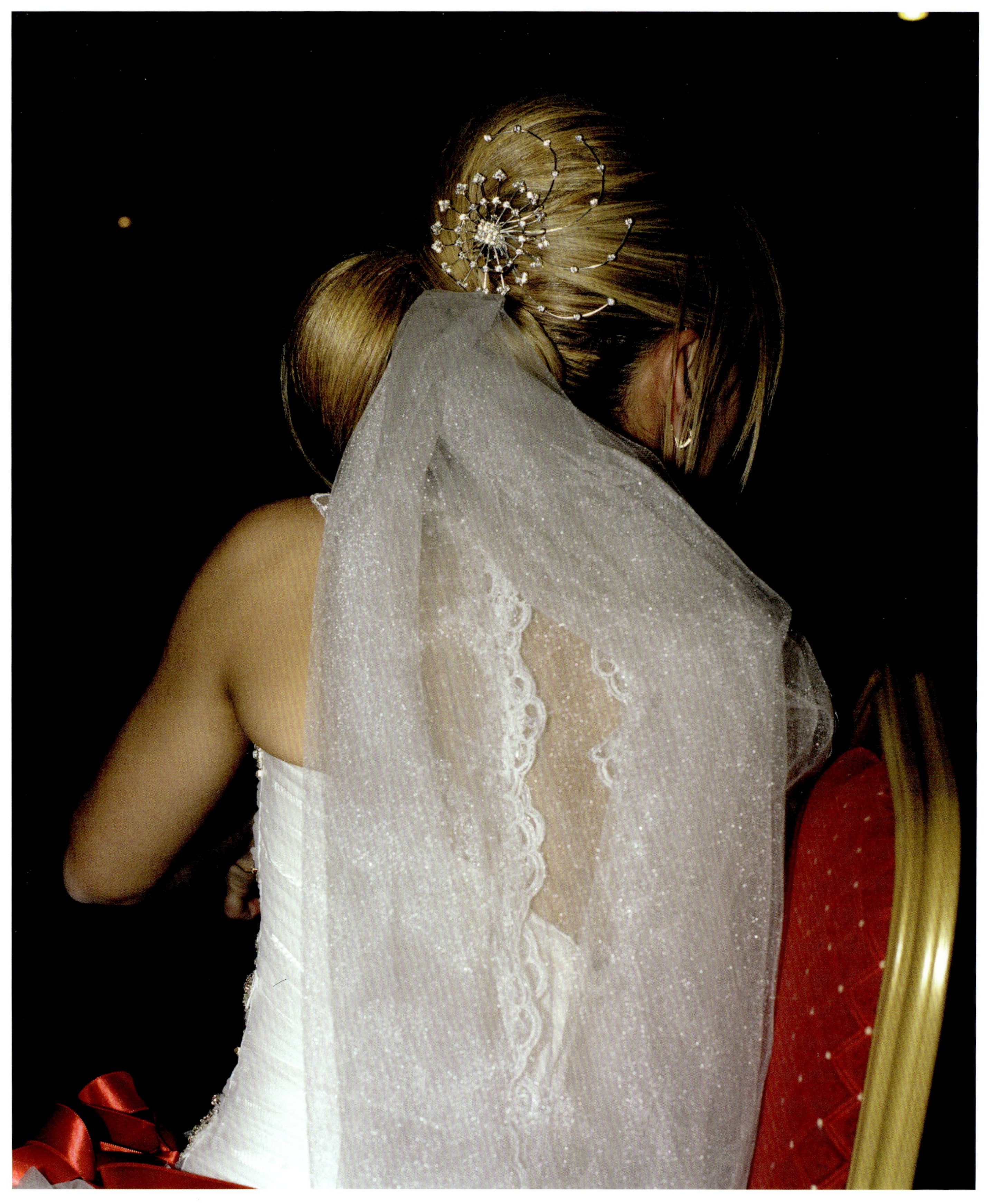

Untitled, 2012
from the *Untitled (2012)* series
inkjet print
128.5 x 105 cm

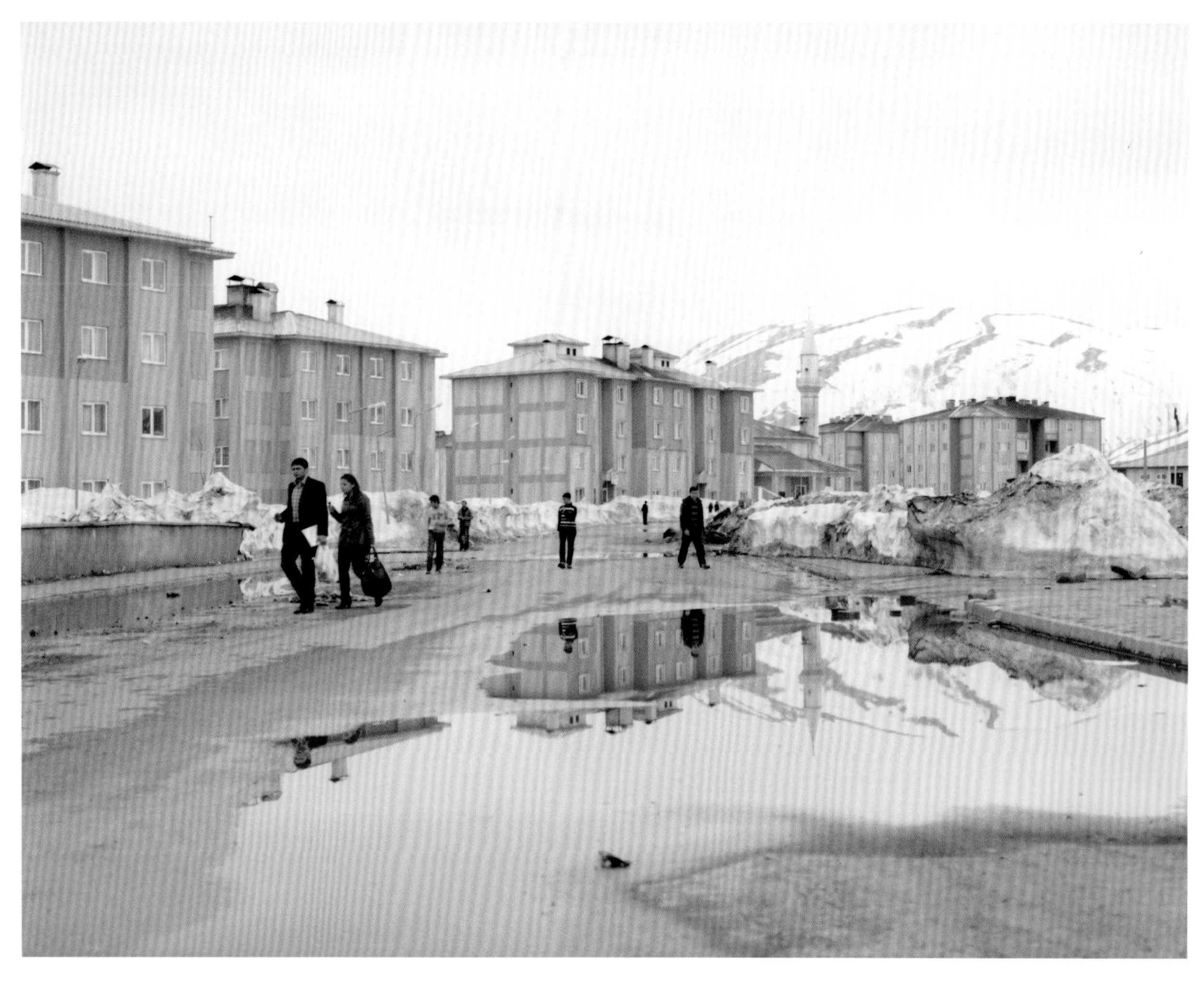

Untitled, 2012
from the *Untitled (2012)* series
inkjet print
17.5 x 20 cm

Ilkka Halso

Ilkka Halso (Orimattila, 1965) belongs to the original group of the so-called Helsinki School: a moniker coined in 2003 by Boris Hohmeyer in an article that appeared in *ART Kunstmagazin*, intended to denote that group of artists – at the time belonging to three different generations – who trained at the Department of Photography of the Aalto University School of Arts, Design and Architecture in Helsinki (until 2009: the University of Art and Design). The Helsinki School definition has lasted over time, acquiring prestige and encompassing new members; furthermore, it has become a model in the field of education, based on a conceptual use of photography, on collaboration and dialogue amongst all of its members, and on the promotion of individual approaches. Although the works of the artists belonging to the group cannot be classified under one single genre or style, there are a number of aspects that are common in their approach, including a marked interest in nature. It is a focus that has its source in the very culture of Finland, a scarcely populated country in which the natural landscape continues to play a significant role. Even before completing his Master's in 1992, Halso was already focusing on the visual imagination of the natural sciences; as he himself states on his website, 'I have the attitude of a joyous scientist, without any obligation for truth or results'.

The works produced in the first decade of his career – such as *De Pterygotis* (1990), *Evolution* (1992), *Cultural Landscape* (1994), *Anatomiche Kabinet* (1997) and *Excavation* (1998) – were followed by *Restoration* (2000–05), a series of night-time photographs with which the artist introduced the theme of the 'restoration' and pro-active care of the natural world, which he would then develop further in subsequent works such as *Museum of Nature* (2003–08), *Tree Works* (2006–10) and *Naturale* (started in 2011 and still underway). While in this latter work, as in *Museum of Nature*, Halso has recourse to 3D technology to integrate rendering and real images, his activity can in general be interpreted as a form of land art of its own. His large-format photographs are the result of direct interventions on the landscape; by investigating the relationship between nature, technology and architecture they offer a reflection on the way in which human beings interact with the natural environment.

The photograph in the collection, *Garden with a View – Inside view*, is the outcome of an installation staged in 2010 at Villa Roosa in Orimattila, the artist's hometown. Around a bunch of trees, Halso built a structure of green netting and tubes (those normally used to erect scaffolding) that constitute visual devices for looking at nature in a different way: no longer as a resource to be exploited to meet human needs but, rather, as a precious asset to be treasured, as a work of art to be conserved and displayed in museums, available to everyone. The scaffolding alludes to the urgent requirement to take responsibility for nature, to preserve and restore it, just as we do with the historic monuments and buildings that constitute our shared heritage.

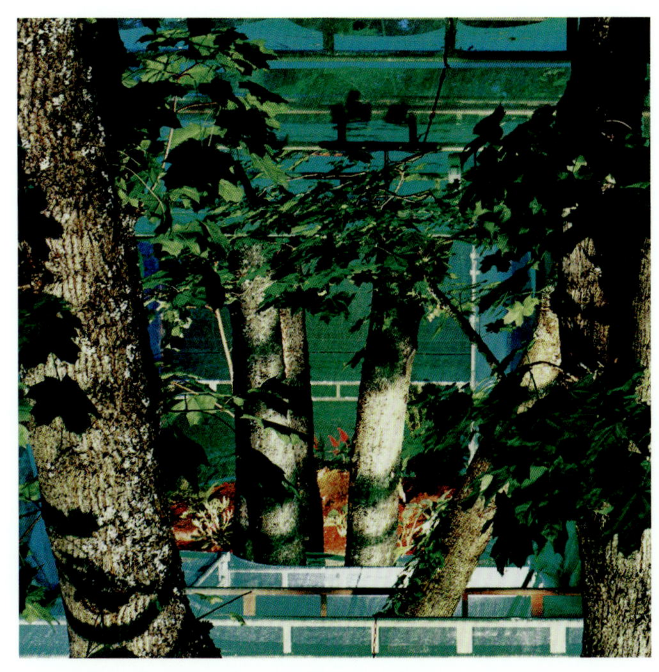

Garden with a View – Inside view, 2010
(detail)

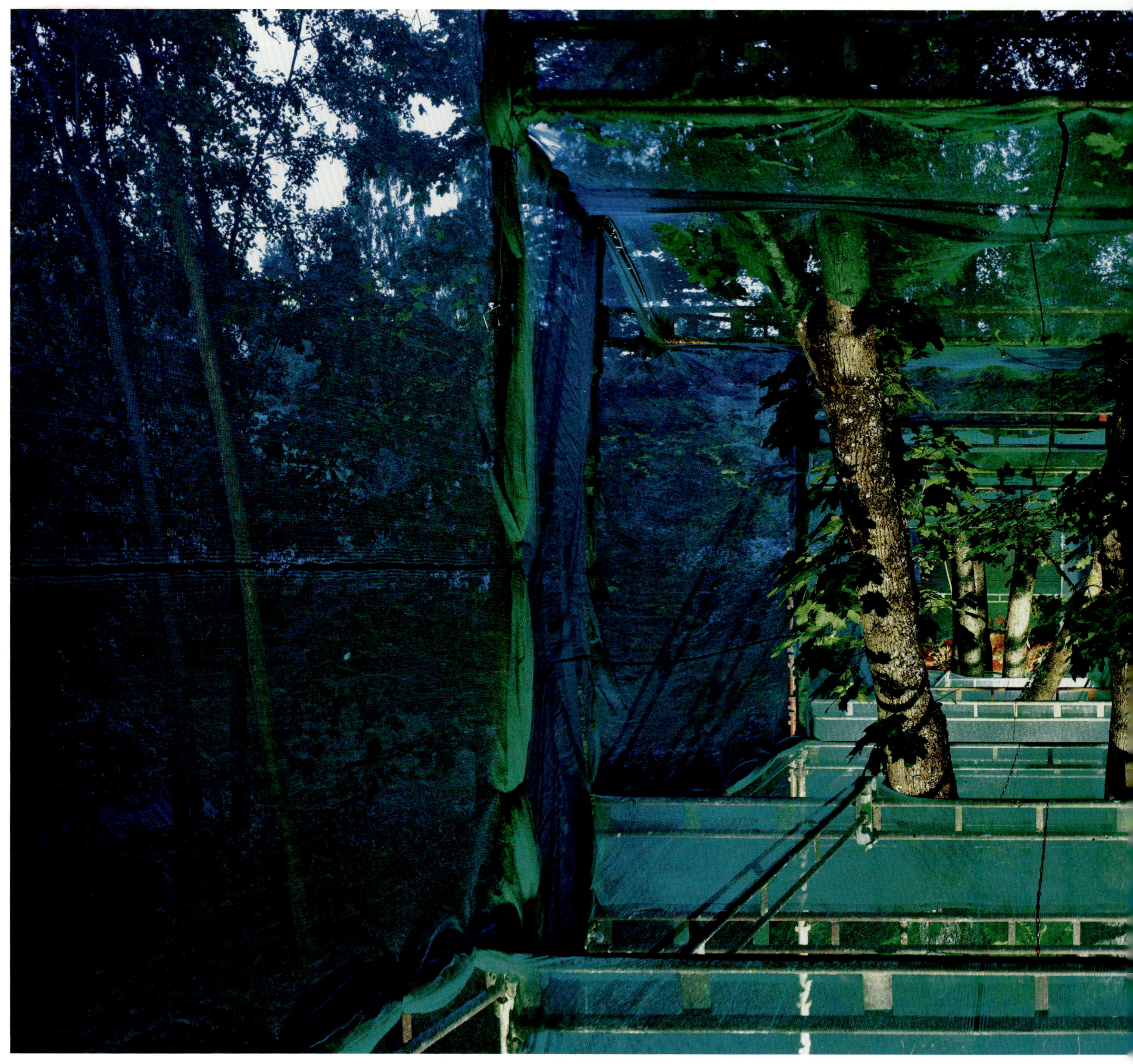

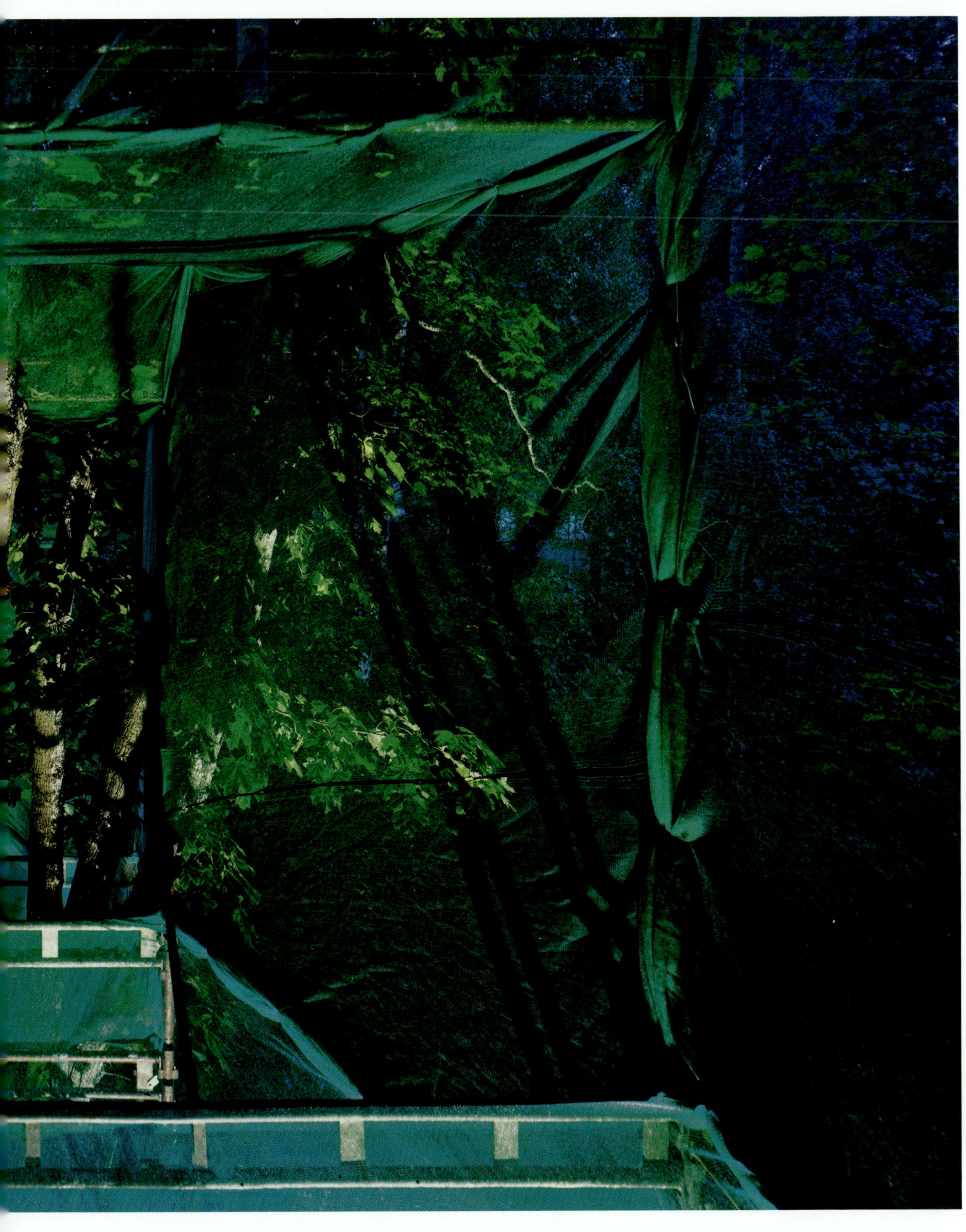

Garden with a View – Inside view, 2010
c-print mounted on Diasec
100 x 189 cm

Sarah Jones

Born in 1959 in London, Sarah Jones still lives in the English capital, where she works as an artist and a Reader in Photography at the Royal College of Art. Her interest in the medium of photography emerged during her studies in Fine Art and Contemporary Dance at Goldsmiths College (which she began in 1978, graduating in 1981). It was there that she realised the dark room was her congenial workspace; fascinated by the limits of photography, she focused on exploring the specific nature of the photographic language and the relationship it establishes with experience, reality and the everyday. In 1994, she returned to Goldsmiths College and, two years later, completed her Master's degree in Fine Arts. There, she was exposed to the psychoanalytical theories of Sigmund Freud and Jacques Lacan and began work on a photographic series dedicated to psychoanalysts' couches and offices; the style of these photographs – documentary in nature, but also pared down and enigmatic – soon garnered her considerable international acclaim.

As the artist stated in a conversation with A. M. Homes, published in her monograph *Sarah Jones* (Violette, 2013), 'Photography allows us to scrutinize something; like putting a glass dish over a specimen to look more closely at it. I'm really interested in what can be expressed with the most limited of means or well chosen vocabulary'. In line with this idea, Jones works by means of the serial analysis of a number of carefully selected subjects and across a number of themes, exploring the formal aspects of photography, such as measuring, transcription onto the photographic surface, and light.

Her works include portraits of young women in domestic settings or in city parks, studies of life models and of places associated with psychoanalysis or art. Her very recent *Cabinet* series of still lifes depicts found objects assembled in the studio.

A major part of the artist's recent work has been constituted by portraits of horses and rose plants, both emerging out of a reflection on stereographic photography. Attracted by the variance between the two images that compose stereographs, Jones worked on the concept of mirroring, photographing roses in a London park both frontally and from behind, investigating the relationship between camera, subject and viewer, and between real space and photographic space. In these works, characterised by a nocturnal atmosphere even though the shots were taken during the day, lighting performs a central role. Produced using studio lights that only illuminate the foreground of the scene, the photographs make the subjects appear isolated, standing out against a black background that seems to squash and flatten the roses onto the photographic surface, evoking pressed flowers conserved as a memento between the pages of a book. Although the series on horses also includes diptychs of mirrored photographs, *Horse (profile) (black) (I)* 2010 is a single image in which light again plays a fundamental role. It is light that delineates the mane of a black horse, positioned against a black photographic backdrop, tracing out its musculature and illuminating the blue of its eye. As well as containing a reference to the history of photography, recalling the black horse immortalised by Muybridge in his studies of movement, the work is a homage to photography itself and to the visual capacity that an intelligent handling of the material can make it possible to exploit.

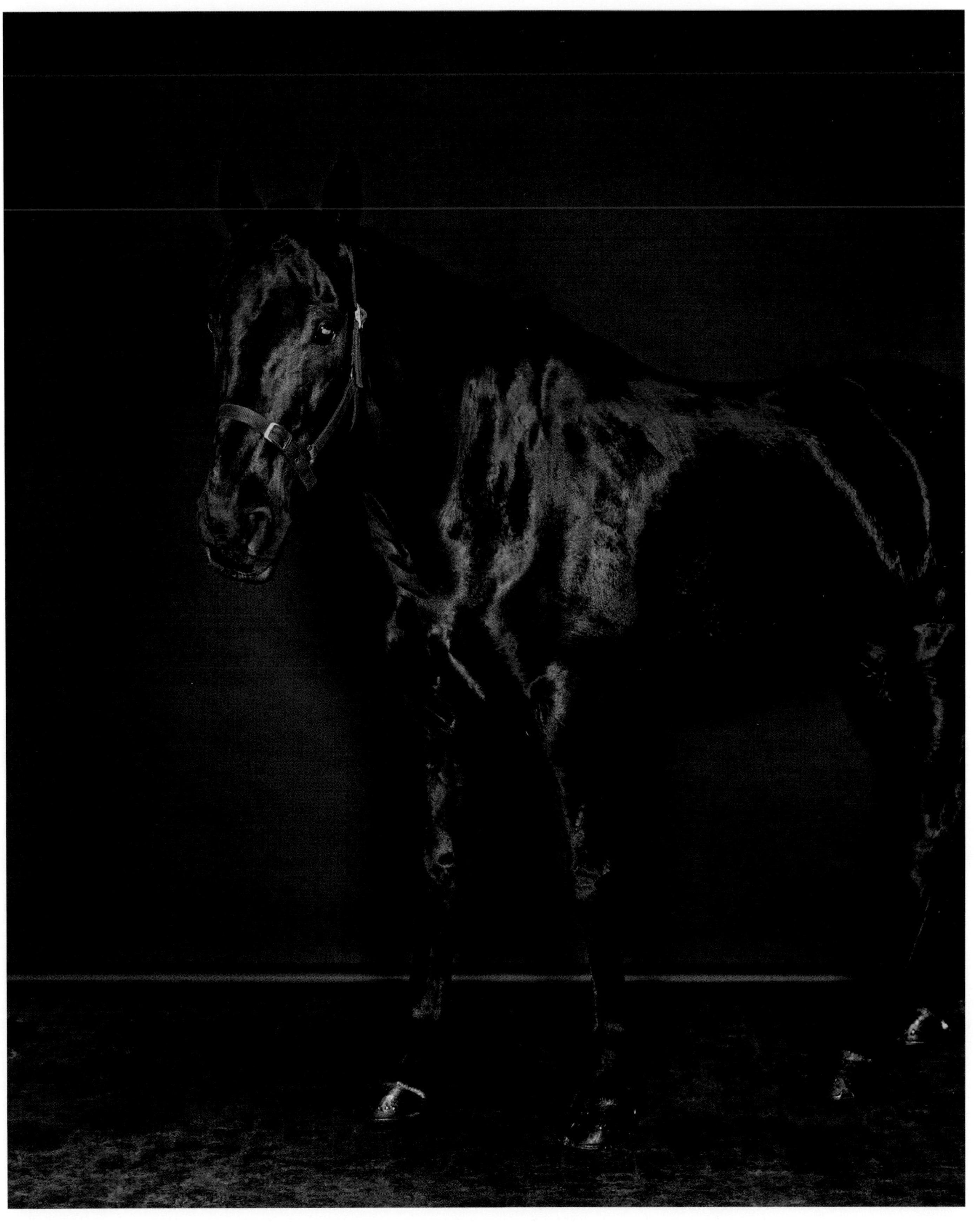

Horse (profile) (black) (I), 2010
c-print
152 x 122 cm

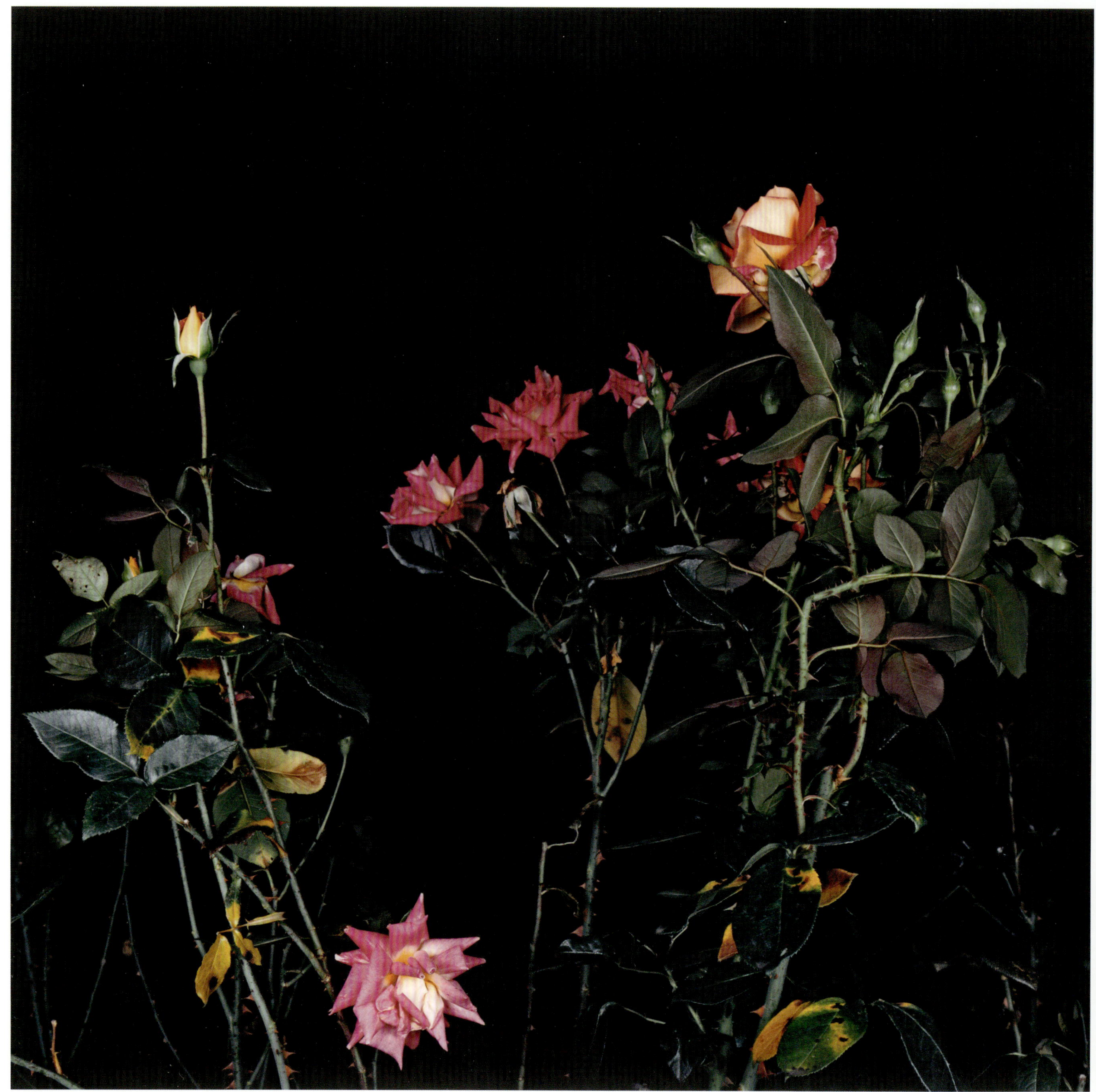

The Rose Gardens (Orange) (I), 2002
c-print
150 x 150 cm

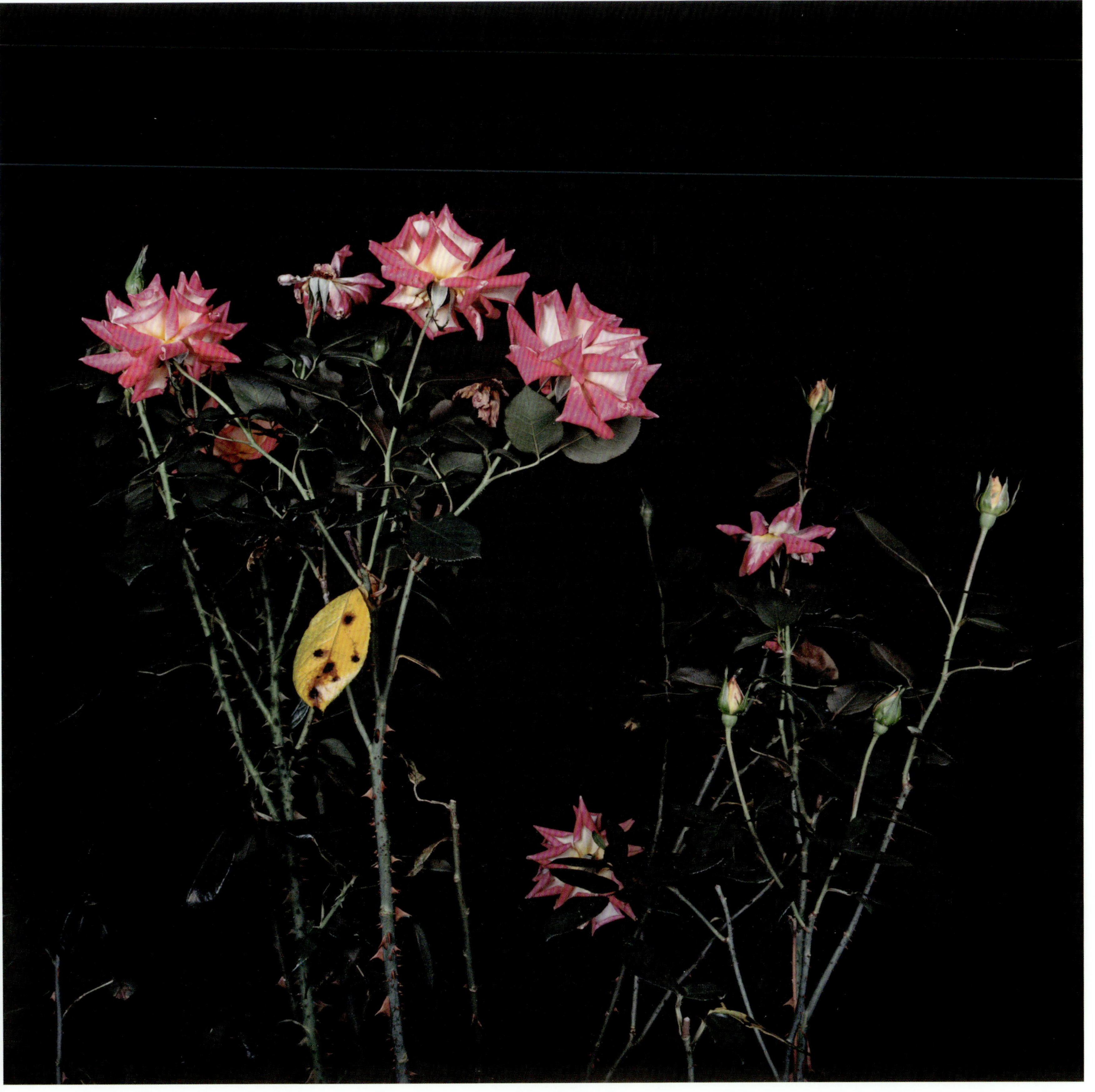

The Rose Gardens (Magenta) (I), 2002
c-print
150 x 150 cm

Sanna Kannisto

The Finnish artist Sanna Kannisto studied photography at the Turku School of Art and Communication and, subsequently, at the renowned Aalto University School of Arts, Design and Architecture in Helsinki (at the time still named University of Art and Design), which for years has been a leading institution for the training of photographers – so much so that the celebrated Helsinki School was born within it.

Born in Hämeenlinna in 1974, Kannisto lives in the Finnish capital, but since 1997 has spent long periods in countries such as Brazil, Costa Rica, Peru and French Guyana, studying the luxuriant natural environment of the rainforests alongside scientists and biologists. In line with her training, which was oriented towards the conceptual use of photography, interdisciplinary collaboration and expressive freedom, Kannisto deals with the natural world through different approaches and perspectives, investigating the way in which it is represented by art and science. While she has often derived her research theories and methods from the scientific field, her work is not lacking in references to conceptual artistic practices in their turn based on quasi-scientific methods, nor in connections to the still-life traditions of the seventeenth and eighteenth centuries and to Romanticism. Her works, all characterized by a high level of aesthetic rigour, take on a multitude of forms: from images that capture animals or natural elements in their original context, through compositions assembled in sets constructed on site, the structures of which often appear within frames, all the way to larger images that include the artist herself portrayed in the act of observing, immersed in nature or surrounded by her research tools.

Working with teams of researchers at biological field-stations, Kannisto has participated in projects that involve the capture and study of birds and bats. Many series are dedicated to hummingbirds, which have fascinated the artist since she found out she was able to observe them up-close and with her own specific tools. As Kannisto explains: 'I like the fact that in the *Act of Flying* series the bird's stopped motion is so sculptural. It's a fully charged force. I feel that the hummingbird is like a sculptural object and I'm able to rotate it in space by means of photography. The speed of the bird is really challenging to frame'. The white background used for *Act of Flying* (2006) is a reference to scientific visualisation, as well as to minimalist still-life photography. The lighting, the isolation of the subject and the white space of the studio all help to focus the viewer's attention, creating metaphorically the same type of situation as a museum. This intermingling of disciplinary fields and representative modes is the cornerstone of Kannisto's entire endeavour; in the interaction between art and science – in the awareness of their respective limits and through the tapping of their potential – she succeeds in giving life to works that are surprisingly balanced between rationality and astonishment, lucid observation and perceptive emotion.

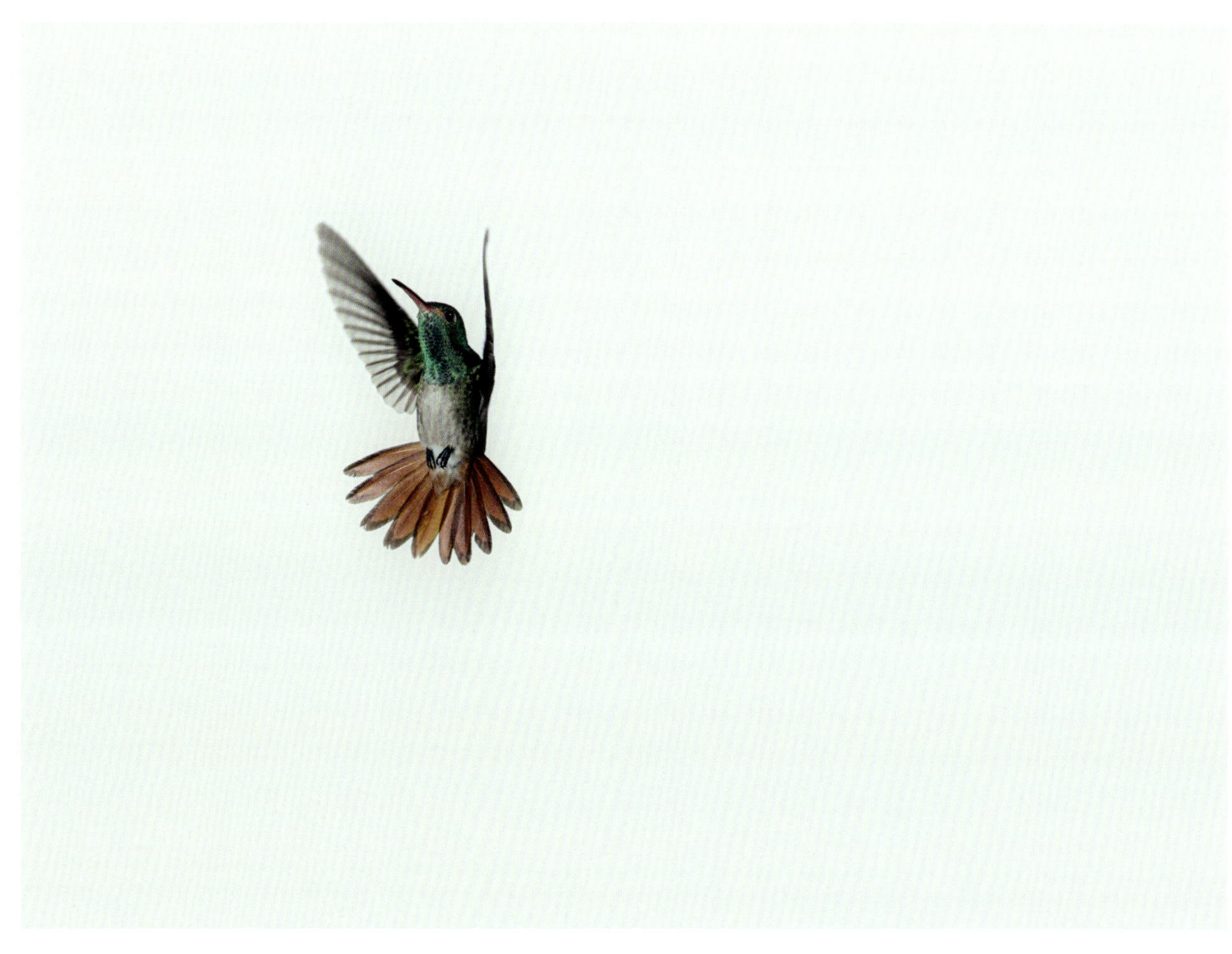

Act of Flying 16, 2006
from the *Act of Flying* series
c-print mounted on Diasec
42 x 56 cm

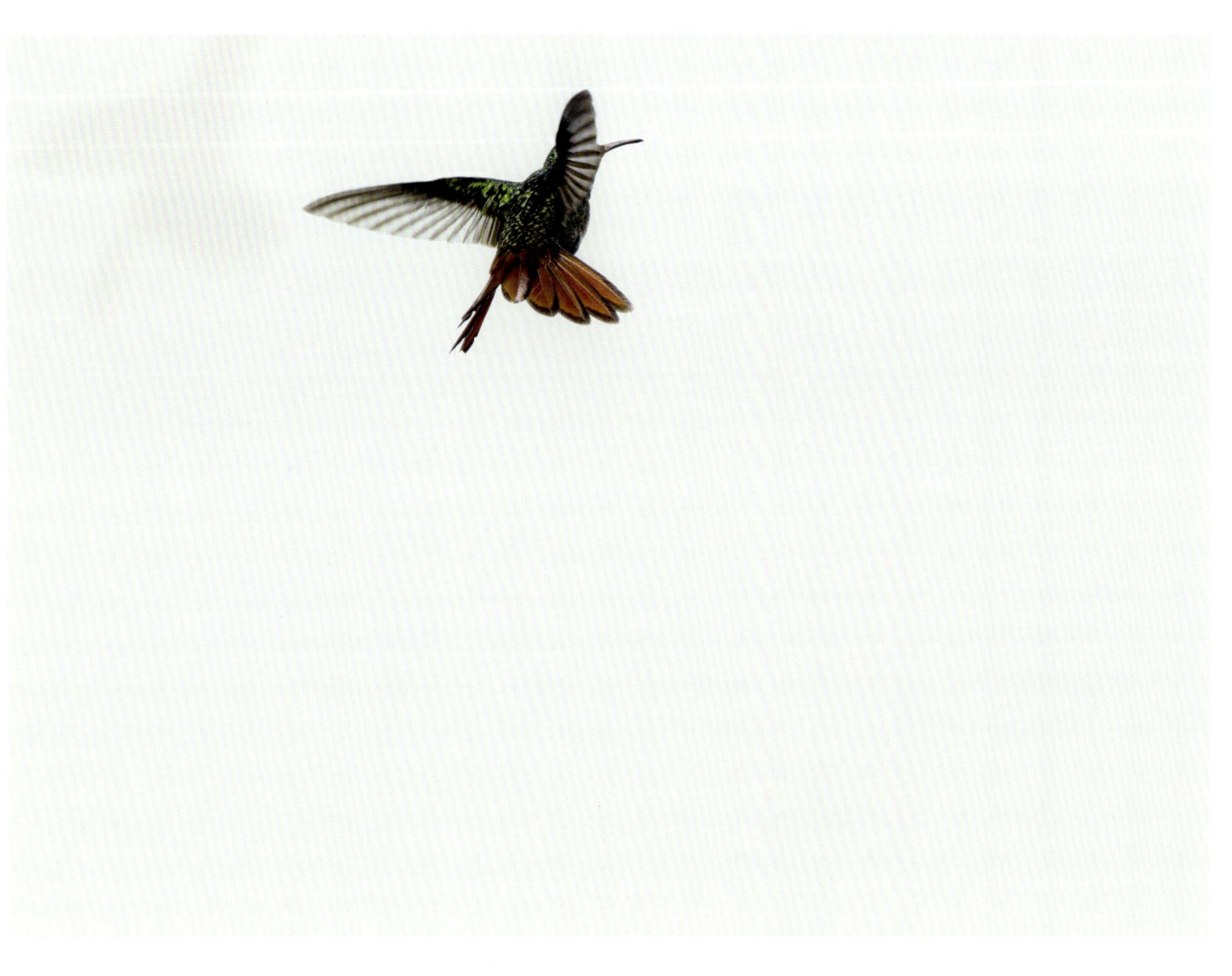

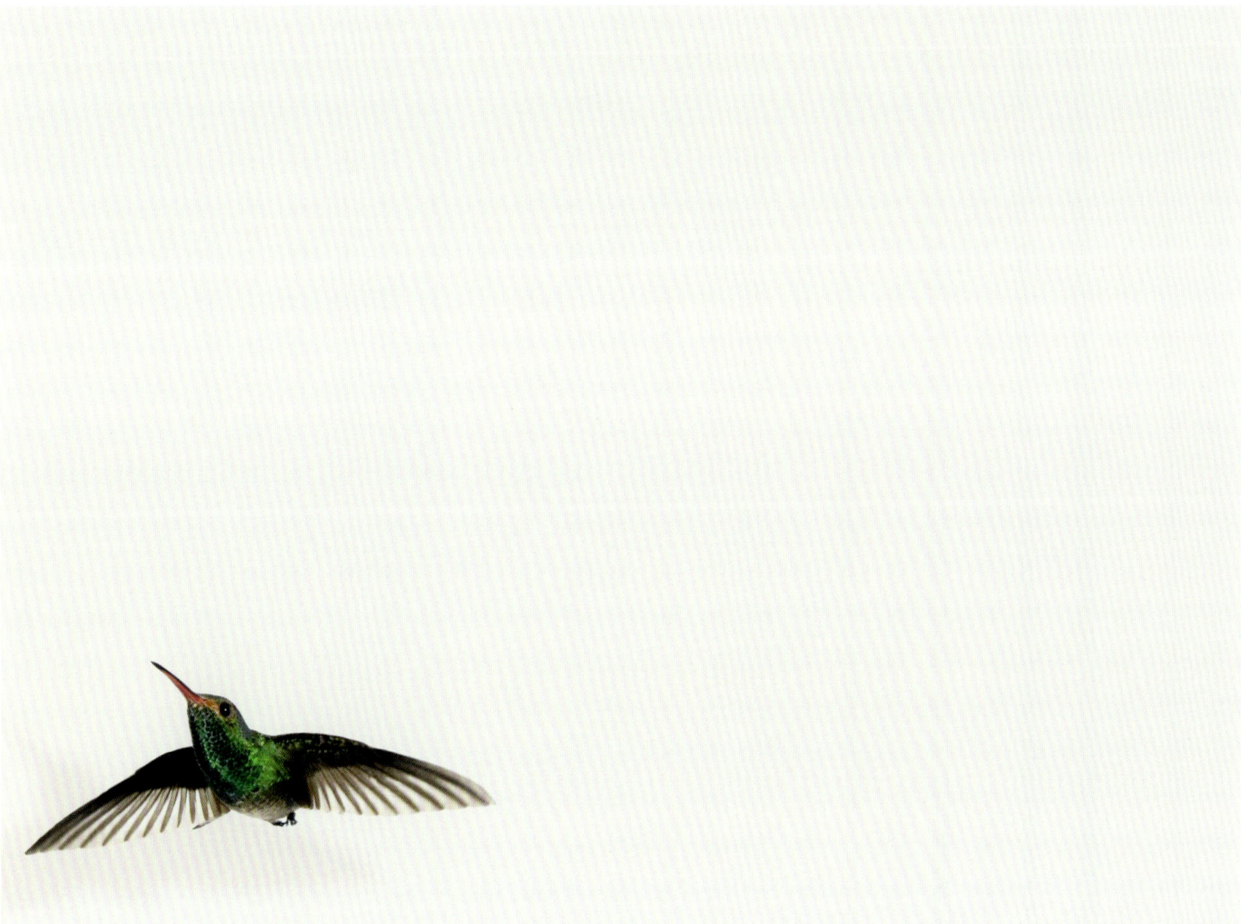

Act of Flying 6, 2006
from the *Act of Flying* series
c-print mounted on Diasec
42 x 56 cm

Act of Flying 21, 2006
from the *Act of Flying* series
c-print mounted on Diasec
42 x 56 cm

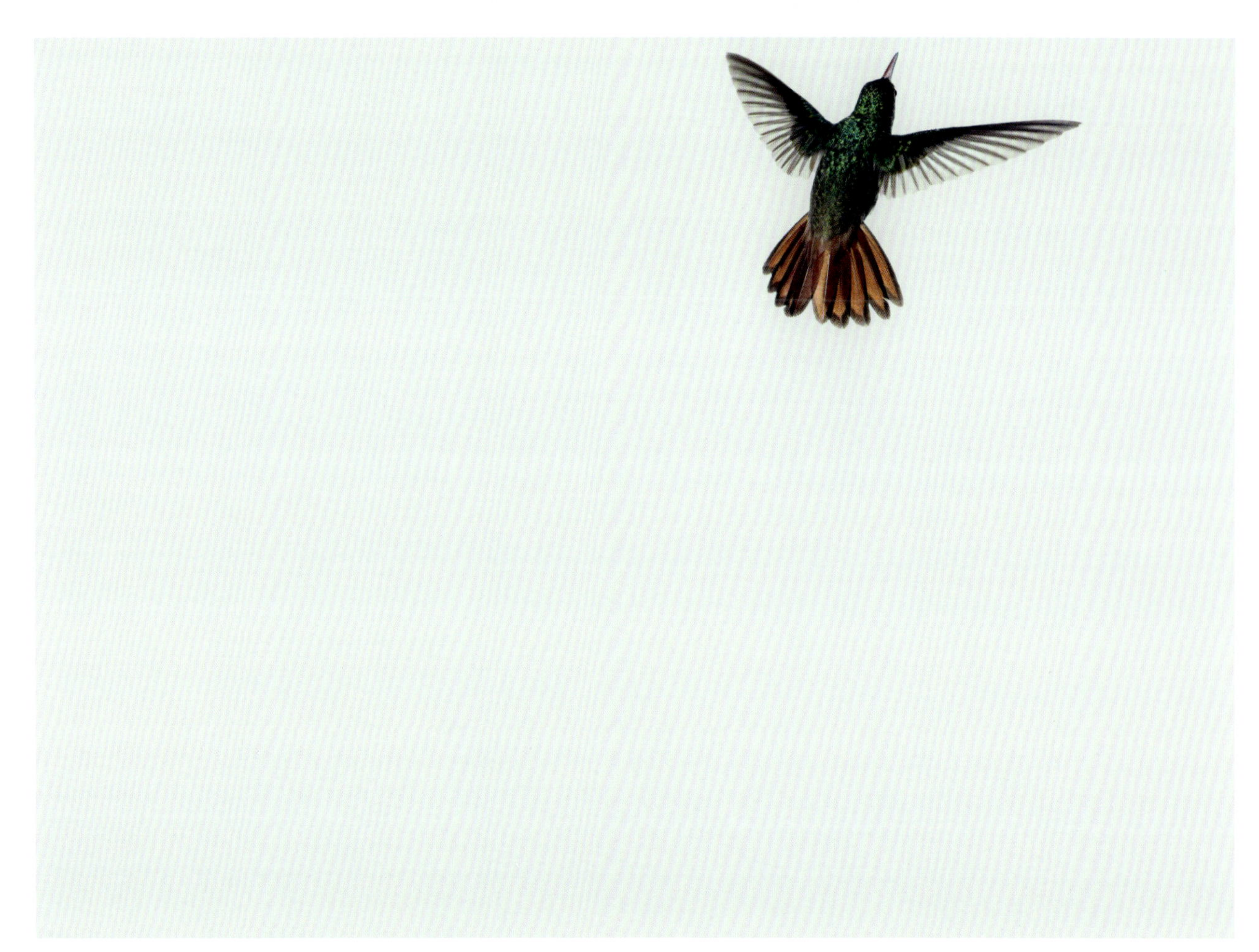

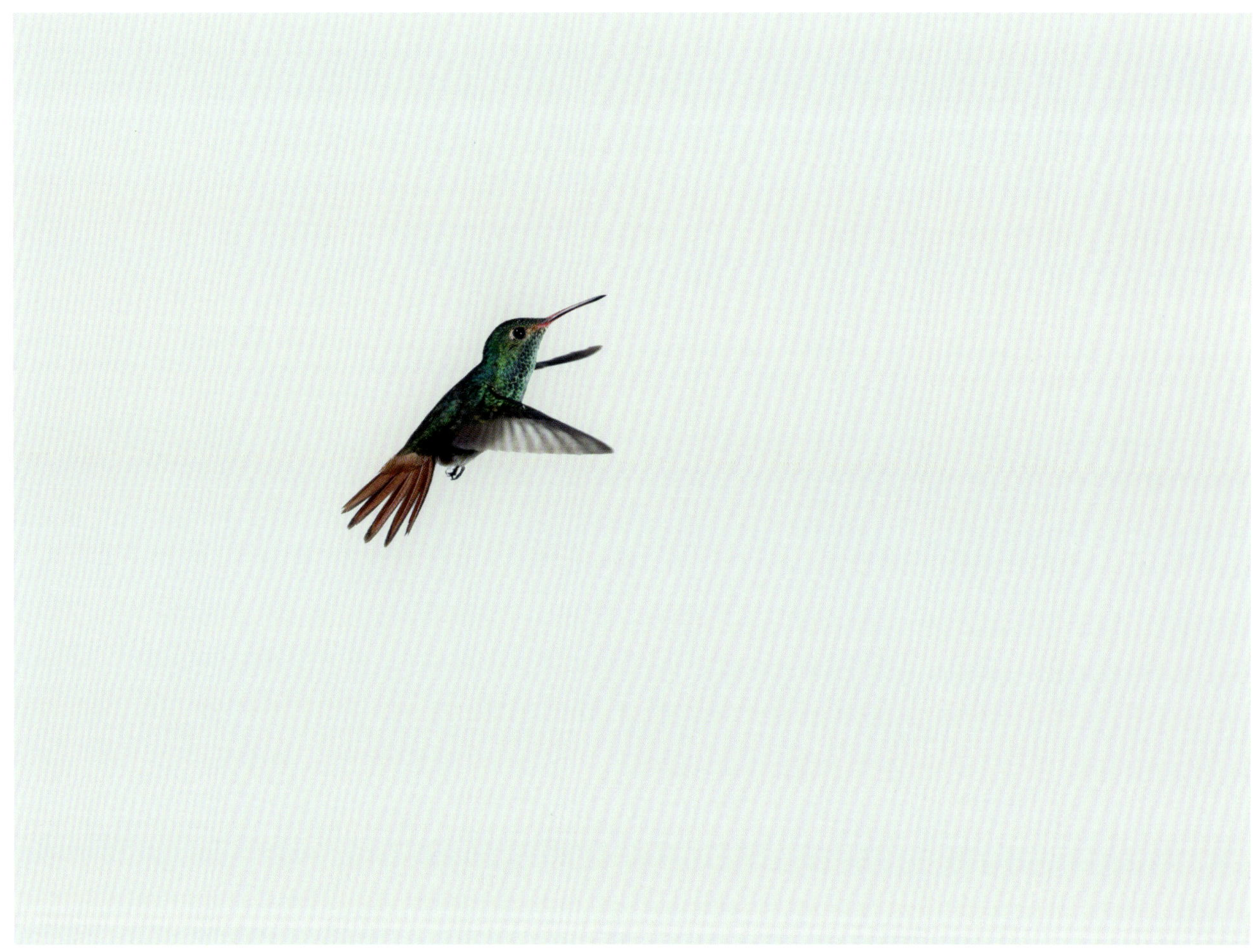

Act of Flying 9, 2006
from the *Act of Flying* series
c-print mounted on Diasec
42 x 56 cm

Act of Flying 14, 2006
from the *Act of Flying* series
c-print mounted on Diasec
42 x 56 cm

Sandra Kantanen

A member of the Helsinki School, Sandra Kantanen graduated from the University of Art and Design (today the Aalto University School of Arts, Design and Architecture) in 2003. During her Master's, she spent a year in Beijing as an exchange student at the city's Central Academy of Fine Arts. Her studies led her to explore the theme of nature through a peculiar approach, which combines a typically Finnish attitude towards the subject with the tradition of Chinese landscape painting. Committed to investigating the Oriental perspective in more depth, Kantanen visited China in 2000, describing the experience in the following words, taken from Alistair Hicks's essay in *Sandra Kantanen. Landscapes* (Hatje Cantz, 2011): 'As I found out, most of the holy mountains they had been depicting for thousands of years were almost destroyed by pollution or otherwise turned into tourist hotspots. It became for me a search for a landscape that doesn't really exist, an idealised picture'.

Since then, Kantanen has focused on the creation of an idyllic world through works that – produced in various countries, including Tibet, Japan, Croatia and Finland itself – hint at Oriental atmospheres without belonging to any particular place or time.

The idealised character of these landscapes is underlined by the specific technique developed by the artist, which makes the most of the properties of digital pigment printing to achieve an original hybrid of photography and painting. Her images are characterised by a sort of aesthetic ambiguity that prompts the viewer to question their origin. Here, photography is no longer a means of bearing witness to a given reality; rather, it provides the basis for experimentally depicting an untainted, paradisiacal natural world, which may have existed in a far-off past, and can perhaps still be found in the most uncontaminated parts of the world or perhaps, in truth, is only ever accessible through the imagination. But the artist, whose presence is made clear by the signs of her intervention on the surface of the paper, serves as the conduit through which this Arcadia becomes possible, constituted as it is by delicate flowers and soft mists, stretches of water and reflections of light, and seasons mixed together like the autumn colours that stain the leaves.

The three works in the collection, all rigorously *Untitled* in order to stress their lack of spatial and temporal reference points, invite the viewer to come face-to-face with this world, to imagine its fragrances and to savour its suspended sense of time, wishing that such a Utopia could exist in some remote place and time.

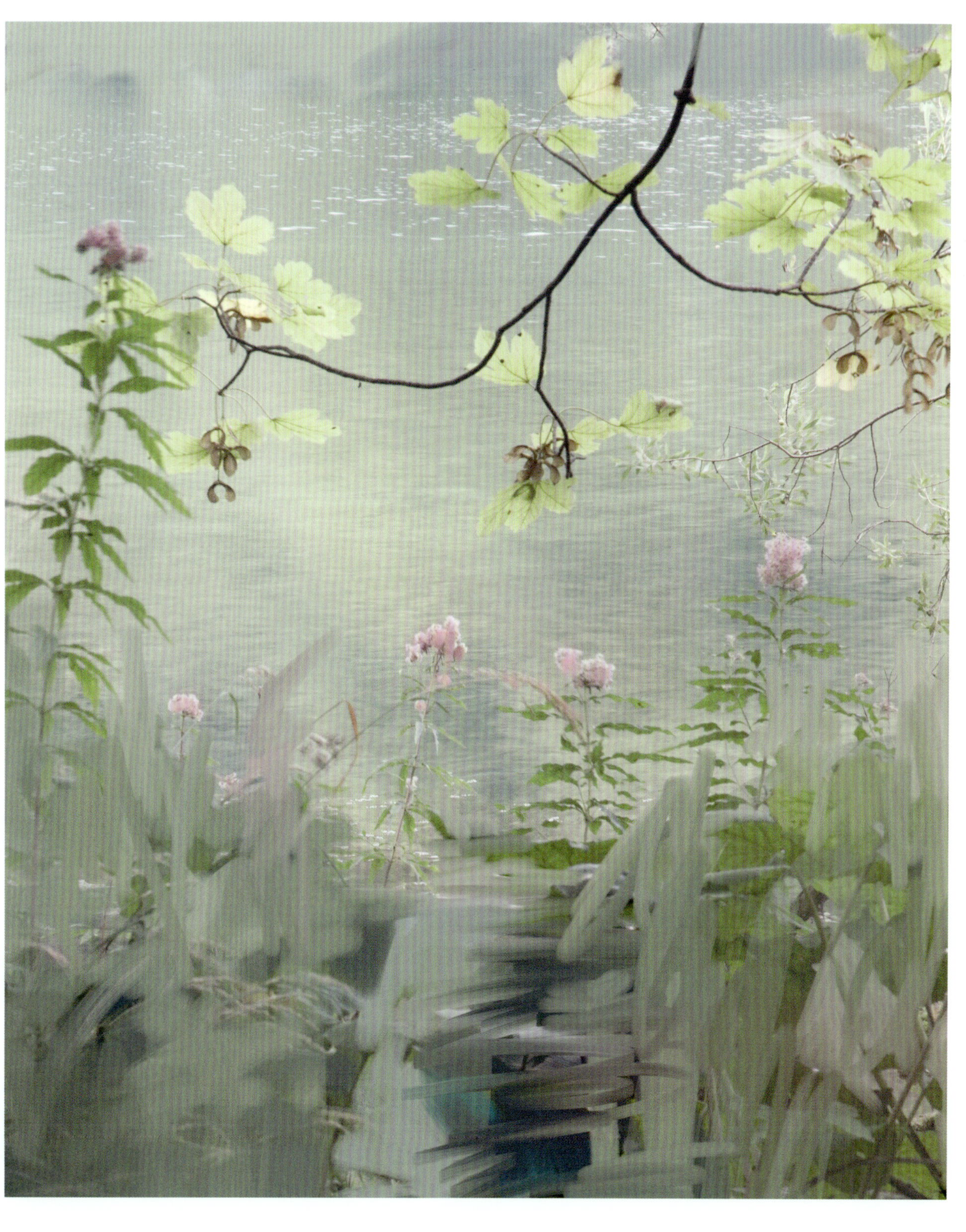

Untitled (Pink Flowers), 2013
pigment print
44 x 36 cm

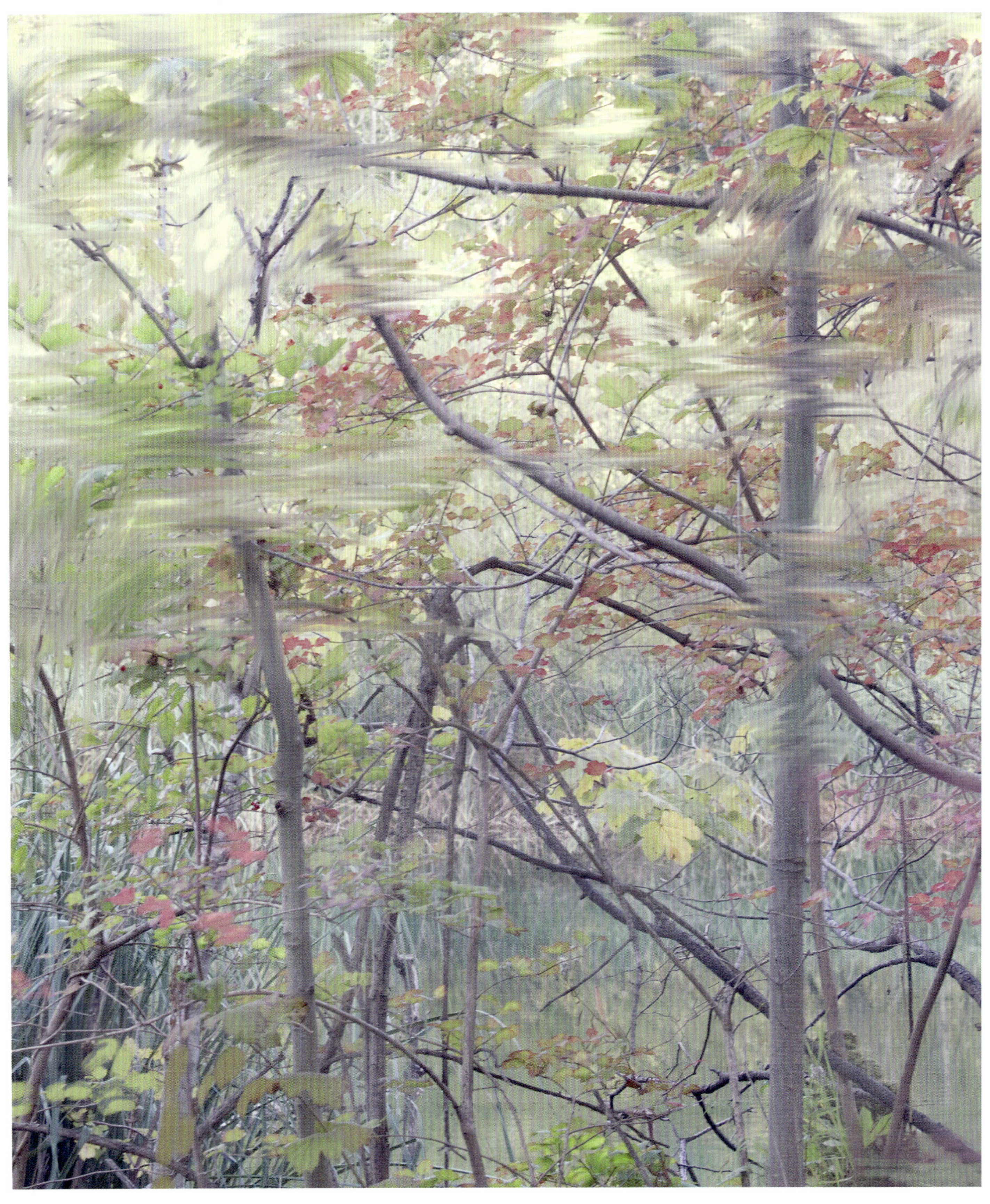

Untitled (Lake 10), 2012
pigment print
82 x 70 cm

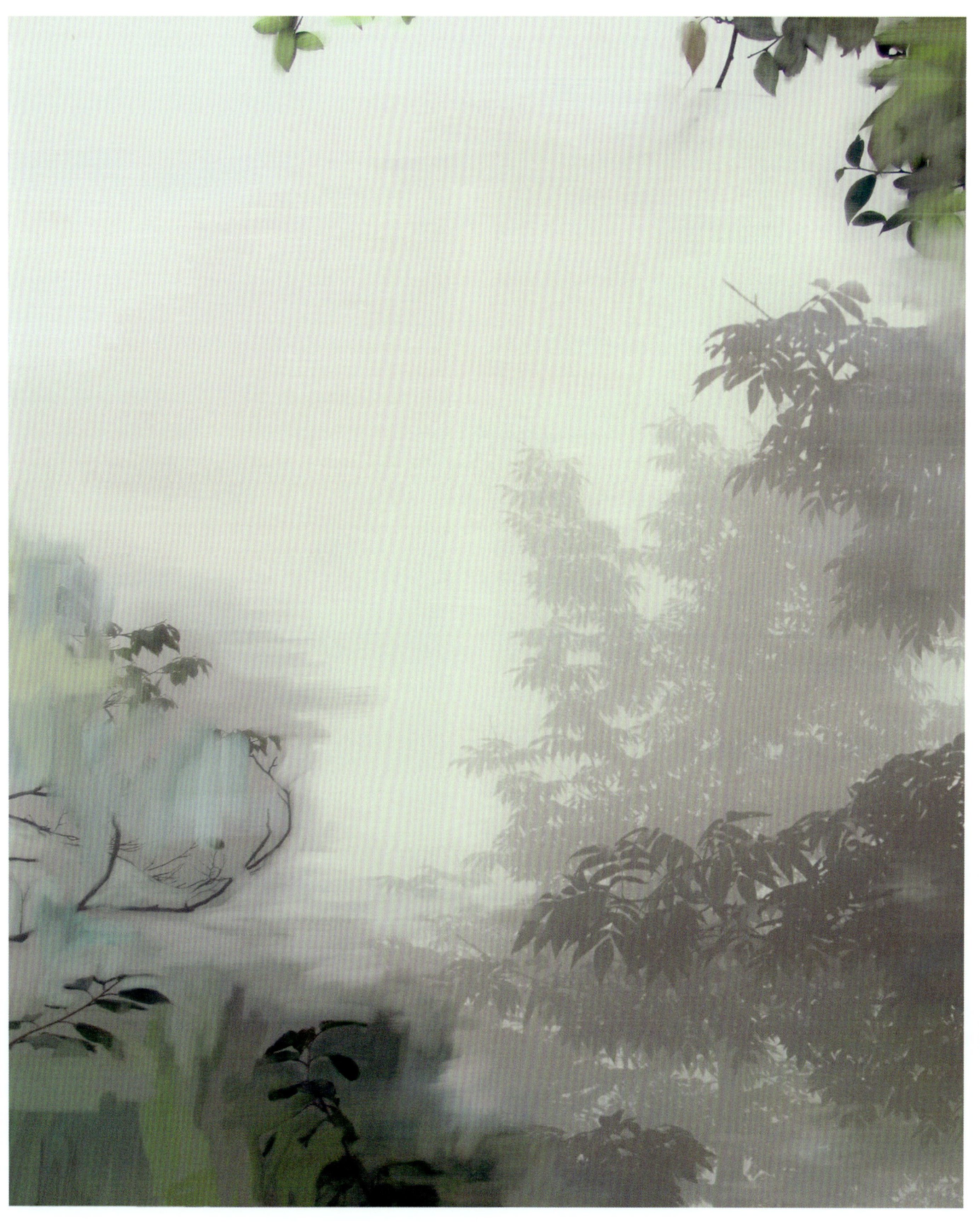

Untitled (Mountain 6), 2010
pigment print
82 x 70 cm

Astrid Kruse Jensen

Born in Aarhus in 1975, Astrid Kruse Jensen started to study photography in her hometown in the mid-1990s. From 1998 to 2000, she attended the Gerrit Rietveld Academie in Amsterdam, and in 2002 she completed her training with the two-year photography course at The Glasgow School of Art. Through the use of the photographic medium, her art explores the border between what is manifest and what is hidden, and the relationship between the real and the imaginary.

For more than a decade, the Danish artist has worked exclusively in nocturnal environments. Some of her series have been made using the artificial light found on site, such as *Imaginary Realities* (1998–2004), where isolated female figures inhabit the urban landscape creating a strong sense of psychological tension, and *Hypernatural* (2003–05), in which deserted spa pools appear like visions located somewhere between the surreal and the hyper-real. Other series, such as *Parallel Landscapes* (2005–07), exploit natural light while still maintaining the same theatrical atmosphere, whereas in *The Construction of Memory* (2006–10) for the first time the illumination is provided artificially, in line with the artist's new approach directed towards controlling every detail of the scene depicted. With this series, in which she reconstructed dream-like and paradoxical memories of childhood, Kruse Jensen introduced a theme that would go on to be central to her subsequent work – memory, its processes and the relationship

that has always linked it to photography. *Disappearing into the Past* (2010–12), to which the works in the collection belong, investigates the concept of memory and signals a turning point in the artist's work: not only is the darkness of the night abandoned in favour of daylight, but the decision to use expired Polaroid film – no longer in production since 2008 – makes the photographic material itself a crucial element in the exploration of the theme. The unpredictability of the outcomes upon development of the films retraces the process of the construction of memory: a fragmented, unstable process that constantly recombines real visions and imaginary evocations arising from the subconscious mind.

Marked by the traces of the chemical reactions and characterised by the soft tones of the Polaroid film, the photographs show a female figure first as a child and then as an adult, the interior of a house and woodlands, a lake, a jetty emerging from it and a boat floating on it as if suspended, composing a story that, while enigmatic, certainly leads back to childhood memories.

With these fragments of ambiguous recollections that cannot be slotted into a linear narrative – the clarity of which is always compromised by the randomness of the chemical process – Kruse Jensen challenges the idea of photography as a medium capable of freezing time and objectively archiving memory, highlighting in contrast its nature as a living, erratic process. Just like memory itself.

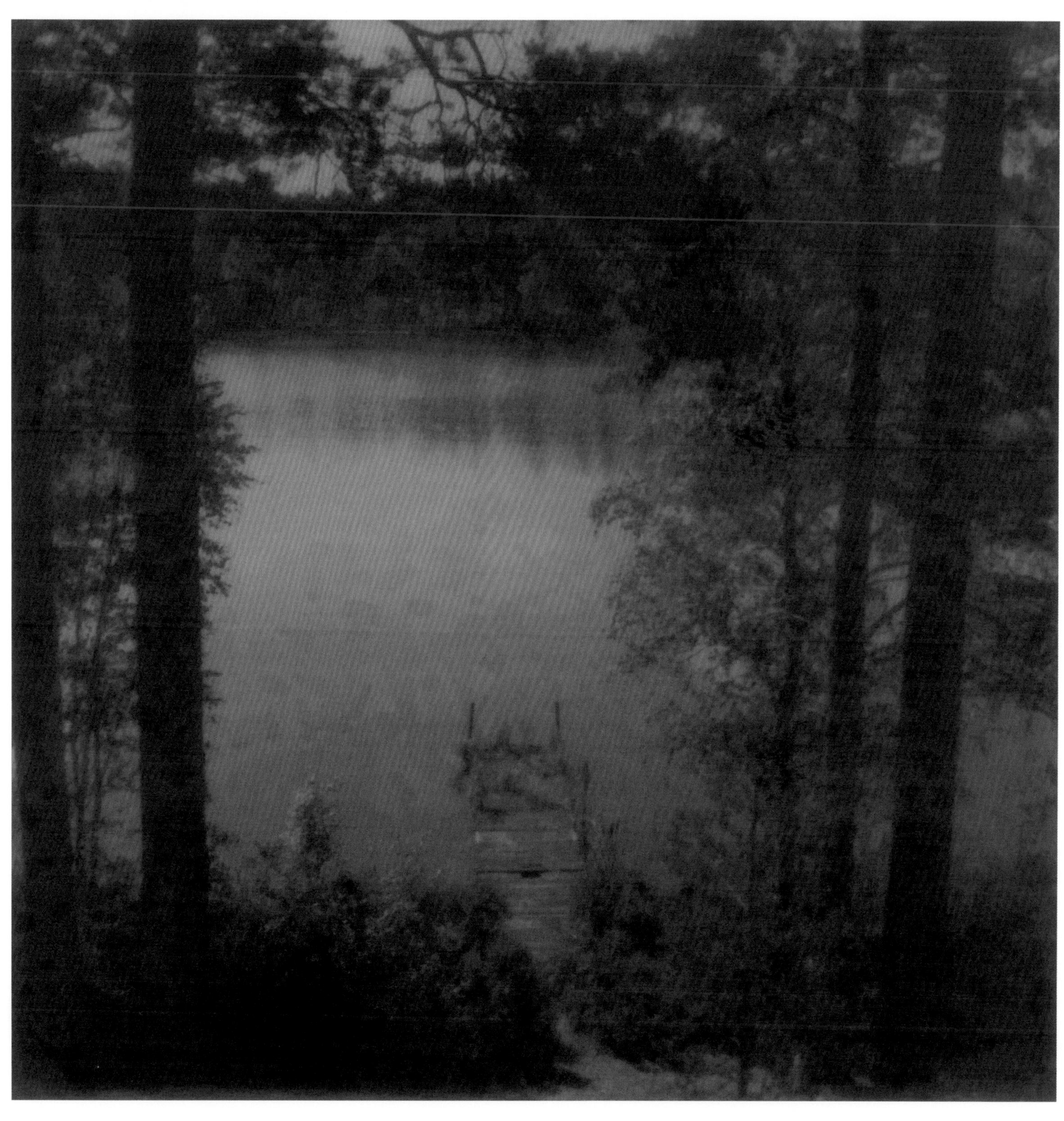

Disappearing into the Past #54, 2012
from the series *Disappearing into the Past*
pigment inkjet print
82 x 80 cm

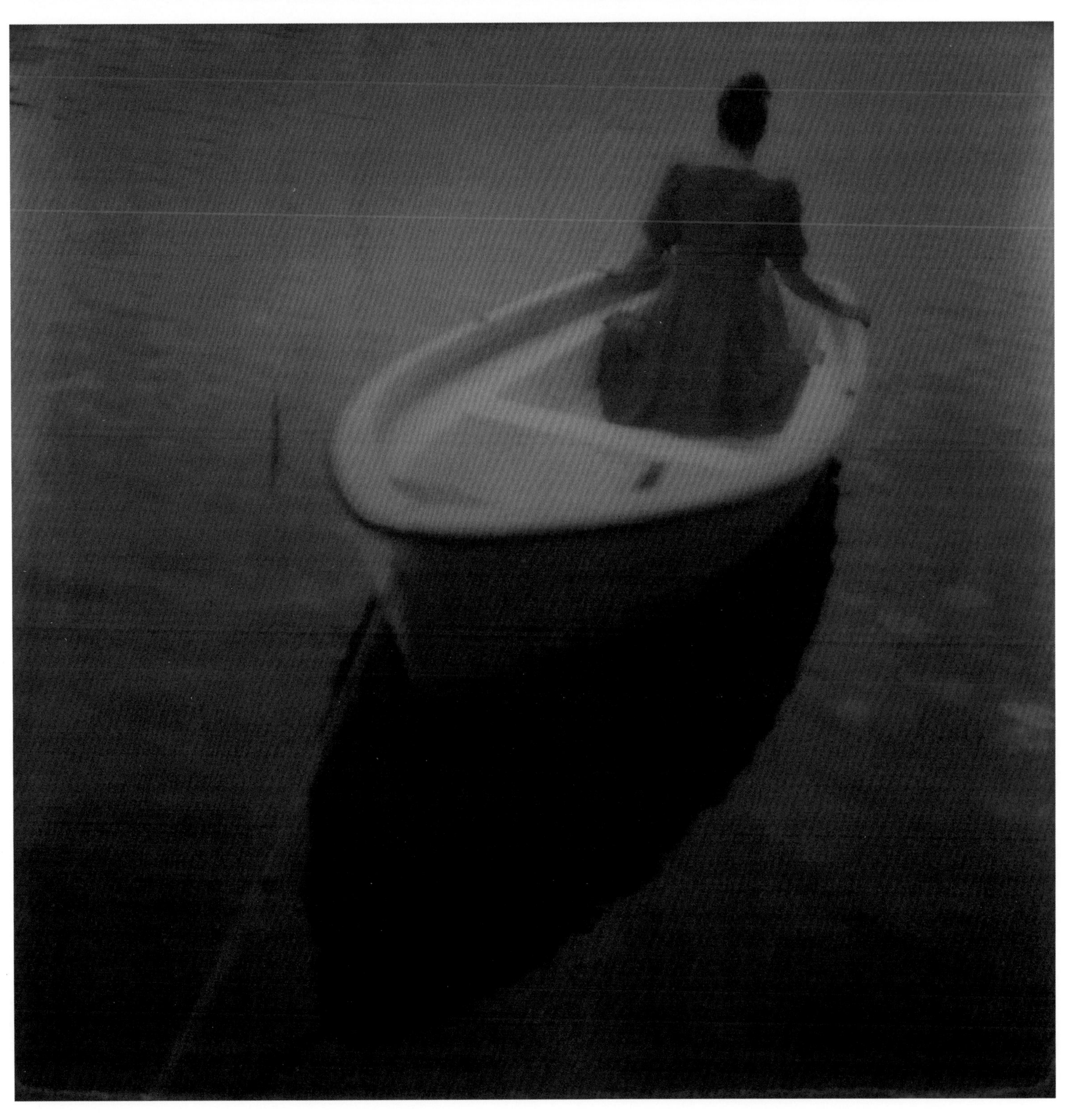

Disappearing into the Past #55, 2012
from the series *Disappearing into the Past*
pigment inkjet print
82 x 80 cm

Lilly Lulay

Born in Frankfurt in 1985, Lilly Lulay studied visual communication at the Hochschule für Gestaltung Offenbach, focusing on the study of photography, sculpture and the sociology of the media. She chose photography as the privileged medium for her artistic research: viewing it as a technique that forms an integral part of daily life, Lulay has explored its technological evolution and the influence that, on the basis of those changes, it has had over time on social behaviours and mechanisms of individual and collective perception. Perfectly aware of the overproduction of images that is a feature of our time, only rarely does the artist produce new photographs: she makes use for the most part of found images, given to her by friends or purchased from second-hand markets or on the internet, which she then processes using a variety of techniques ranging from cropping to embroidery, from installation to collage. Regardless of the specific subject of the individual pieces, all of her work, which she defines as manual post-production, is targeted towards examining and questioning the theoretical foundations of the photographic medium.

The *Mindscapes* series, begun in 2007 and still ongoing, is made exclusively using found photographs sourced from different places and times. Cropped and recombined by the artist, these images that once belonged to others become abstract compositions, 'scenes of an inner world of memory and imagination to which no camera has access: *Mind-scapes*', as Lulay declared. If seen from a certain distance, the collages recall subjects such as mountains, panoramas, urban buildings, whereas from closer up they reveal a plethora of fragments: small portions of reality that someone else has voluntarily framed or included casually in their photographs, shot and then sold, abandoned or lost.

The series entitled *Zeitreisende*, or time travellers (2011–12) is a trip through the techniques and the uses made of photographs in the past and in the present. Every collage is composed of two images: a found photograph, analogue and in black-and-white, and a cropped digital colour image, which Lulay has manipulated to reveal the pixels that form its structure. The artist explains: 'As a result the *time travellers* are portraits that do not depict identifiable individuals any longer. Rather, they raise questions about the materiality and the circulation of private photographs'.

As in many of Lulay's works, the *Zeitreisende* create a constant shifting between the private sphere – that of those who shot the images and that of the artist, who through manipulation confers new meanings upon these otherwise forgotten photographs – and the public dimension relating to the modes of production, circulation and use of images in the present day.

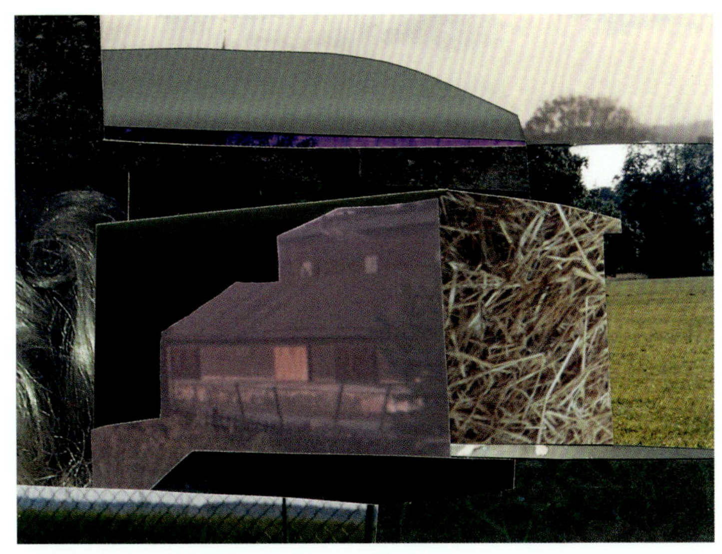

Mindscapes No. 14, 2007
from the *Mindscapes* series
photo collage: gelatin silver print
and c-print
7 x 9 cm

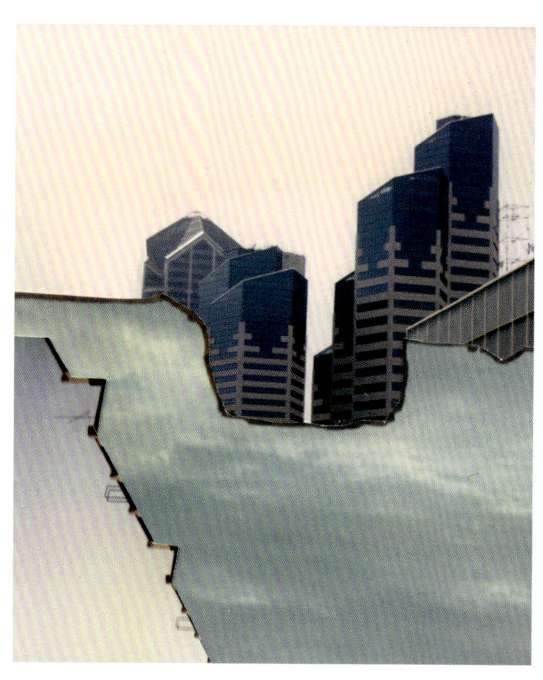

Mindscapes No. 54, 2010
from the *Mindscapes* series
photo collage: gelatin silver print
and c-print
8.5 x 7 cm

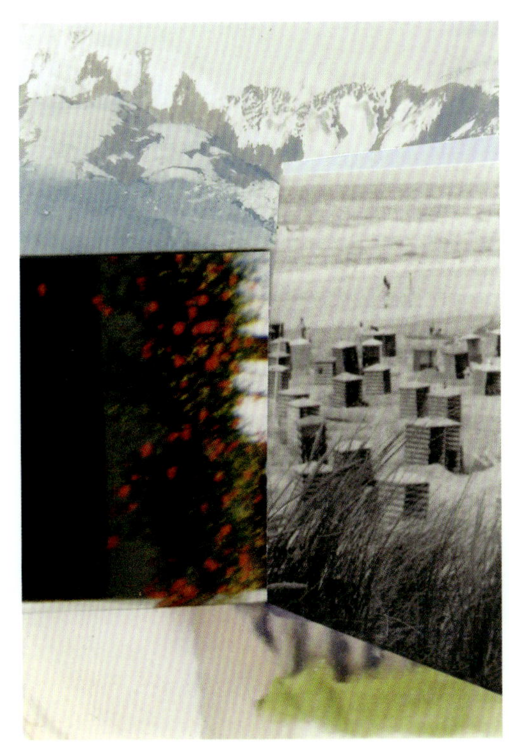

Mindscapes No. 66, 2013
from the *Mindscapes* series
photo collage: gelatin silver print
and c-print
9.5 x 6.5 cm

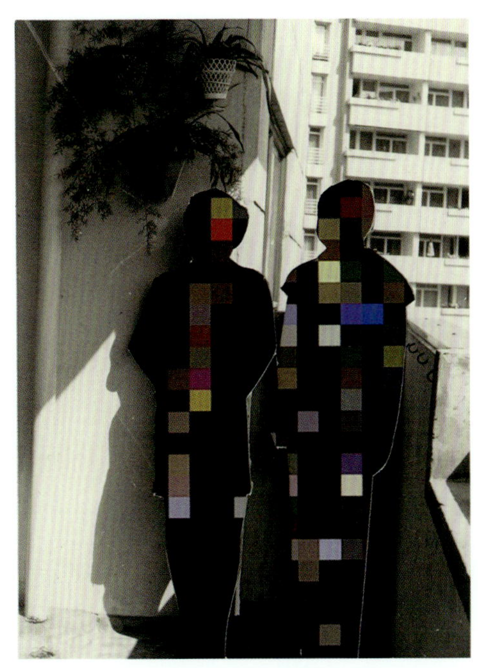

Zeitreisende j22abh7403s0b.jpg, 2011
from the *Zeitreisende* series
photo collage: gelatin silver print
and c-print
10 x 7 cm

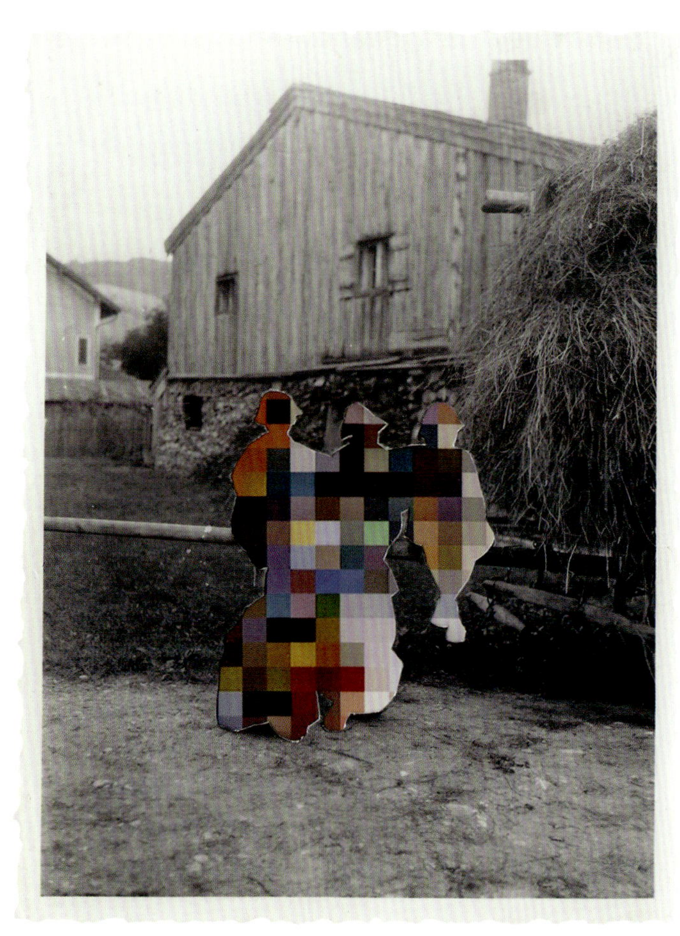

Zeitreisende gr56kivstr07br.jpg, 2012
from the *Zeitreisende* series
photo collage: gelatin silver print
and c-print
12 x 9 cm

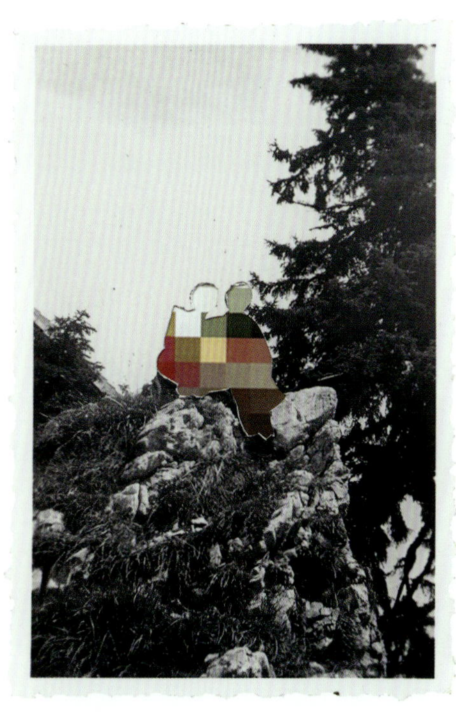

Zeitreisende pä020ab57gr.jpg, 2011
from the *Zeitreisende* series
photo collage: gelatin silver print
and c-print
8.5 x 5.5 cm

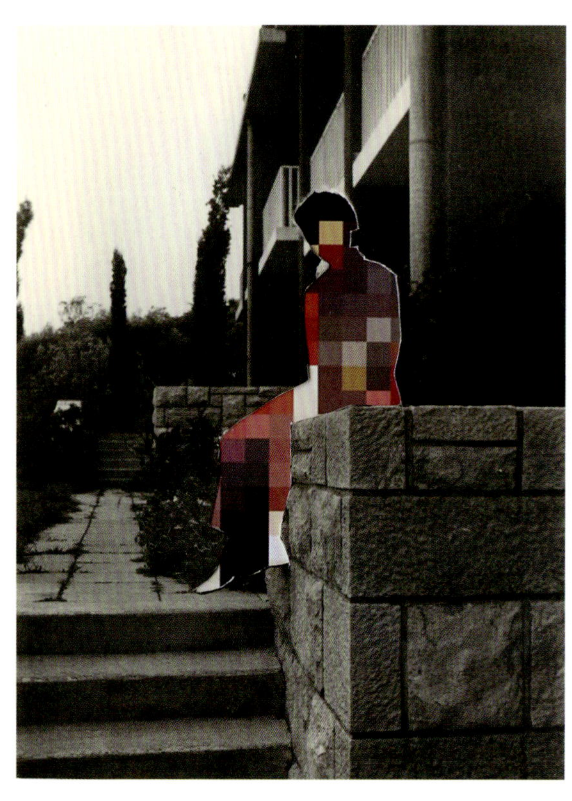

Zeitreisende m1atrp09ro.jpg, 2012
from the *Zeitreisende* series
photo collage: gelatin silver print
and c-print
10 x 7.5 cm

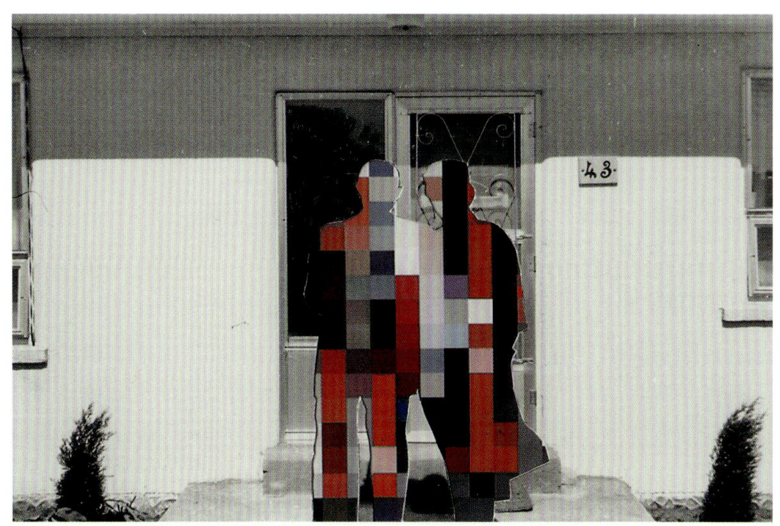

Zeitreisende pa23vh50wro.jpg, 2012
from the *Zeitreisende* series
photo collage: gelatin silver print
and c-print
7 x 10.5 cm

Melissa Moore

Born in Nottingham in 1978, Melissa Moore studied at Manchester Metropolitan University, the Kunstuniversität Linz and the Royal College of Art in London, where she attained a Master's degree with distinction for Research. She is currently a Lecturer at the University of the Arts London.

Her photographs have always arisen from performative actions, carried out for the benefit of the camera, in which her body serves as a conduit for an exploration of public and private spaces. Her whole work takes the form, then, of an investigation into places, and is shot through with an unconventional approach aimed to question the conformism that pervades the modern world and the predominant modes of interpreting it.

The images of the *Land Ends* series were taken on Hornby Island, one of the small Northern Gulf Islands in the Strait of Georgia, Canada. Only reachable through a long, arduous journey, in the 1970s the island was a favoured destination of youngsters in search of alternative lifestyles; fleeing from the frenetic pace of life on the mainland, they found here a self-sufficient natural paradise of peace and freedom. The artist first visited it in 1999, driven by her interest in vernacular architecture. Since then, she has returned time and again and *Land Ends* is the outcome of her numerous stays on the island.

Constituted by still lifes, landscapes and records of performances, the images resonate equally with Henry David Thoreau's *Walden* and Annie Dillard's *Pilgrim at Tinker Creek*, encapsulating the atmosphere of a place where, as Moore explains, 'away from an overabundance of human artifice, the cacophony of all other living things is perceived'. In *Portal*, crouching in a tree, the artist looks out towards a tangle of branches and bushes that foretells the presence of a hidden, isolated world. Viewed from behind, she seems about to jump in: could we follow her? If *Lights* reassures us about the possibility of entering into the magic of this world, *Talisman* poses a number of new questions: is the talisman of the title the skull that the woman has on her back, or is it that sort of mandala resting on the window, or is it hiding amongst the kitchen items? The woman seems to be engaged on some banal task, an everyday gesture, but one being carried out in a place that is out of the ordinary: what is this woman's life like? Who lives with her? As *Occupation* suggests, the very architectural structure seems to be an organic part of this mysterious and welcoming world.

The interstices of the building are spaces in which the body can feel comfortable, finding protection and refuge inside a time that passes slowly, far from the frenzied rhythms we are so accustomed to now.

As the artist explains, 'I nestled into the landscape and the communal dreams of the island … as if trying to mend rusty dreams of utopia'. Although the utopias that gave form to the myth of Hornby Island are now but a distant echo, still the entire universe described by *Land Ends* seems capable of offering the body a shelter, a place in which to regenerate energies in order to go back to the world and tune in to it in a new and unconventional way.

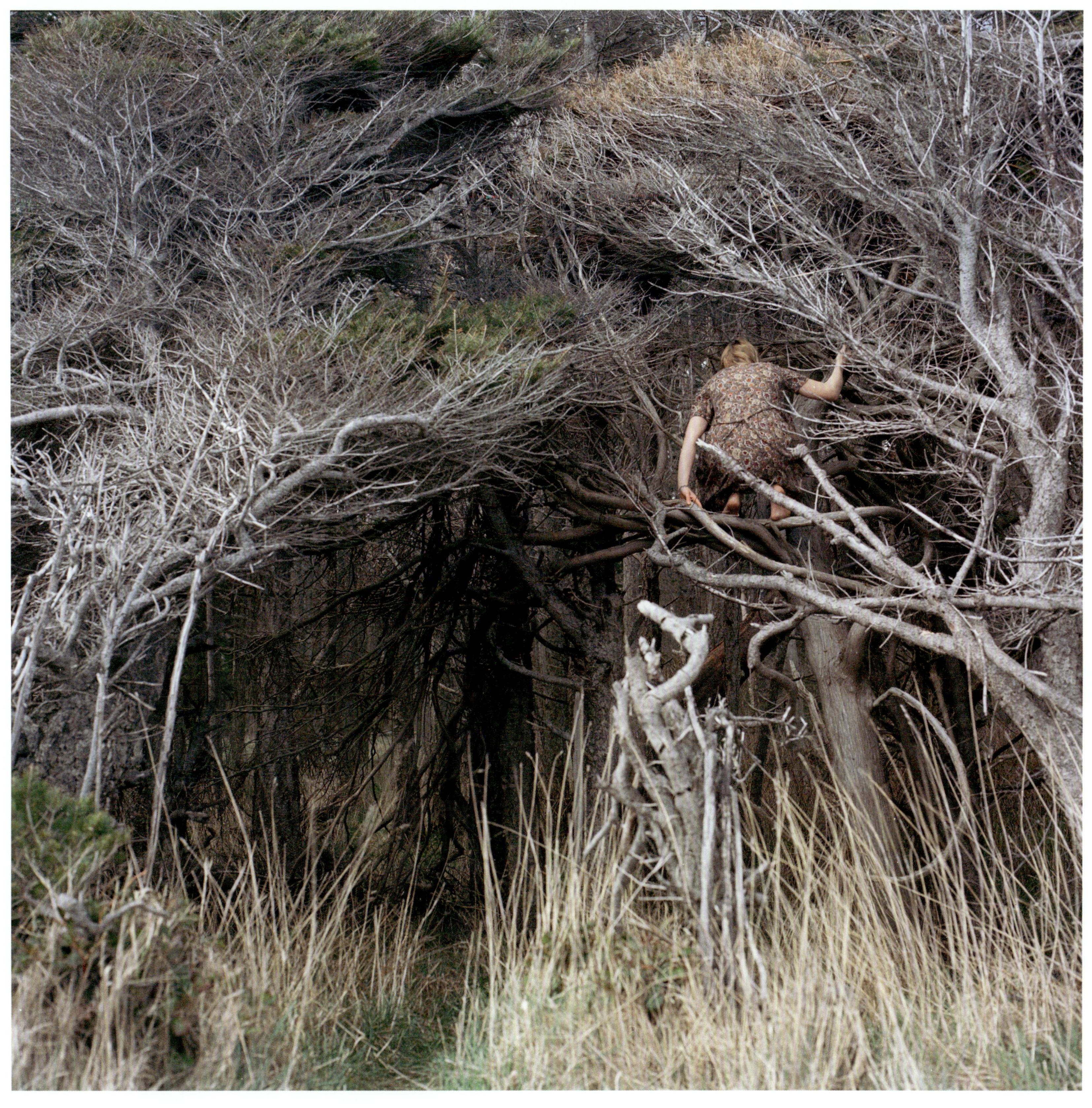

Portal, 2011
from the *Land Ends* series
c-print
90 x 90 cm

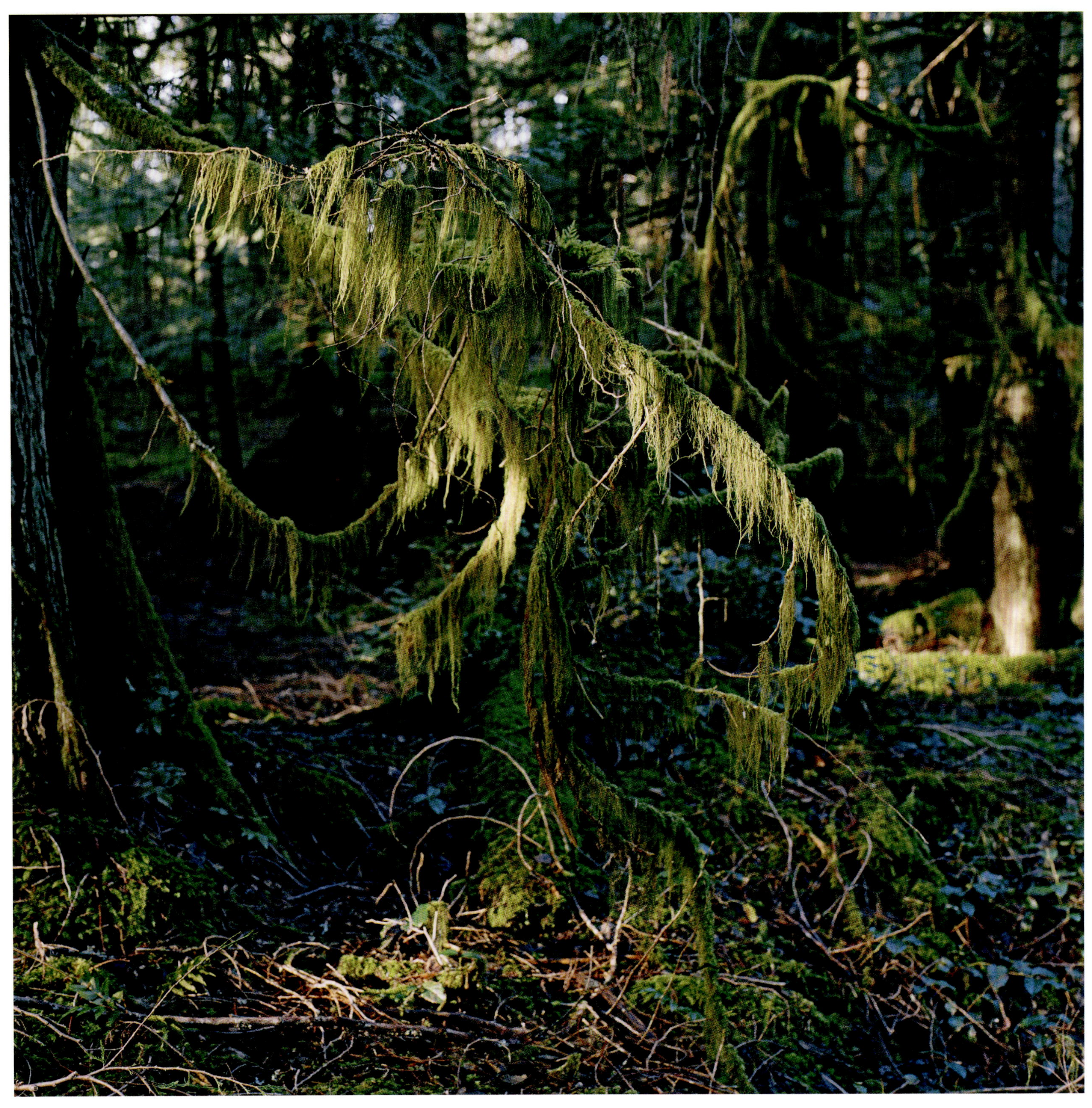

Lights, 2011
from the *Land Ends* series
c-print
90 x 90 cm

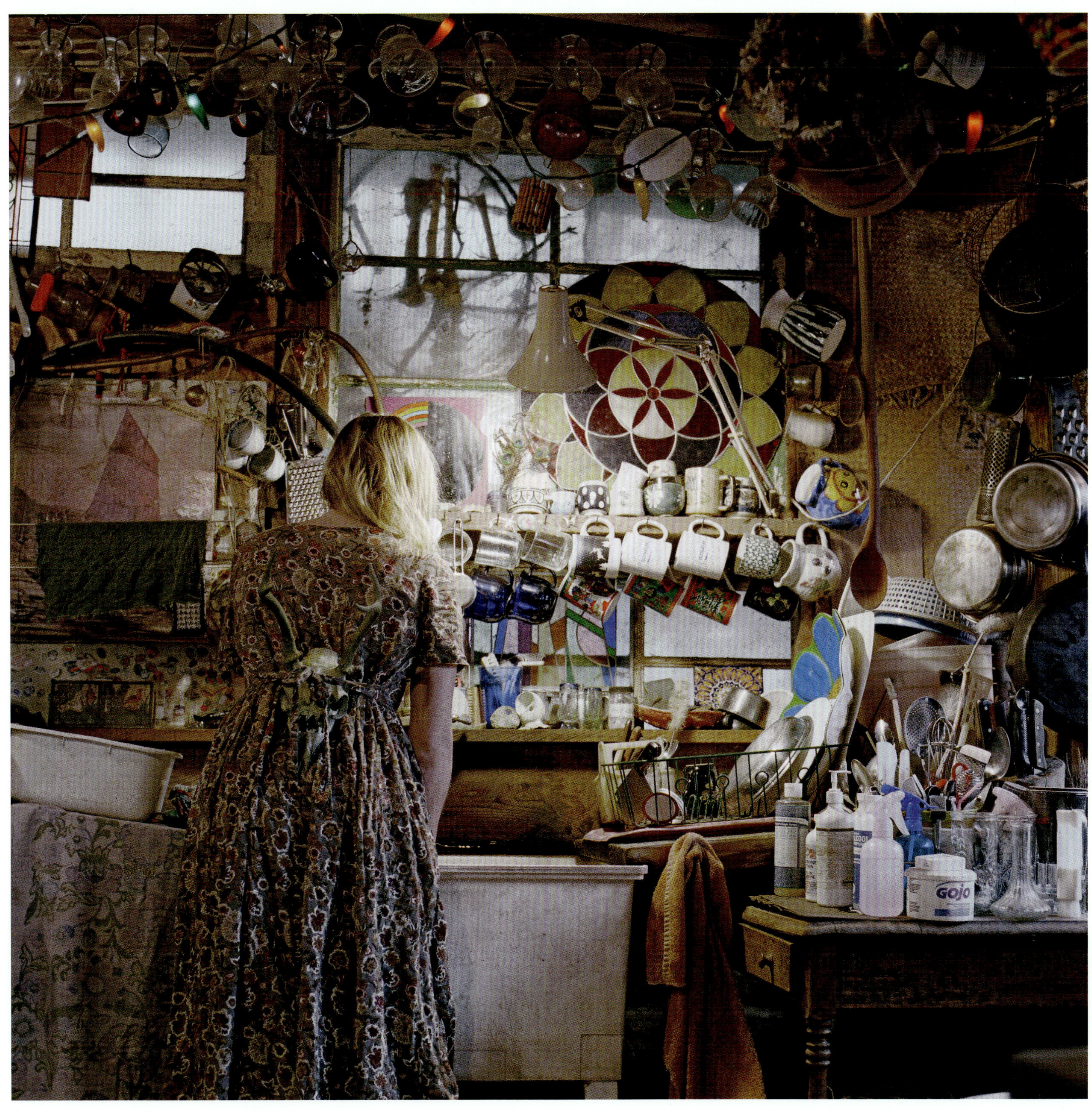

Talisman, 2011
from the *Land Ends* series
c-print
90 x 90 cm

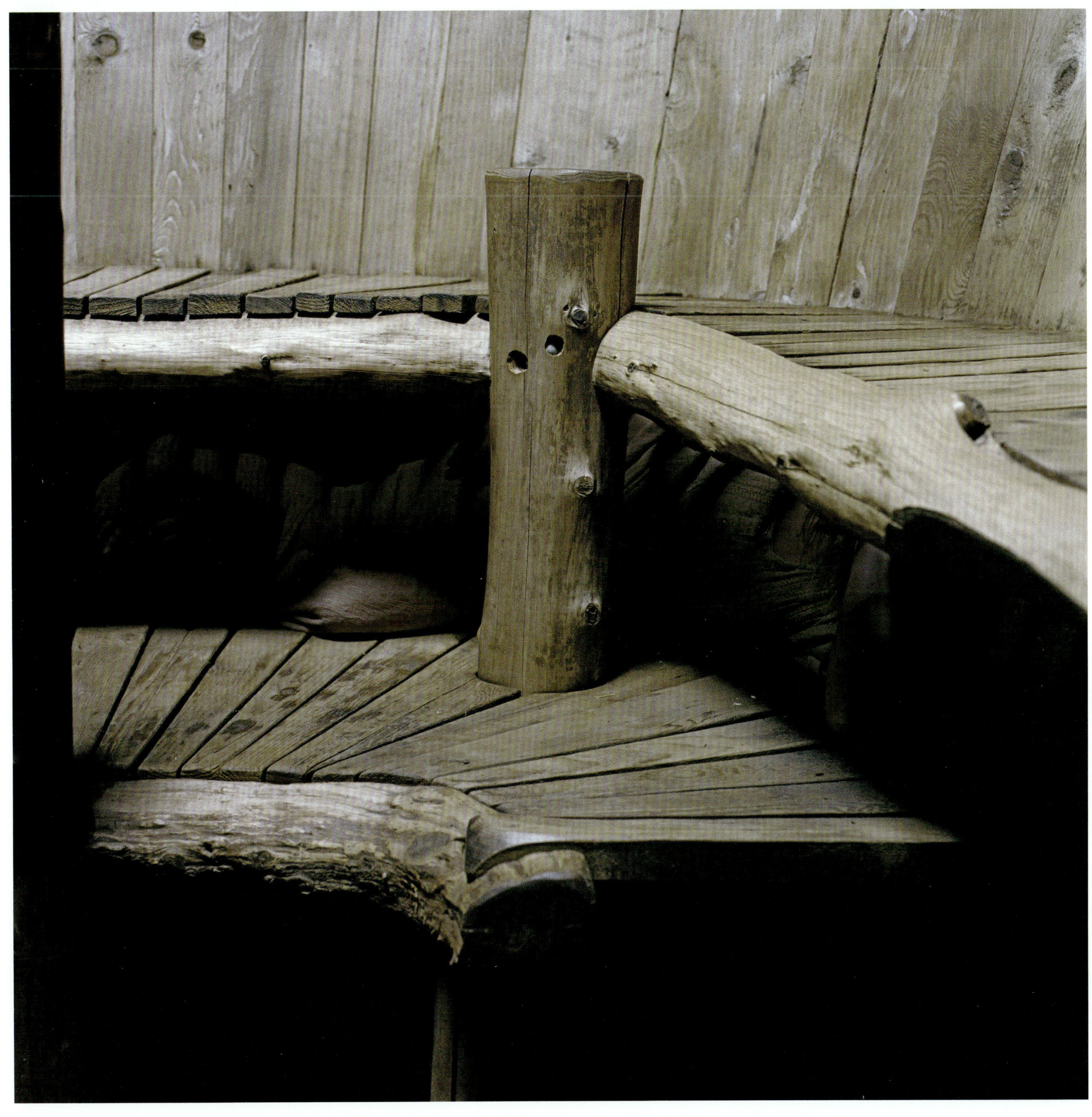

Occupation, 2011
from the *Land Ends* series
c-print
90 x 90 cm

Barbara Probst

From the very outset, German artist Barbara Probst has devoted her research to the analysis of the mechanisms of the photographic medium and to the questioning of its basic elements: from light, through film grain, all the way to the roles of the photographer and the viewer, via the categories of subject and object. Born in Munich in 1964, since the late 1990s she has been based in Germany and New York. In 2000, on a terrace on Eighth Avenue in Manhattan, she set up her first experiment of a series of works still in progress, each of which features the word *Exposure* in the title, followed by an indication of the place, date and time in which it was produced. In *Exposure #1, 545 8th Avenue, 01.07.00, 10:37 p.m.*, a simple event – a leap made by Probst in the centre of the terrace – was shot from twelve different angles, opening up a whole universe of possibilities on which the artist could work. Since then, the multiplication of points of view in the act of representing an event has become the common thread of her entire work. Thanks to a system of remote control that makes it possible to synchronise various cameras, Probst produces groups of images that share neither a theme nor a style but are linked by the fact that they have been taken in the same instant and they all relate to the same banal event. While in the initial experiment it was the artist herself who was at the centre of the action, in the subsequent works she decided to make use of a limited number of recurring models in order to enhance the sense of impersonality of the works: what matters is not the identity of the people involved, nor the specific nature of their gestures – what is important is the extent to which photography can represent reality. Like some of Probst's other works, *Exposure #6a, N.Y.C., Central Park, 06.04.01, 2:44 p.m.* came about thanks to the participation of various photographers who, clutching their cameras, appear while shooting each from his or her individual point of view. As Probst explains, this work 'displays in a very clear way my affinity for the Brechtian notion of art, namely art which is supposed to reveal the principles of its own construction'. The multiplicity of the points of view and their simultaneity force the viewer into an active game, the aim of which is to reconstruct the spatial and relational map of the situation that gave rise to the images. But these same characteristics also bring into question the credibility of photography as a documentary tool, demonstrating that the truth expressed by an image is only partial, incomplete and never neutral. Composed of two or more photographs, produced in the studio or outdoors combining carefully controlled plans with the randomness of the street, and shot using colour or black-and-white films at different heights and from different perspectives, the 'exposures' create a variety of images, encompassing all of the possible fields of photography – from amateur to fashion, from documentary to publicity – and definitively undermining, for each of those fields, the very concept of photographic truth.

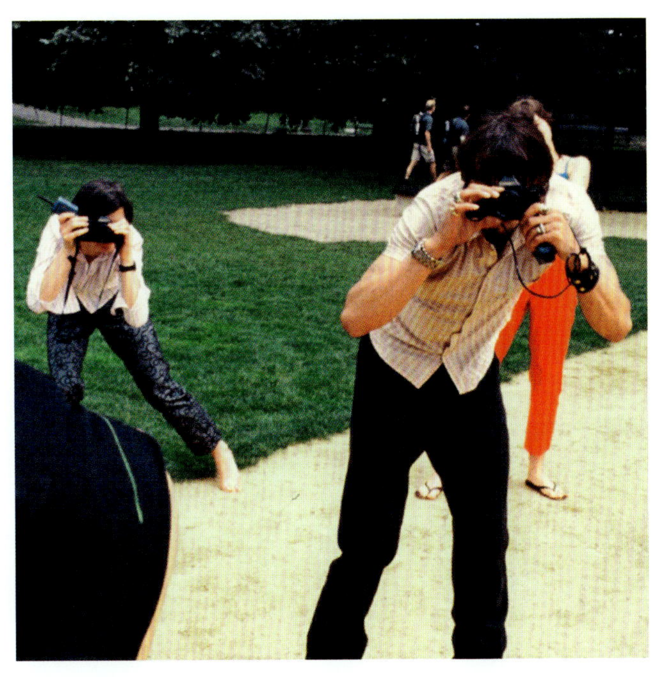

Exposure #6a, N.Y.C., Central Park,
06.04.01, 2:44 p.m., 2001
(detail)

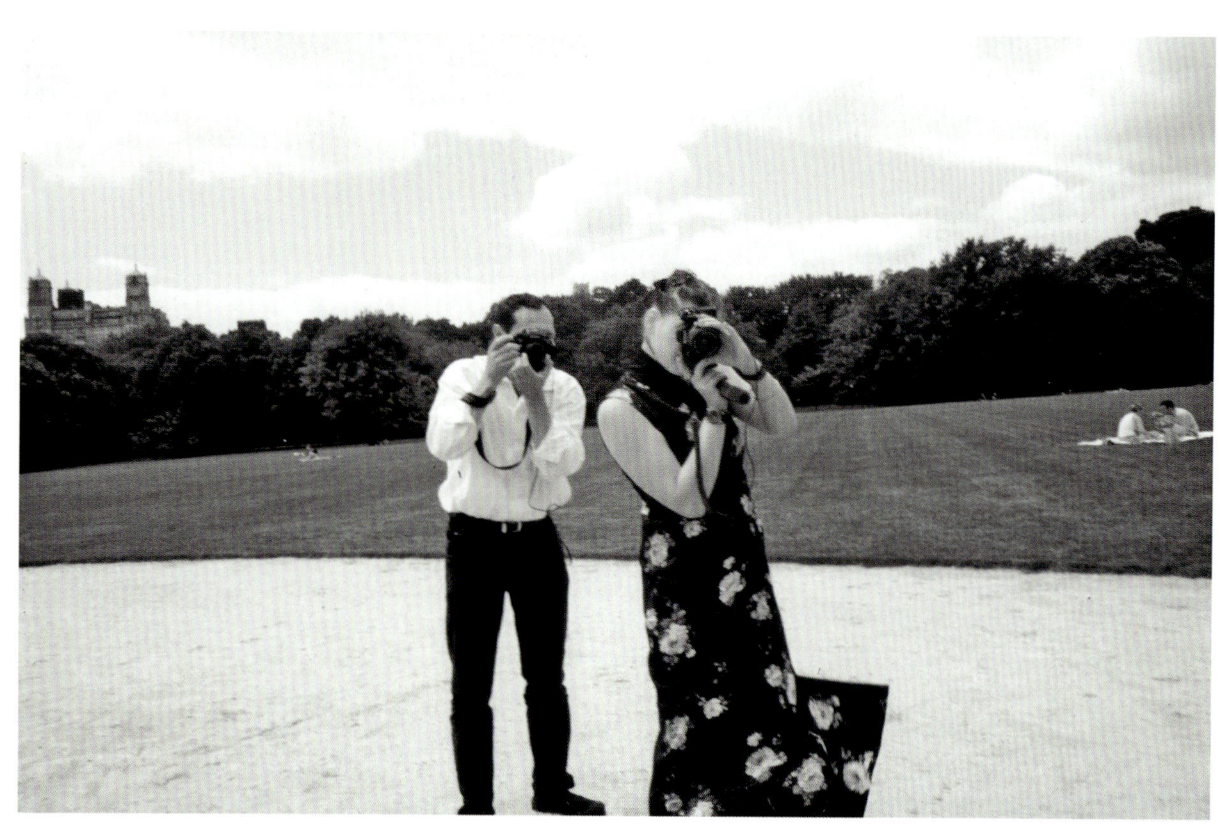
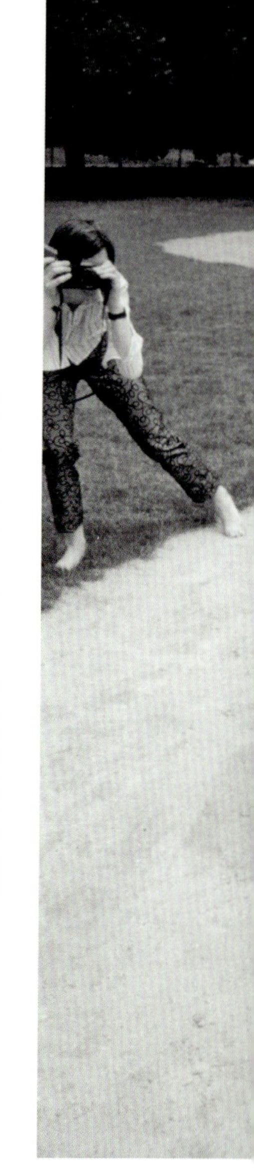
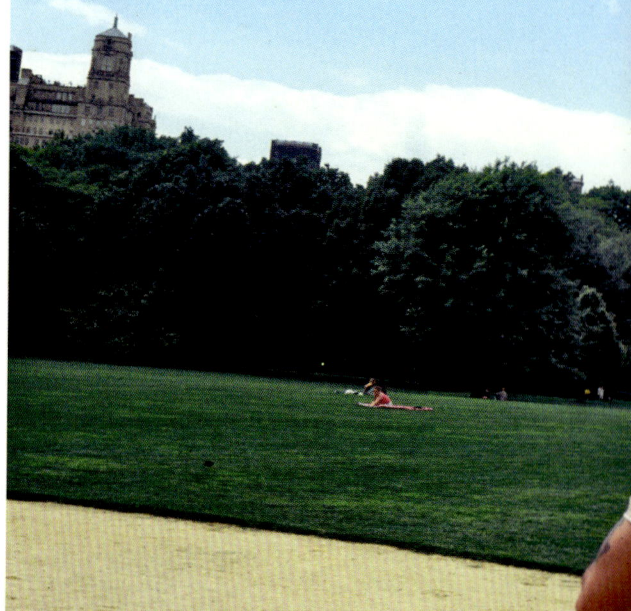

Exposure #6a, N.Y.C., Central Park,
06.04.01, 2:44 p.m., 2001
installation of 5 pigment inkjet prints
70 x 105 / 105 x 70 cm each

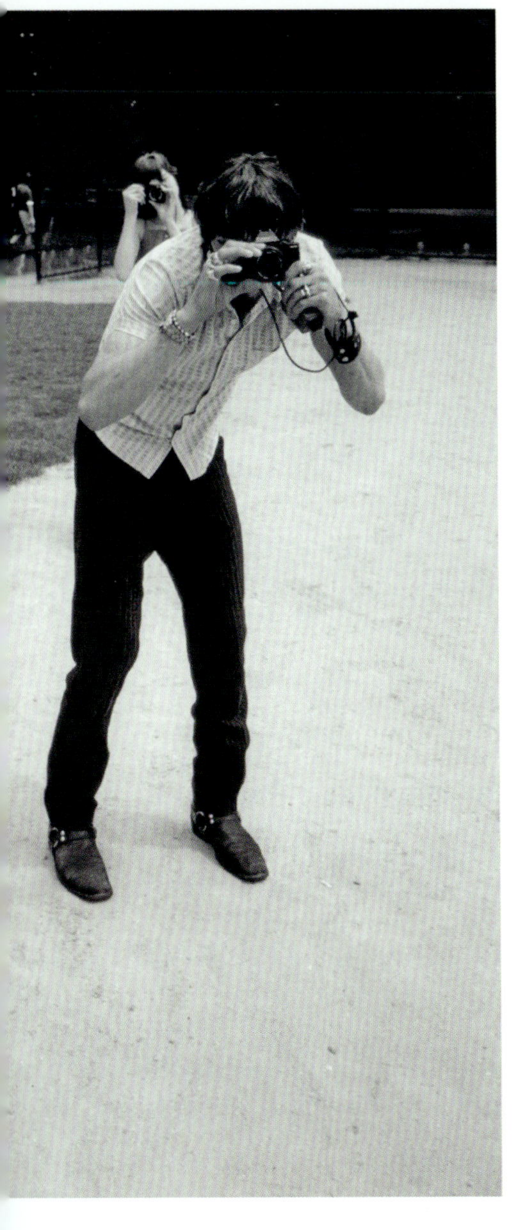
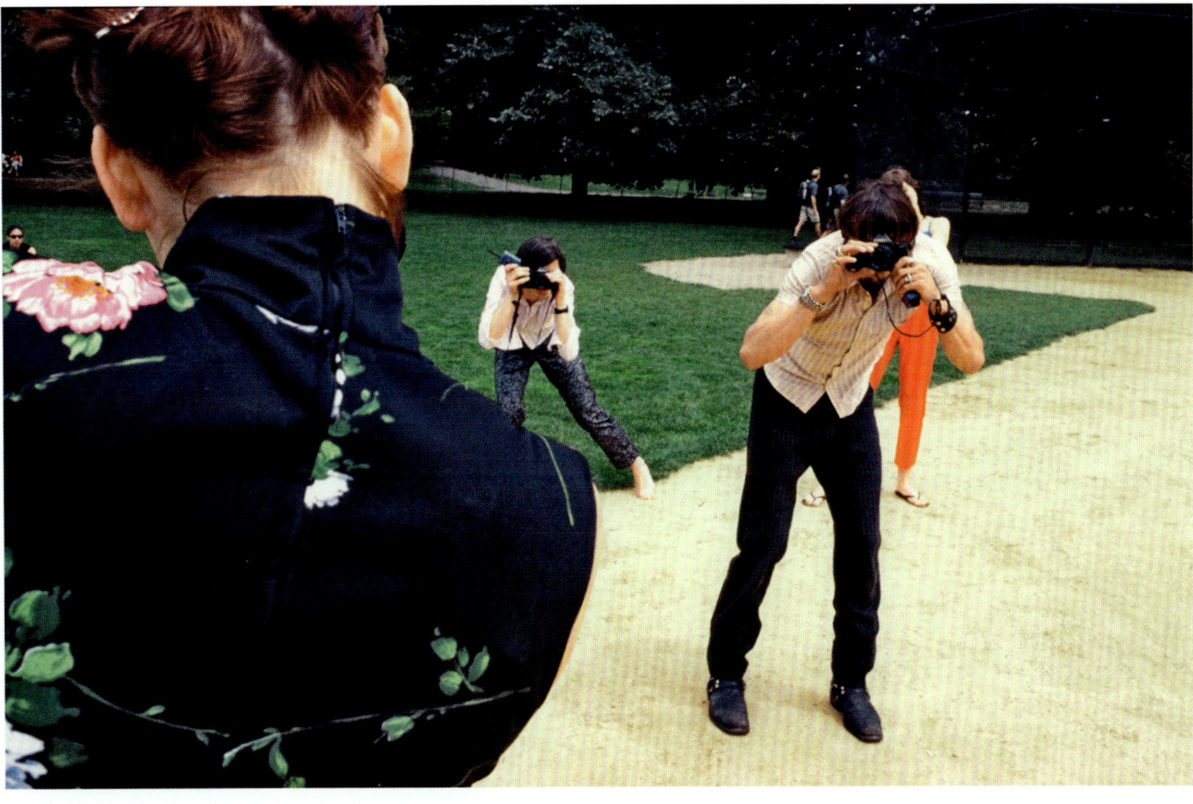
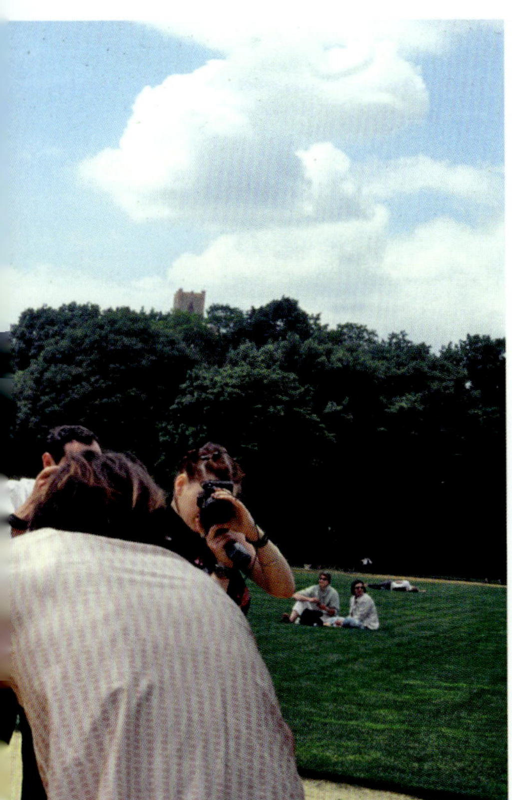
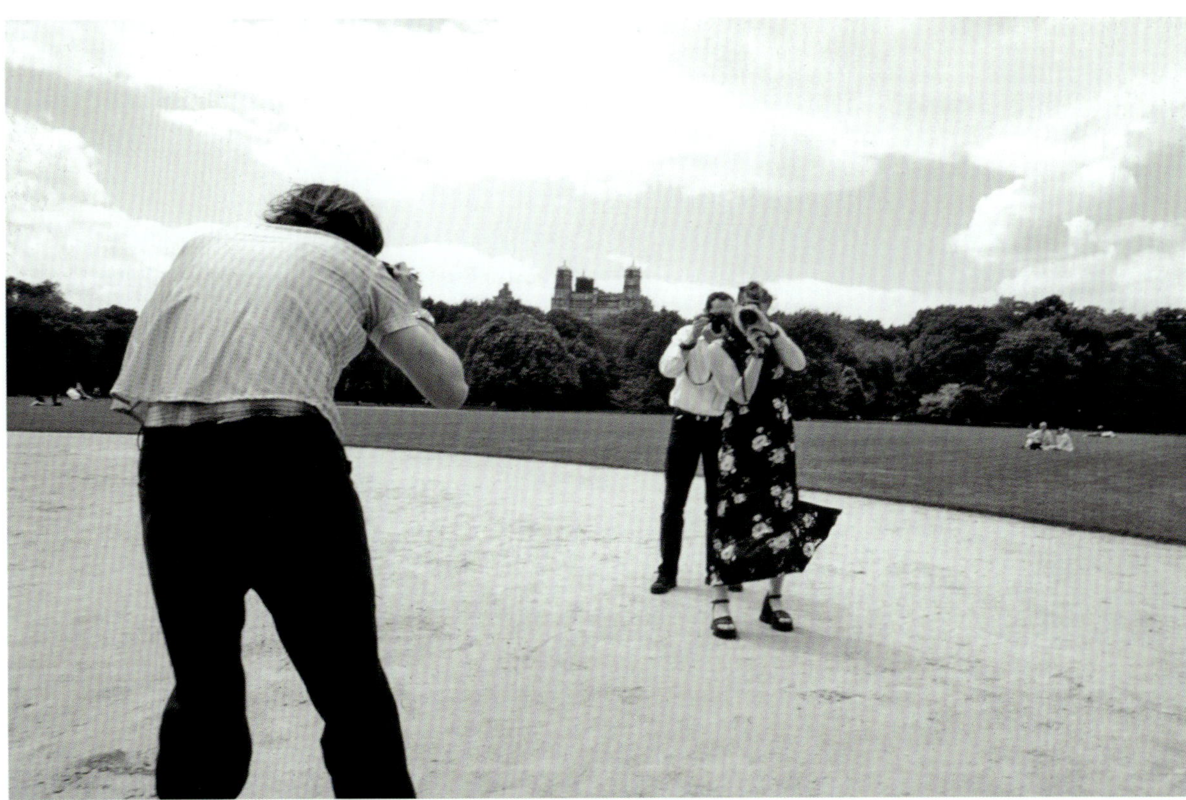

Olivier Richon

Born in Lausanne in 1956, Olivier Richon has lived in London since 1976. In the late 1970s, he studied at the Polytechnic of Central London where he was taught by Victor Burgin; then, alongside his artistic career, he became a teacher and in 1997 was appointed director of the Department of Photography at the Royal College of Art – a role he retains to this day. In his early years in London, he produced together with Karen Knorr a photographic series on the world of youth subculture, presented for the first time at The Photographers' Gallery in 1978 and published recently in the volume *Punk* (GOST Books, 2013). From the 1980s onwards, he concentrated on the still life genre, which he reinterpreted in line with the artistic theories and practices that in those years attempted to redefine the concept of allegory. More than mere visual expressions, images are to be considered as 'scripts', rebuses to decipher, constructs generated by the accumulation and stratification of signs and signifieds; for this reason they are open to multiple readings and interpretations.

Richon's work involves the study and arrangement of objects and animal subjects, which participate in the construction of the scene, emphasising the overall theatricality of the representation. His photographs are allegorical images rich in references to history and to the history of art, to literature and to psychoanalytical, social and philosophical theories. *After Joseph Wright of Derby, Arkwright Mills at Night* and *After Pieter Saenredam, The Buurkerk at Utrecht* (both produced in 1990) appear emblematic in this respect; both are based on the use of pre-existing paintings, which serve as backdrops: Pieter Saenredam's painting shows the sober interiors of a Protestant church, whereas *Arkwright Mills at Night* by Joseph Wright of Derby depicts one of the first English industrial cotton mills, the night-time illumination of which testifies to its non-stop production cycle. The relationship between the two works alludes to the connection between Labour and Protestantism, while the fact that the paintings have been inserted into the photographs by means of frontal projection is a direct reference to cinema, which used that same technique to achieve background scenes. This method of projection also relies on light, as a way to produce images. Both photographs, moreover, include the figure of a monkey, depicted in the act of contemplating the projected paintings. Like many elements in Richon's works, its presence could generate various different readings: in a Jungian key we could consider it a projection of our condition as human beings, otherwise we could see it as an emblem for the visual practice of imitation that photography has partly inherited from the Renaissance – a period to which the chessboard floor and the stage curtains seem to refer as well. Resistant to unique, definitive interpretations, Richon's works highlight the allegorical potential of photography, emphasising its power as a means of reflection and knowledge.

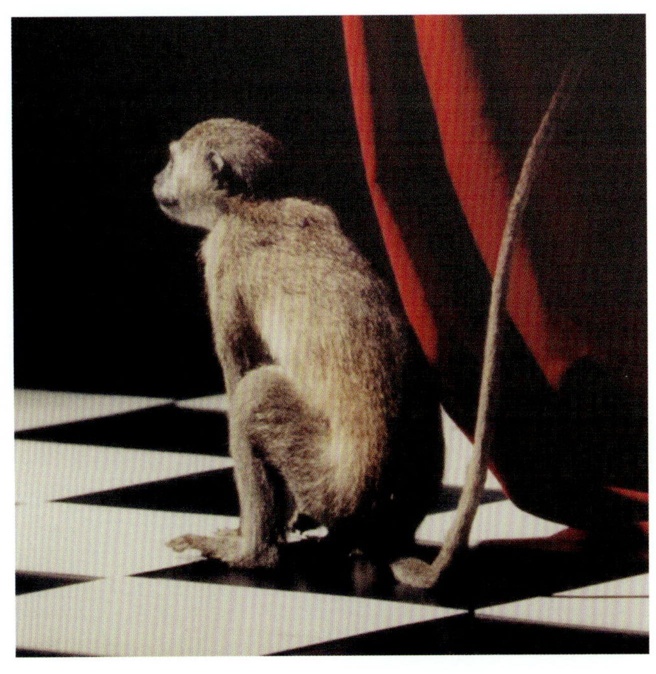

*After Joseph Wright of Derby, Arkwright
Mills at Night*, 1990
(detail)

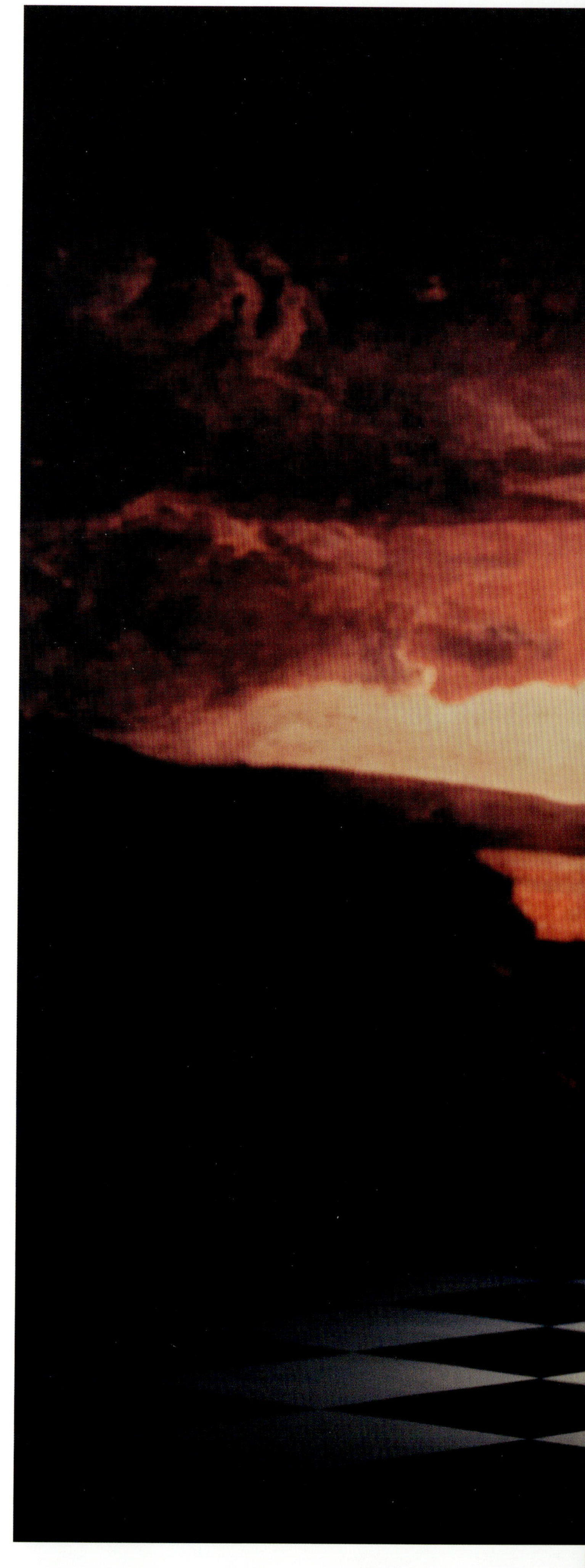

*After Joseph Wright of Derby, Arkwright
Mills at Night*, 1990
c-print
100 x 140 cm

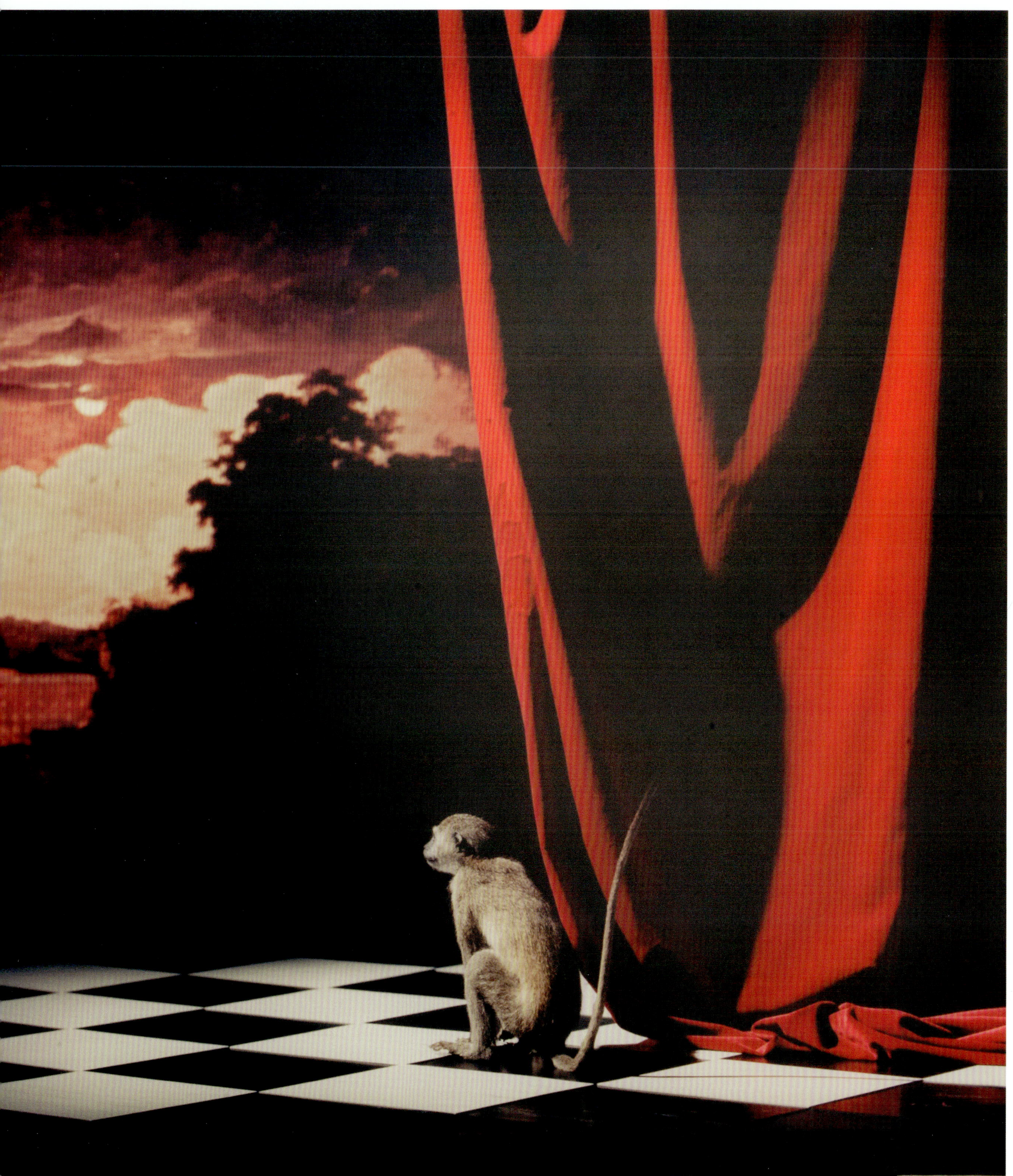

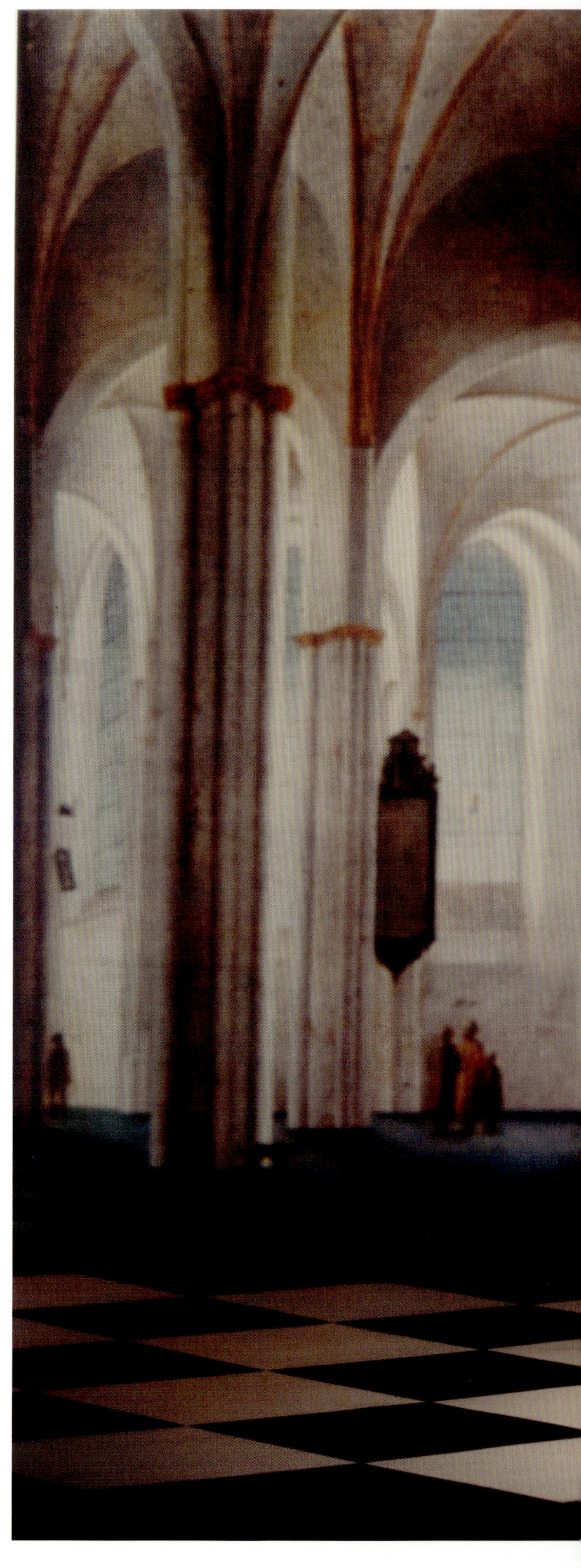

*After Pieter Saenredam, The Buurkerk
at Utrecht*, 1990
c-print
100 x 140 cm

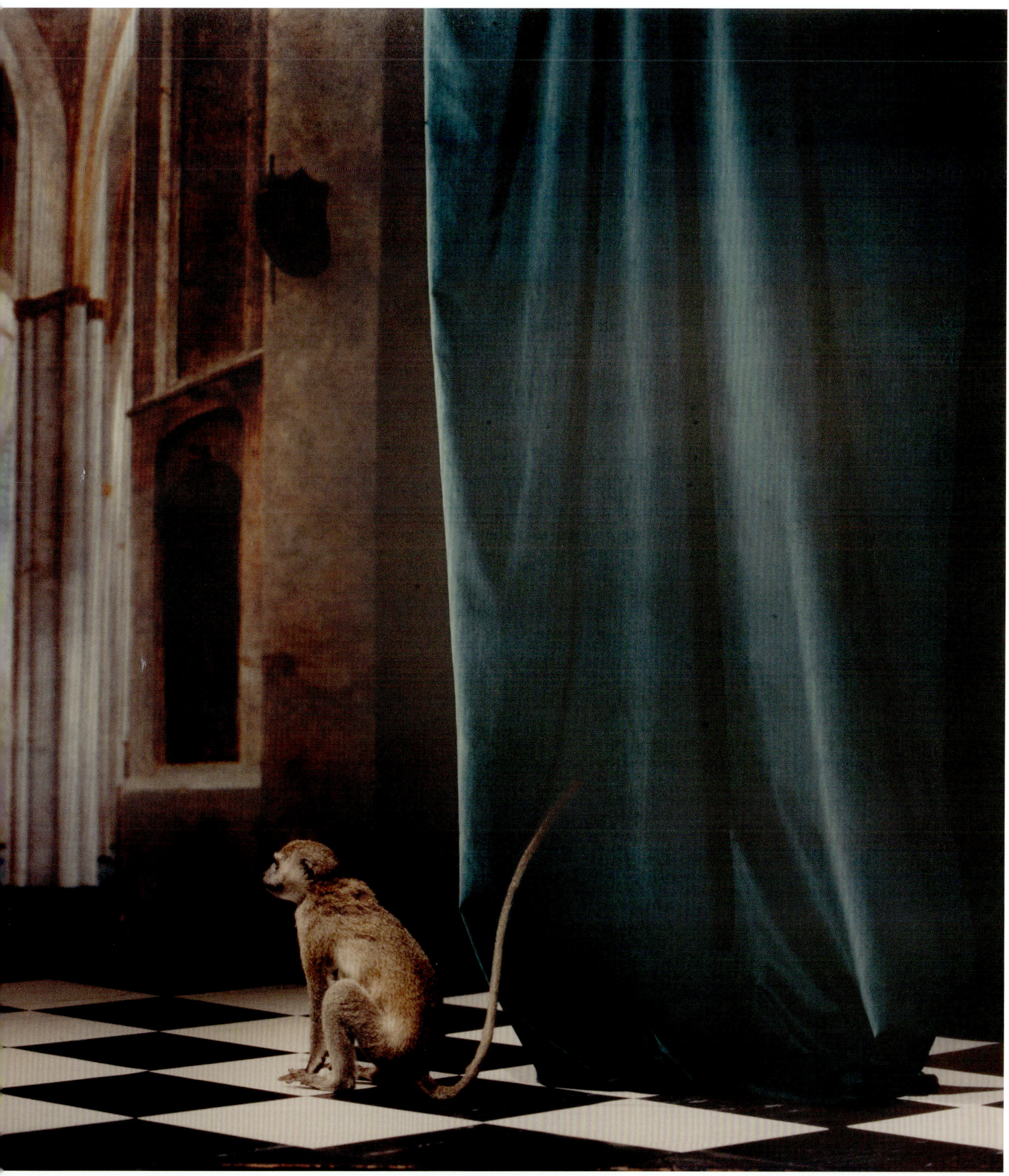

Tom Sandberg

Tom Sandberg, who passed away prematurely in 2014, is one of the most celebrated Norwegian contemporary photographers. Born in Narvik in 1953 and brought up in Oslo, in 2010 he won the Anders Jahre Culture Prize, the most important culture prize awarded in Norway. He had worked in the field of photography since the 1970s, when he studied art in the UK: first at Trent Polytechnic in Nottingham, where he was taught by Thomas J. Cooper and Paul Hill, and then at the Derby College of Art and Technology, where among his teachers was John Blakemore. Following his return to Oslo, in 1977 he participated in the setting up of Fotogalleriet, the country's first non-commercial photo gallery, thus contributing – along with his own work – to the promotion of photography as a form of artistic expression in Norway. The 2007 exhibition at MoMA PS1 entitled *Tom Sandberg: Photographs 1989–2006* brought his work to the attention of the American public and critics, giving an international dimension to a reputation that had already been consolidated in Scandinavia.

In his thirty-year career, Sandberg almost always worked with large formats and black-and-white film, promoting an idea of pure, direct photography that is rooted in the American photographic tradition of the early twentieth century. Without ever lapsing into strict fanaticism, and maintaining at all times a significant expressive freedom, the artist inherited from straight photography an attitude of enhancing the aesthetic qualities of the photographic language and reducing to

a minimum any editing on the images, such as cropping or manipulations at the developing or printing stages. The images in the collection belong to the *Portfolio* published in 2003 by the Galleri Riis in Oslo, containing six photographs taken between 1994 and 2001. In this selection of palladium prints, the artist's poetics emerge with crystal clarity: his focus on a wide range of subjects reveals that, for Sandberg, photography is a means to experiment with the world in an unhindered, non-hierarchical way. Whether the subject matter is a car parked in the street or the sinuous body of a model, the lush greenery of nature or geometric architectural details, his photographs embody a powerful seductive charge, nourished by the sensitivity that has always marked out the artist's perspective. In addition, his works are a reflection on photographic vision itself: the formal purity of the images often moves towards abstraction, exposing the viewer to all of the enigmatic power and the potential for mystery implicit in the act of perception and in every form of representation. A depression in the asphalt can thus become the pretext for fantasising on an eclipse that first obscures the world before returning it to the light, or on the very act of observing, performed from the black depths of a superhuman eye.

In Sandberg's works, the coupling of light and dark echoes other pairings: presence and absence, revelation and concealment, sensuality and death. His entire oeuvre is a tribute to life and to photography as a medium through which to live it.

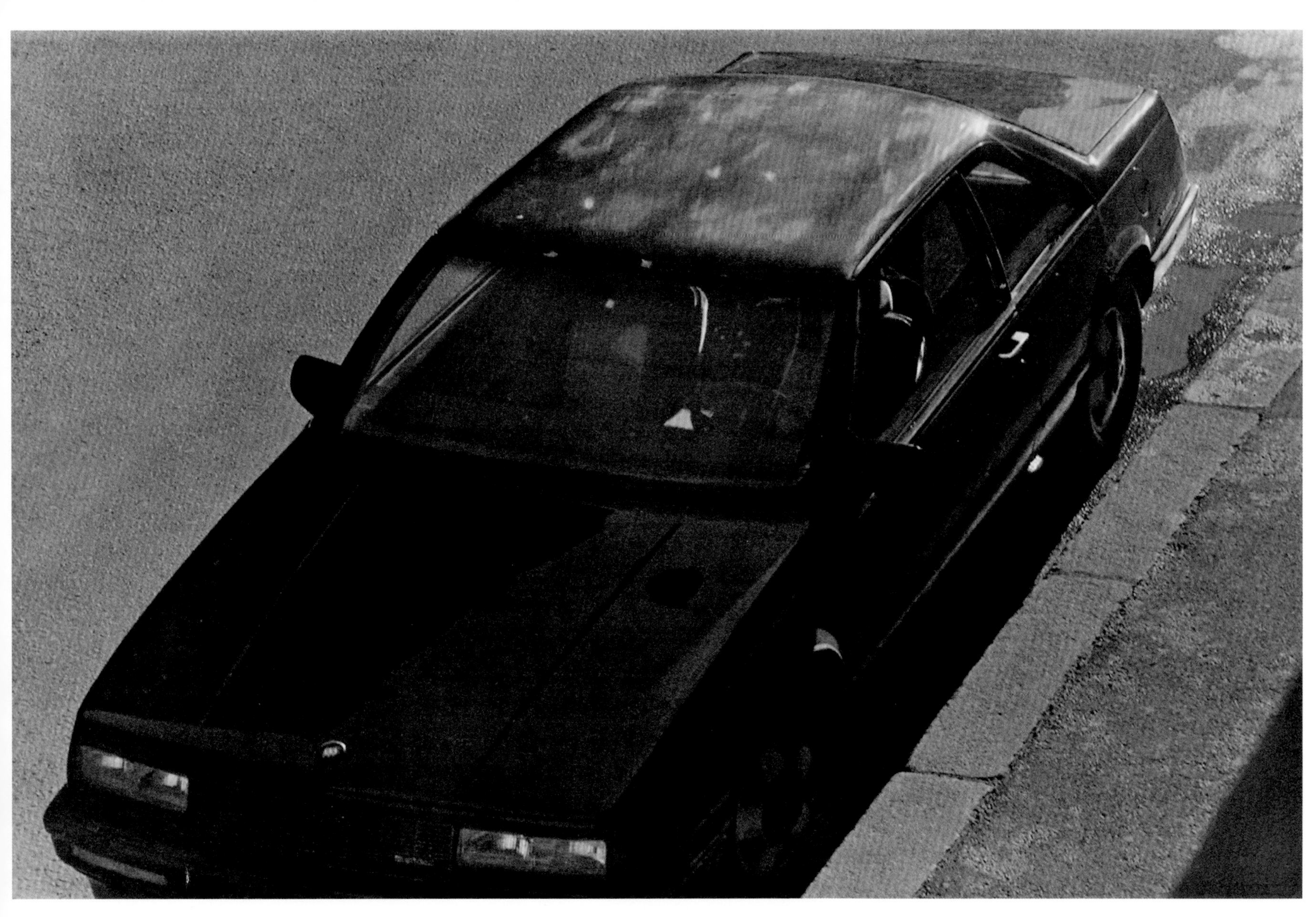

Untitled, 1994–2001
from *Portfolio*, 2003
palladium print
25.5 x 38 cm

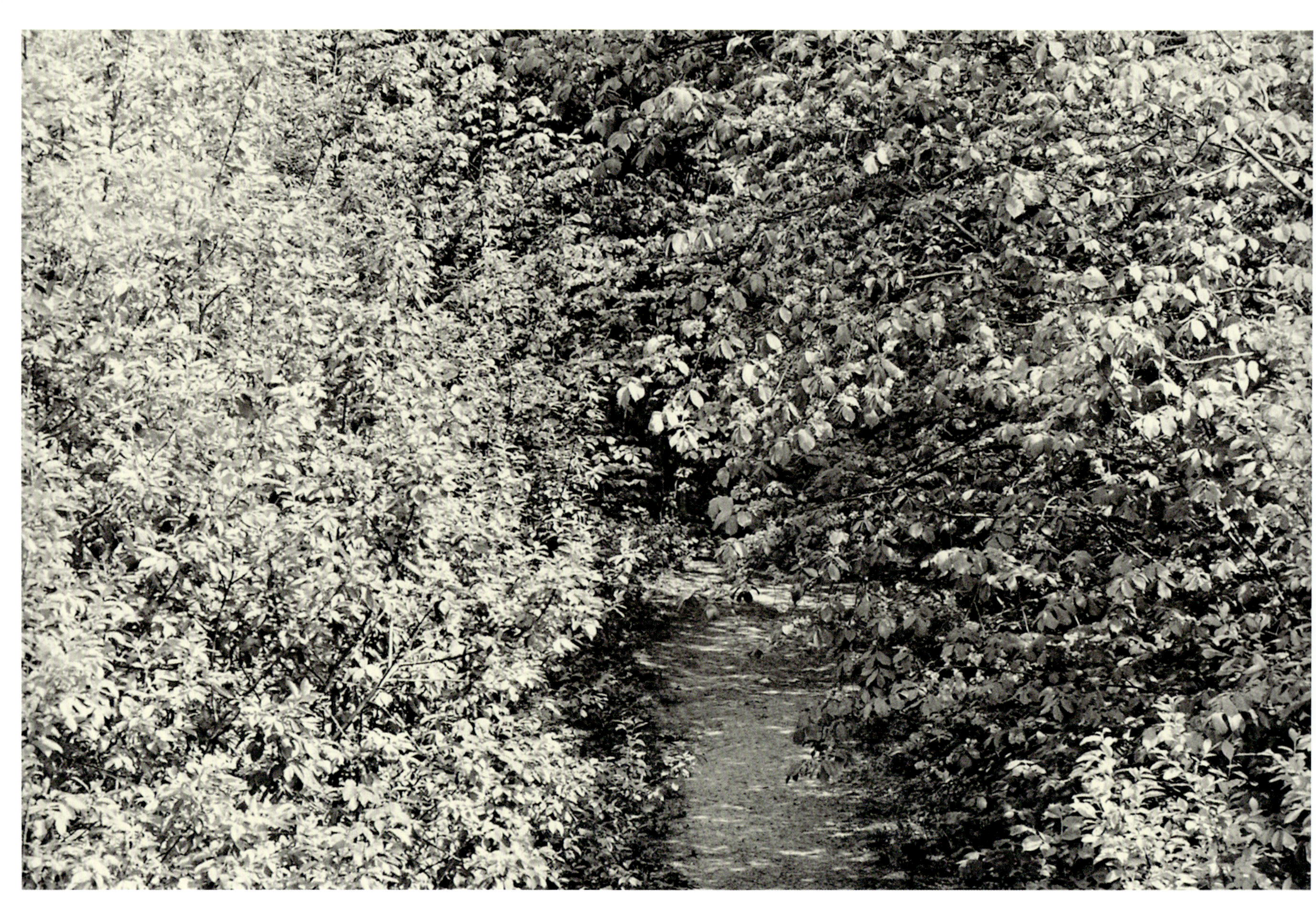

Untitled, 1994–2001
from *Portfolio*, 2003
palladium print
25.5 x 38 cm

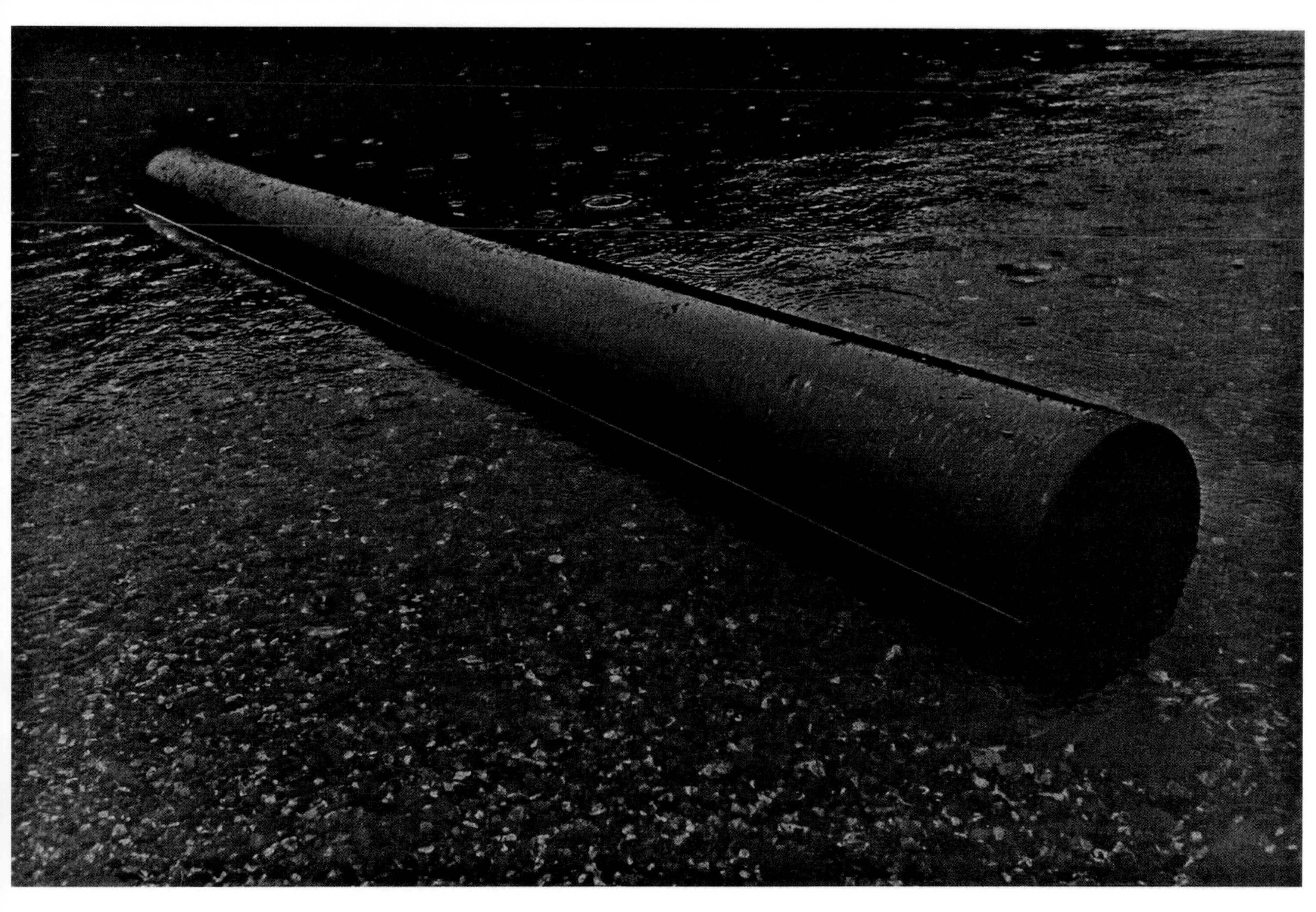

Untitled, 1994–2001
from *Portfolio*, 2003
palladium print
25.5 x 38 cm

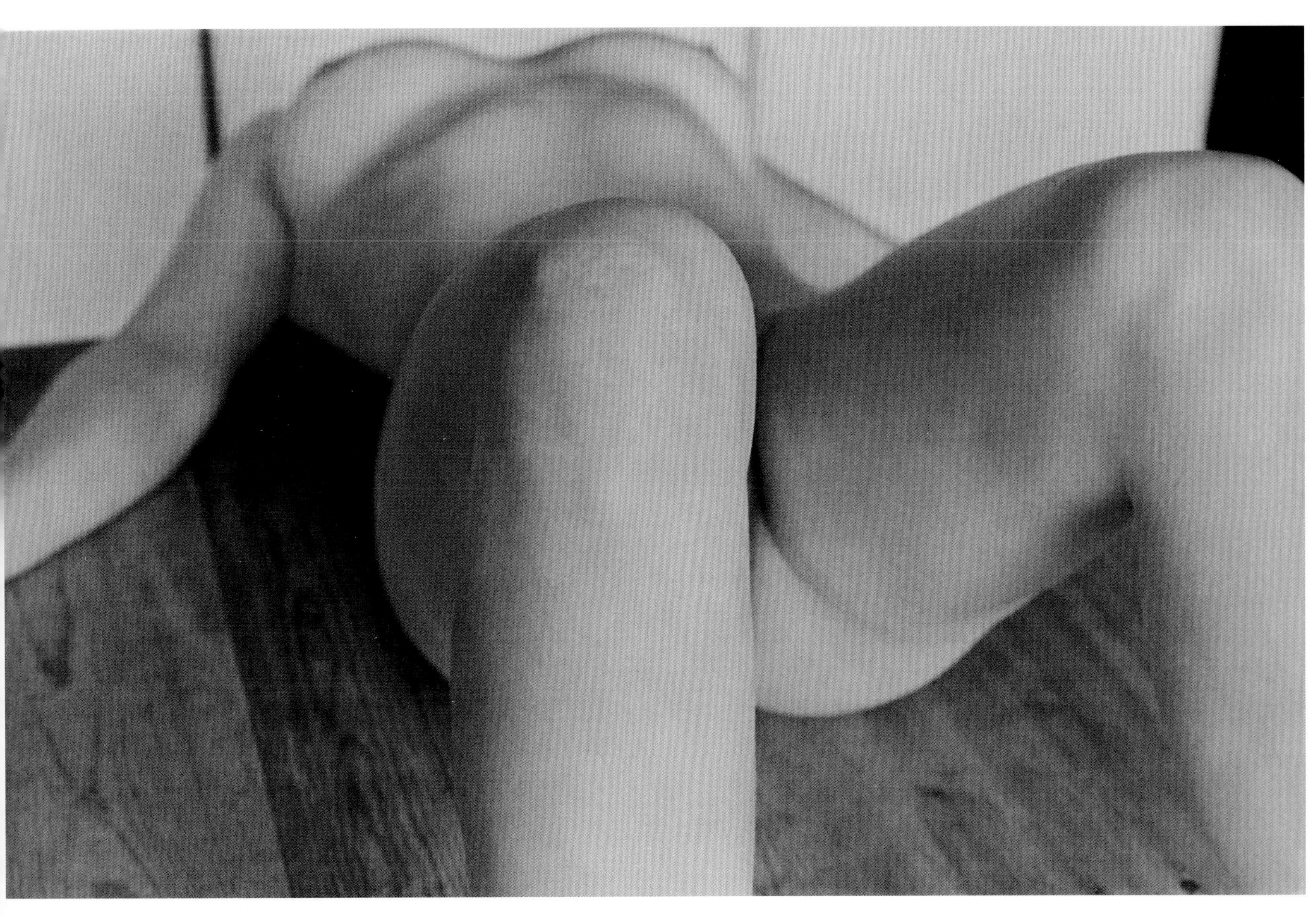

Untitled, 1994–2001
from *Portfolio*, 2003
palladium print
25.5 x 38 cm

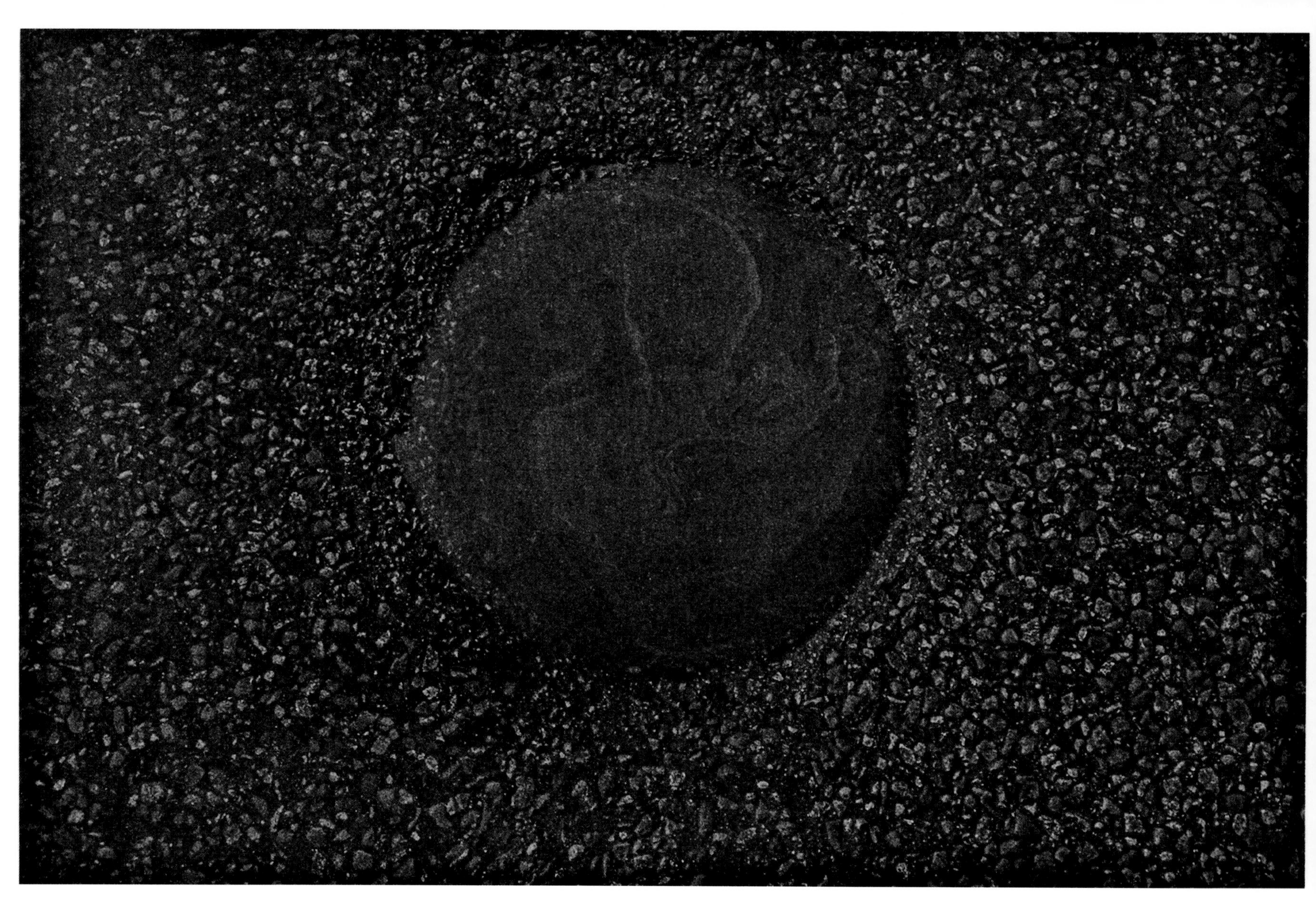

Untitled, 1994–2001
from *Portfolio*, 2003
palladium print
25.5 x 38 cm

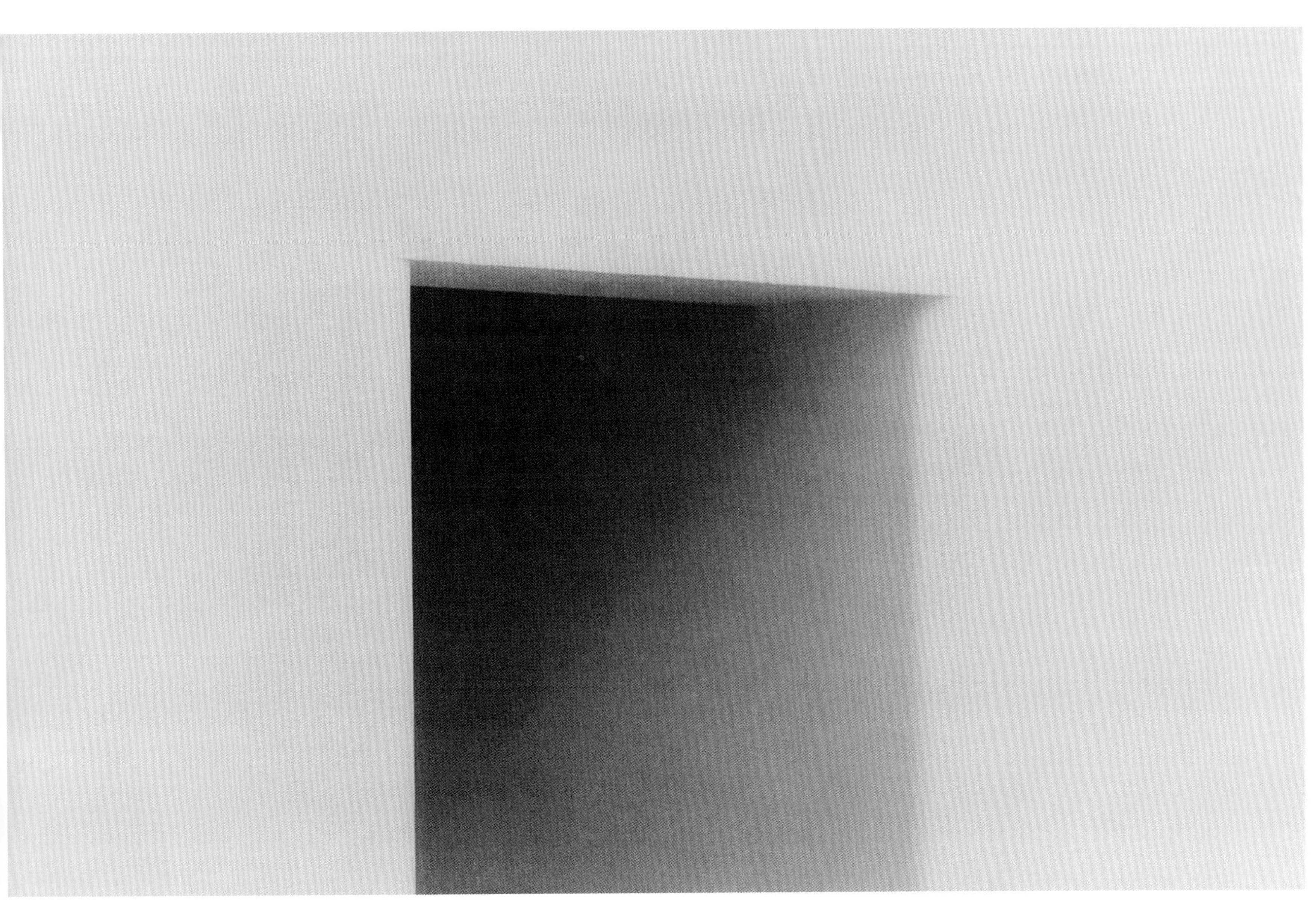

Untitled, 1994–2001
from *Portfolio*, 2003
palladium print
25.5 x 38 cm

Trine Søndergaard

After studying drawing and painting in Aalborg and Copenhagen, Trine Søndergaard (Copenhagen, 1972) completed her studies in 1996 at 'Fatamorgana', the Danish School of Art Photography, before initiating research directed towards the investigation of the photographic medium, its limits and the very nature of the image. In 2000, she won the Albert Renger- Patzsch Award for *Now That You Are Mine* (1997–2000), a series on the world of prostitution in the red-light district of Copenhagen, which has gone on to become a cult book. Capable of ranging from documentary photography, through the diaristic style, all the way to conceptual photography, over recent years she has concentrated on the landscape and portrait genres. The latter has been the subject of a number of series such as *Guldnakke* (2012–13), which takes its name from the gold-embroidered bonnets typically worn by the rural Danish nobility in the nineteenth century; *Strude* (2007–10), in which the models wear the headgear of the popular tradition of the island of Fanø; and *Monochrome Portraits* (2009), showing acquaintances of the artist immersed in their interior world.

Linking the various series is the peculiar approach that Søndergaard reserves for the genre: her subjects are often portrayed from behind or in profile, but in any case they never look at the camera, as if to refuse the game of gazes that traditionally binds subject, photograph and viewer together in this type of photography. Other elements contribute to questioning the portrait genre: although certain clues – such as the bonnets or the contemporary clothes – anchor the images in the past or the present, the photographs are suspended, frozen in time, carriers of a 'duration' that, rather than referring to the exact moment of the shot, speaks of the eternity that photography is able to embody. Traditionally used to represent people in public or private environments, the portrait is transformed by Søndergaard into a means for rendering a mental state visible. These essential, minimalist and elusive images reveal nothing of the identity of the subjects, about their lives or their status: although portrayed, they remain anonymous. In her *Monochrome Portraits* (three works of which are now in the collection), the image of every person, captured in his or her contemplative isolation, is characterised by a specific dark tone that from the photographic surface expands out to the hand-painted frame. Even if chosen by the people photographed, the colours disclose nothing about them, simply contributing to the heightening of the sense of concentration and meditation that, after all, is the true subject of the work. In a way, these non-portraits may also be considered self-portraits: as Søndergaard stated in an interview with Christian Lund published in *Monochrome Portraits* (Hatje Cantz, 2009), 'The portraits … are about finding calm and putting a stop to the thoughts that keep crowding in on me'. Every work, explains the artist, is in part a self-portrait; in each one of them it is possible to catch sight of who is behind the camera: 'Here I show something of myself with an honesty I haven't shown before'.

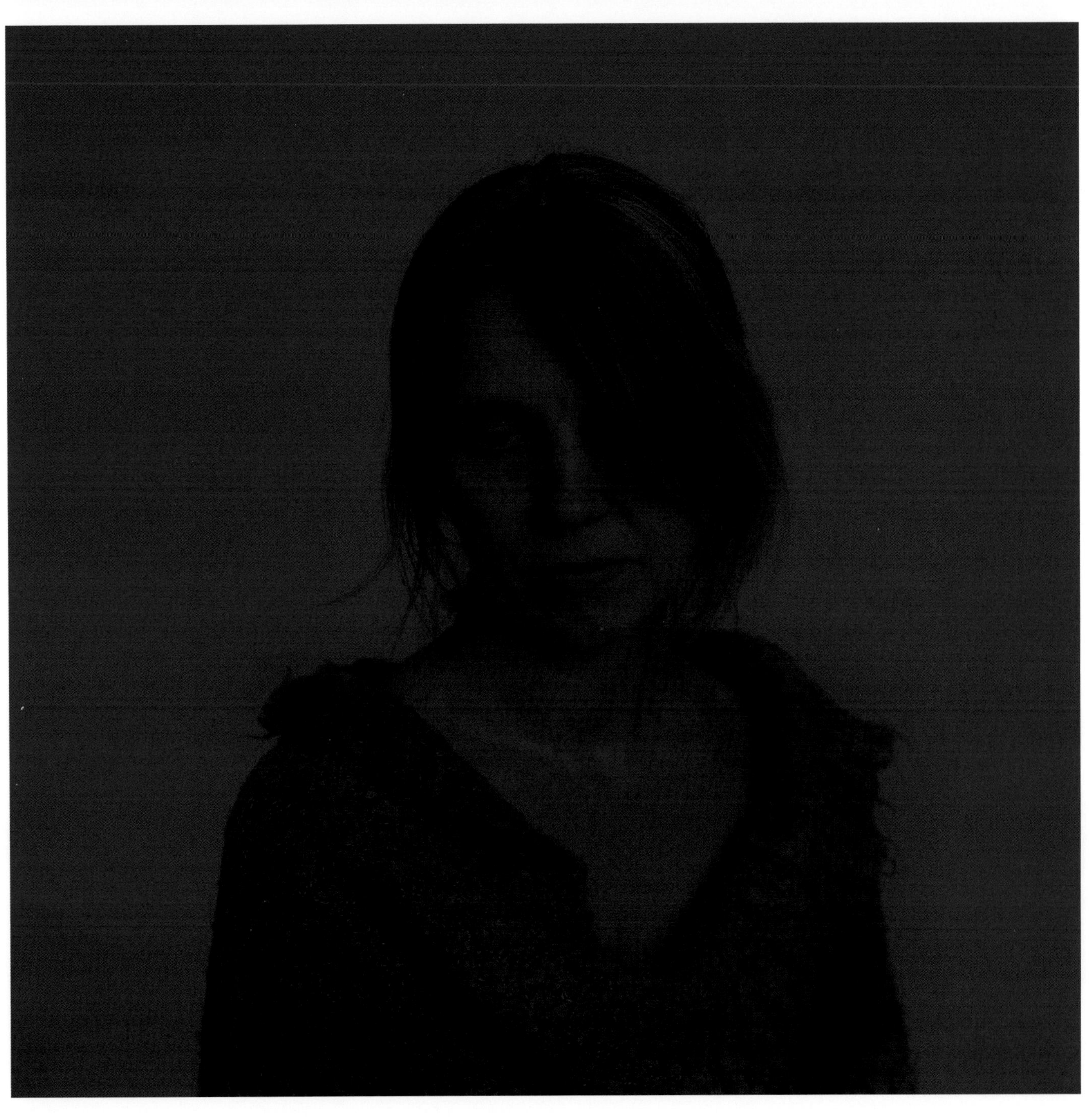

Monochrome Portraits #01, 2009
pigment inkjet print
60 x 60 cm

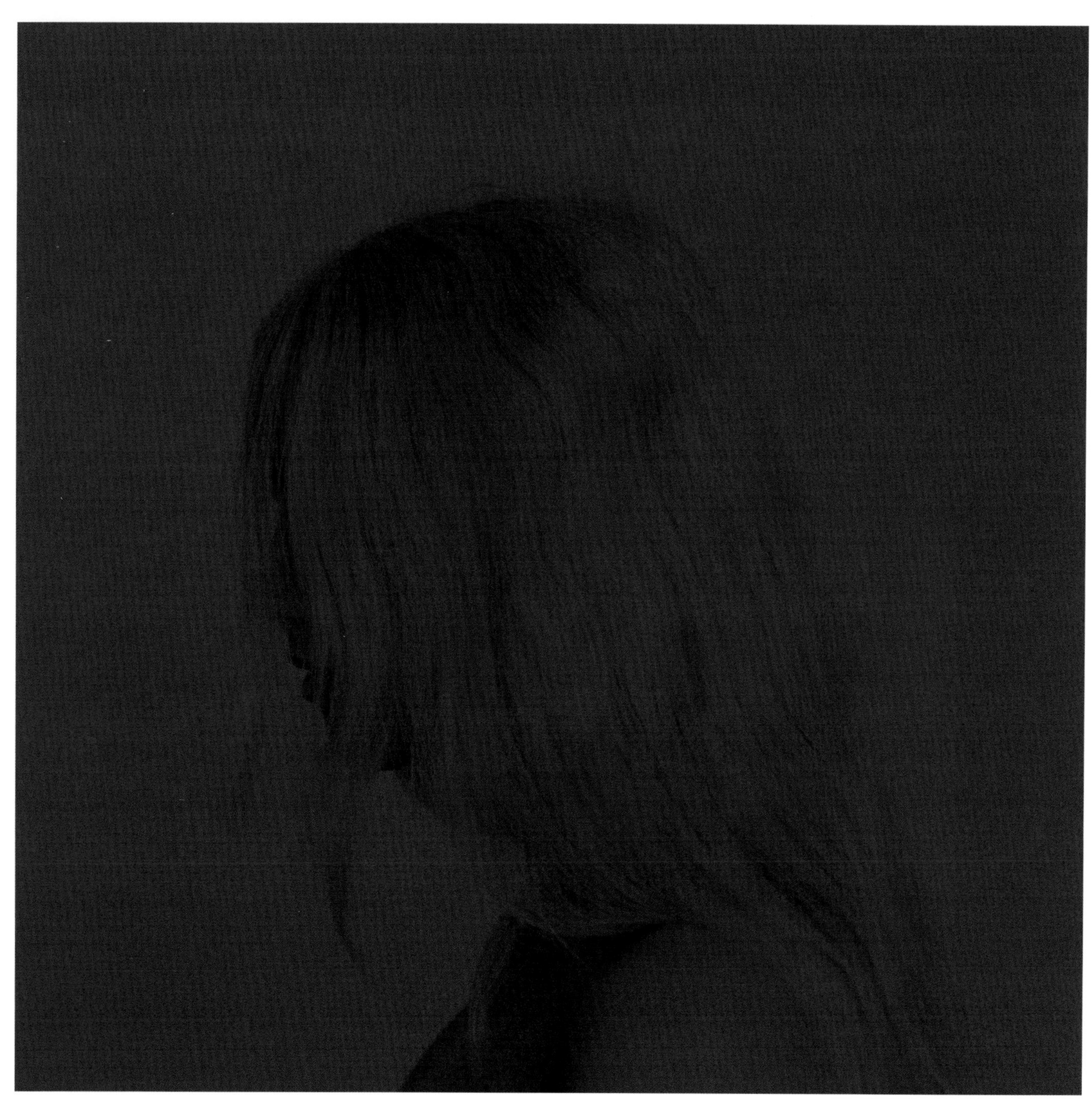

Monochrome Portraits #02, 2009
pigment inkjet print
60 x 60 cm

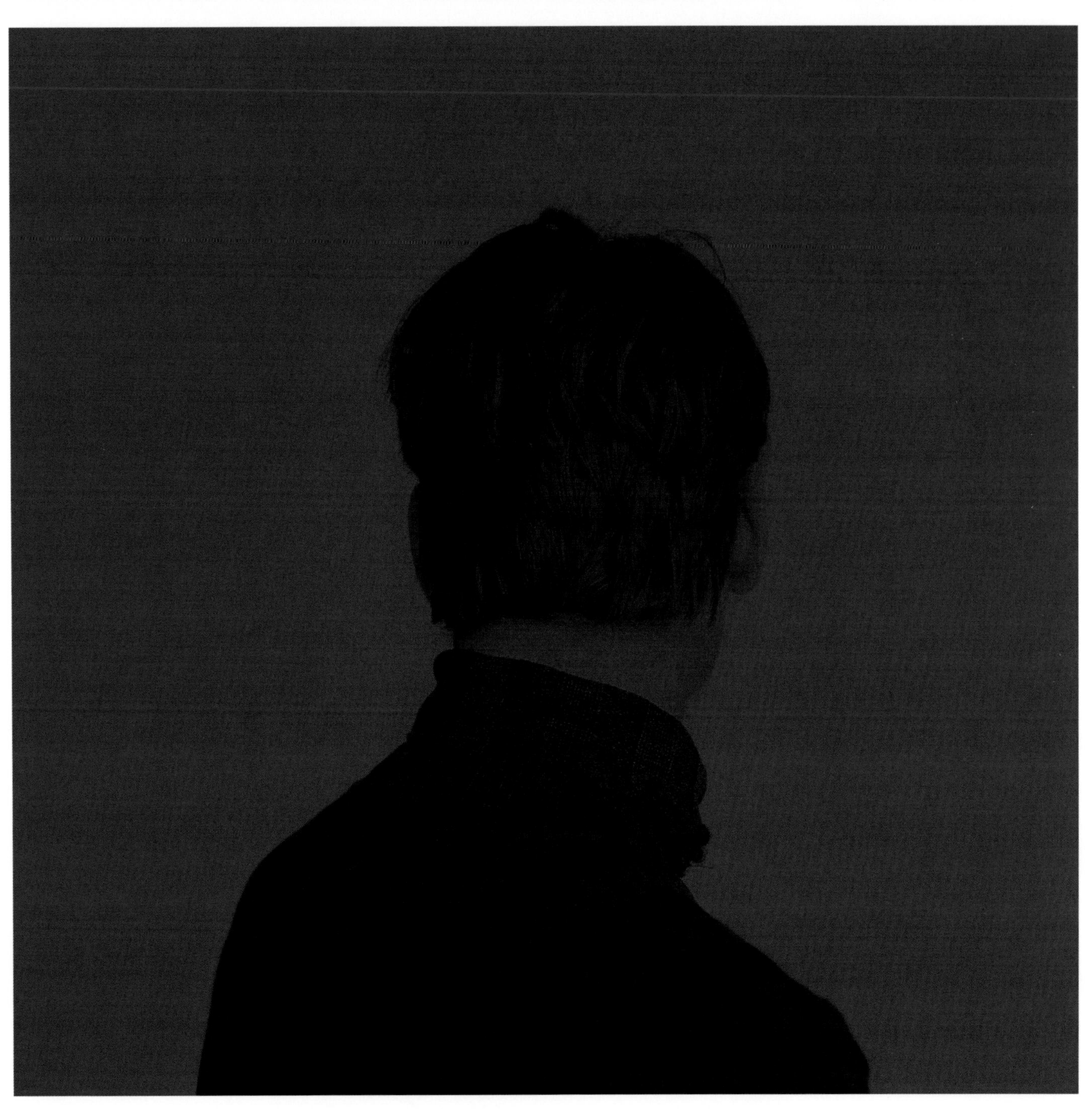

Monochrome Portraits #03, 2009
pigment inkjet print
60 x 60 cm

Wolfgang Tillmans

Even before starting to take photographs, Wolfgang Tillmans entered the orbit of images by manipulating materials taken from magazines and newspapers with a copy machine capable of zooming in by up to 400%. Born and raised in Remscheid, where he graduated in 1987, he moved to Hamburg to carry out his (non-military) national service. There, he continued his experiments and in 1988 exhibited for the first time, at the Café Gnosa, photocopies of images, including a few shots he had taken himself.

One year later, he began taking photographs for magazines such as *Tango*, *Prinz* and *Tempo* and, having moved to London, for UK title *i-D*, a fanzine dedicated to street style that, featuring several of his contributions, would go on to raise the profile of his work.

The images published in those years describe youth sub-cultures and their specific contexts, from Gay Pride marches to religious gatherings and the world of nightclubs and techno music, which in the late 1980s and early 1990s was taking hold throughout Europe. Belonging to this counterculture himself, Tillmans contributed to defining its codes through images that would go on to become iconic. Many of these images were exhibited in 1993 at the Galerie Daniel Buchholz in Cologne. The exhibition not only signalled his entry into the world of art, but also set out the style for which he would become known: images of various sizes and types – photographs, colour photocopies, pages from magazines and ink-jet prints – were shown in a non-hierarchical way, mostly without frames, stuck up with adhesive tape or pins, using grid or linear or random patterns dictated by associations deemed valid by the artist in that space at that particular time. Presenting street photography, portraits, still lifes, landscapes and abstracts, his entire oeuvre takes on the form of a continuously evolving flow of material that renews itself thanks to the open, never-static nature of the images and working processes.

Although linked by the common thread of the sky – a recurring theme in the artist's work – the photographs in the collection are emblematic of the experimental diversity of his output, and of the directions his art has taken over recent decades.

Red Eclipse and *Conquistador III* (both from 2000) bear witness to the artist's interest in abstraction, which first manifested itself in the early 1990s: whereas the former is representative of the type of hybrid images capable of taking us elsewhere while preserving a strong figurative component, the latter belongs to the special editions produced starting from single images that were then rephotographed – the upshot of incidents or errors caused by light or by chemicals during the printing process.

Last but not least, *Lux* (2009) stands as a testament to the return to representation after a decade of abstract experiments through which Tillmans probed the materiality of photography, its chemical processes and its formal aspects, also making use of off-camera practices. Placed in a central position in the book *Neue Welt* (Taschen, 2012) – a reflection on how it is possible today to represent the world – *Lux* is one of the few natural subjects in a series otherwise constituted by architecture, day-to-day scenes, urban landscapes or technological details. Even in this apparently simple image, the tension generated by the play of light between the clouds mirrors the intensity of the entire oeuvre of the artist, characterised by a constant search of balance between randomness and control.

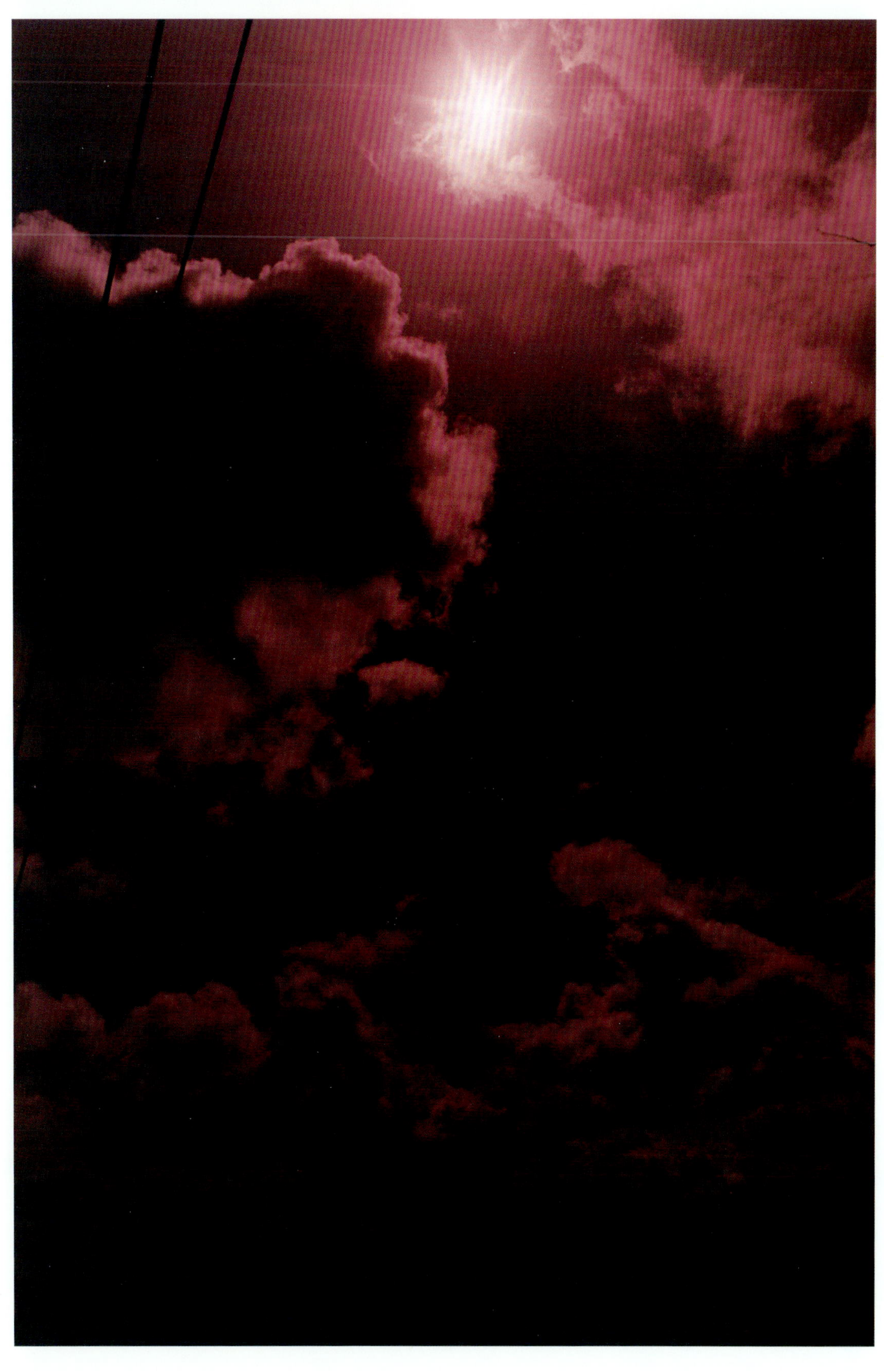

Red Eclipse, 2000
c-print
40.5 x 26.5 cm

Conquistador III, 2000
c-print
61 x 45.5 cm

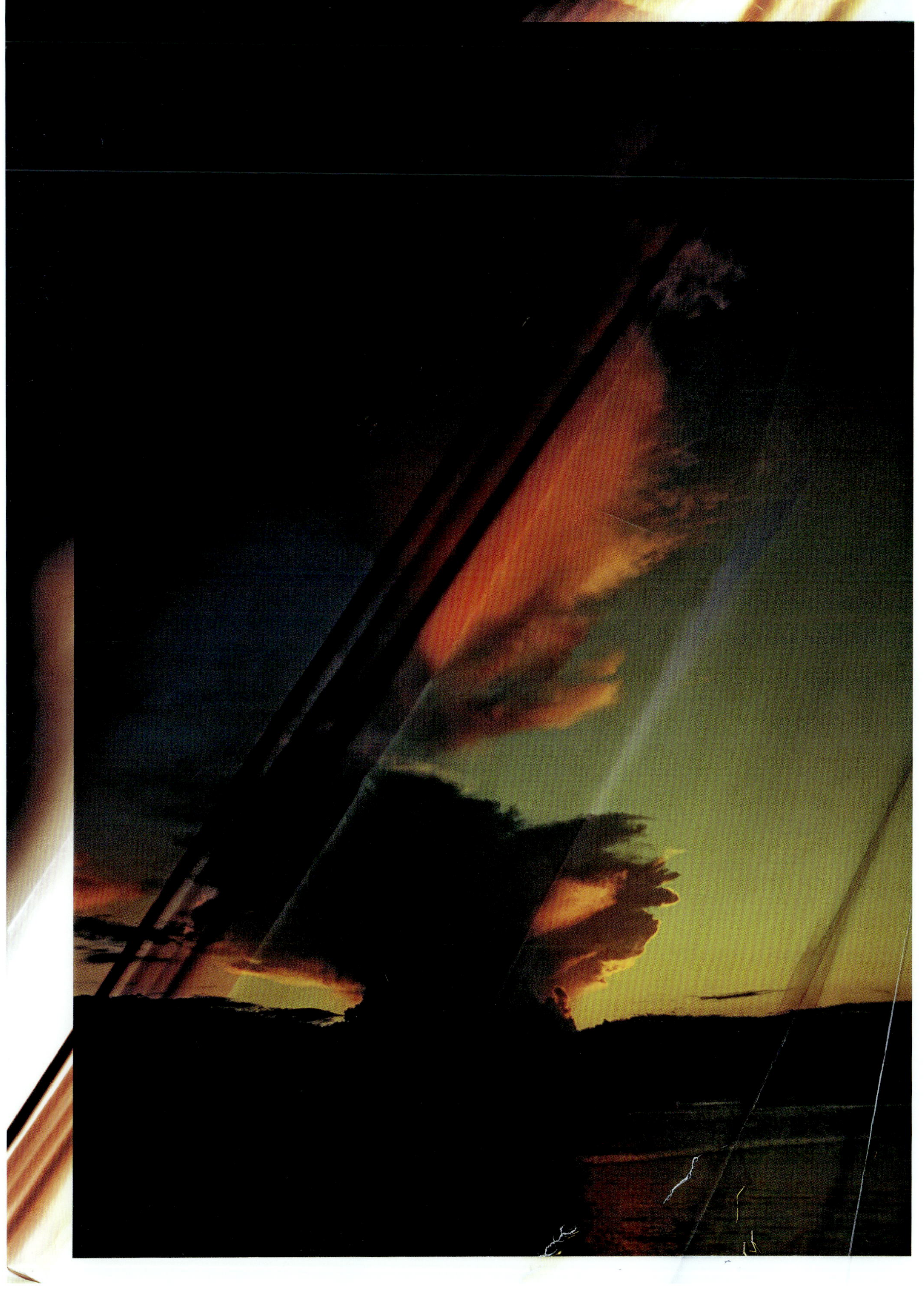

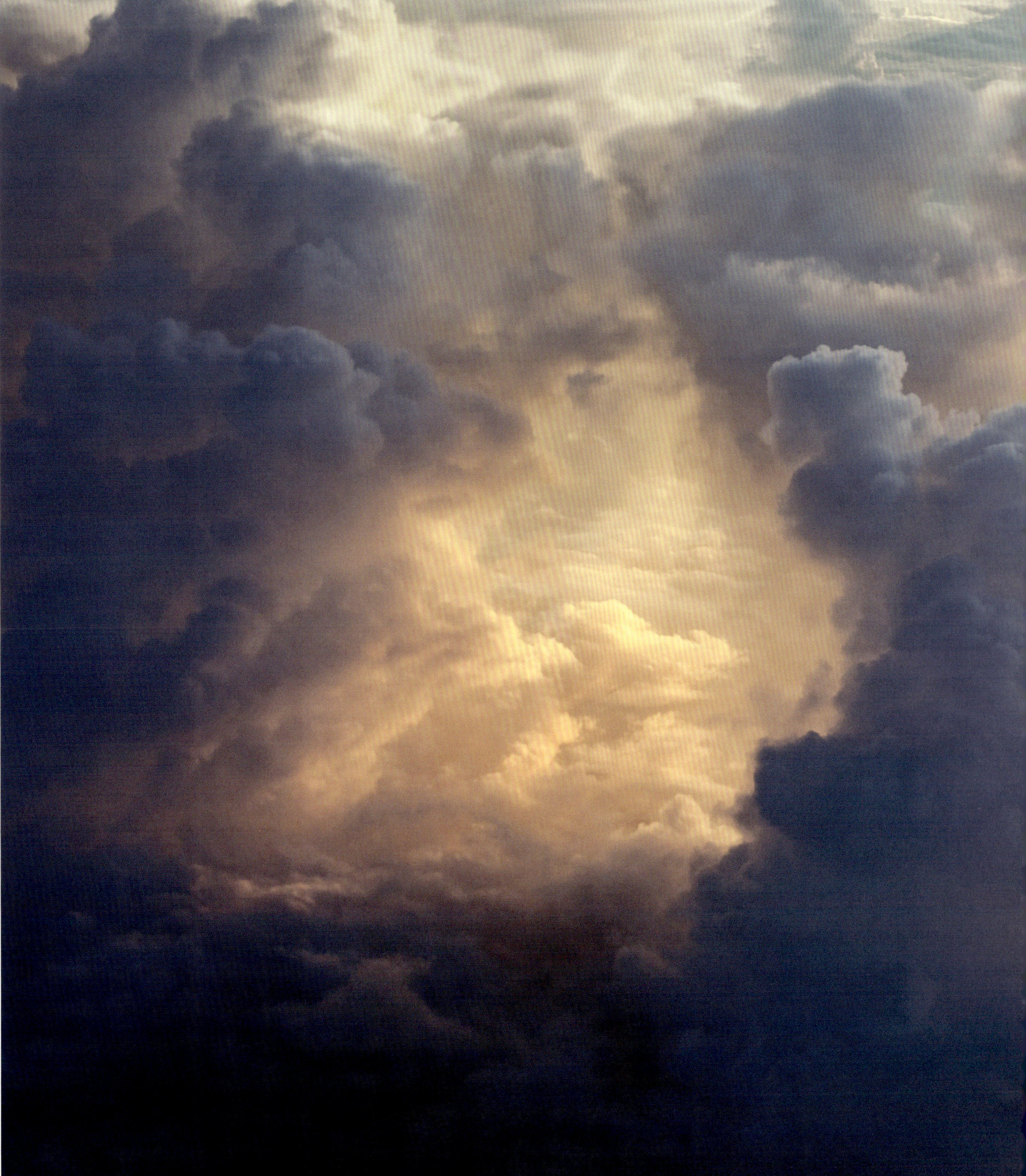

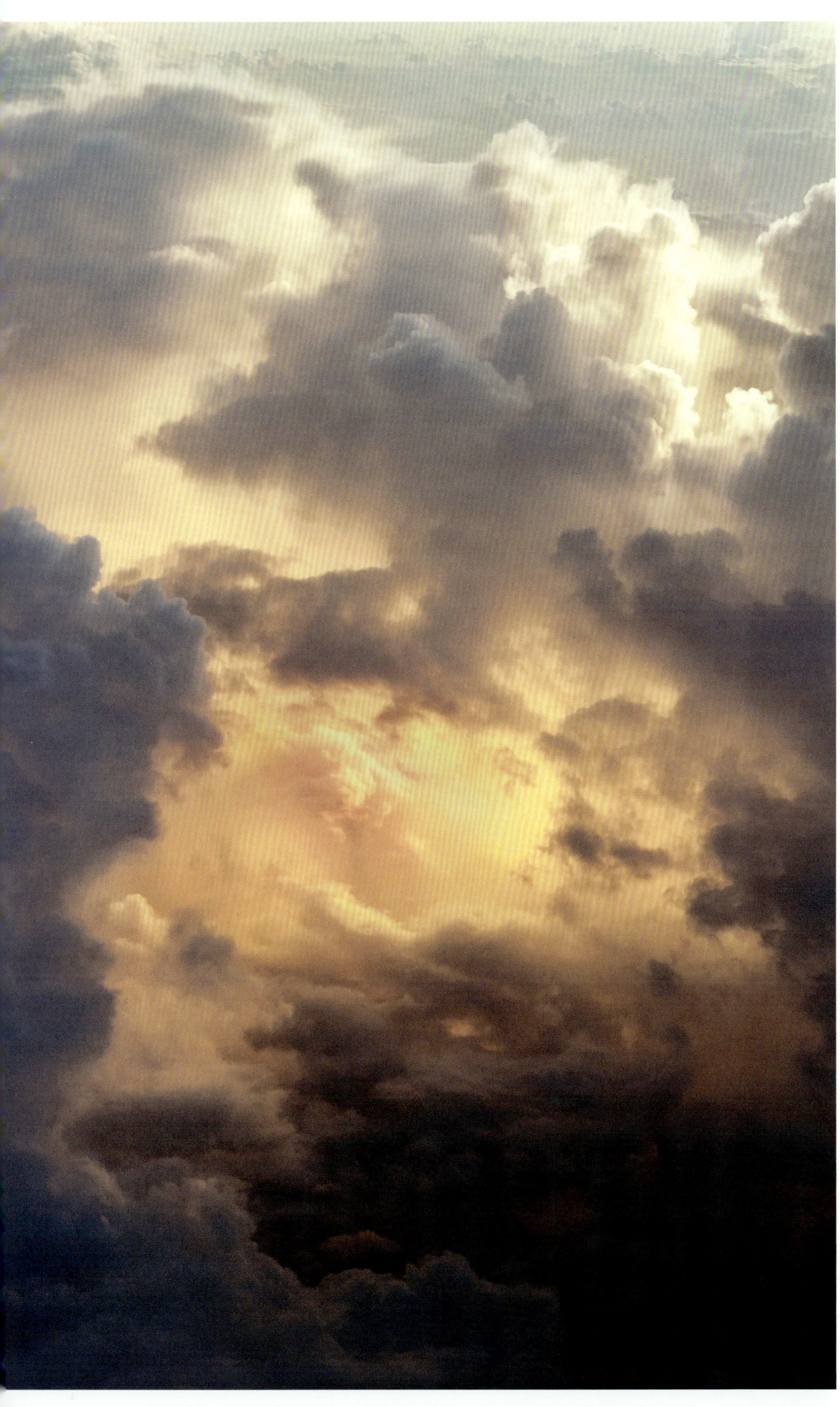

Lux, 2009
inkjet print
26.5 x 40.5 cm

Gillian Wearing

Since the early 1990s, Gillian Wearing (Birmingham, 1963) has been using photography to explore the processes of the construction of the self, its layers, the social norms that define it and its expressive possibilities.

The social slant of her work was immediately evident when, on graduating from Goldsmiths College, she produced *Signs that say what you want them to say and not Signs that say what someone else wants you to say* (1992–93), a series of portraits of people encountered in the street who hold up signs on which, at the artist's request, they wrote their most pressing thoughts. The participatory element of her work was confirmed in subsequent works, in which she started to use video alongside photography: *Confess All On Video. Don't Worry, You Will Be in Disguise. Intrigued? Call Gillian…* (1994) was put together by collecting the confessions of people contacted via a *Time Out* advert (the text of which then became the title of the work); in *Trauma* (2000), men and women recount the experiences that have marked their lives; and in *Secrets and Lies* (2009), unmentionable secrets are made public. A common thread in these works is the use of masks that, clearly false and often rather disturbing, conceal the identities of those making the confessions, allowing them to express themselves freely, thereby affording access to their most intimate thoughts and feelings. The mask takes on a central role in Wearing's work thanks to its function as a bridge between the public and private dimensions of the individual, as well as between the artist and the others.

In the *Album* series (2003–06), the masks became more convincing, produced in partnership with experts trained at Madame Tussauds in London. It was Wearing herself who wore them to impersonate her direct family including her parents, brother, sister, uncle and herself aged 17 – playing out fragments of her family history as passed down through family photographs, used as reference points for the work. In *Album* disguise is used to investigate the mechanisms of memory and the relationships that bind the family group together.

In *Me As Talbot* (2013), which belongs to a series of works started in 2008, Wearing questions herself as an artist and her role as a creator of images. The people impersonated in this series are iconic figures in art and photography considered by Wearing to be her 'spiritual family', such as Diane Arbus, Robert Mapplethorpe, Andy Warhol, Claude Cahun, August Sander, Weegee and, of course, William Henry Fox Talbot, the father of photography and the inventor of the calotype. All of the portraits concern looking or being looked at and often contain relevant objects: for instance, the mask in *Me As Cahun Holding a Mask of My Face* (2012), the Mamiyaflex in *Me As Arbus* (2008) and the small handheld camera used by Talbot.

As in the previous series, the artificiality of the portrayed face is betrayed only by the gaze of the artist that, passing through the mask and the camera, reaches the viewer. Through this revelation, Wearing seems to remind us that the image is not an objective representation but a projection, just like the layered identity of an individual. And photography, the surface *par excellence* where projections are frozen, is nothing but a depository of those stratifications, a meeting point for the self and others, whether they are idols of photography, family members or viewers.

Me As Talbot, 2013
gelatin silver print
148 x 122 cm

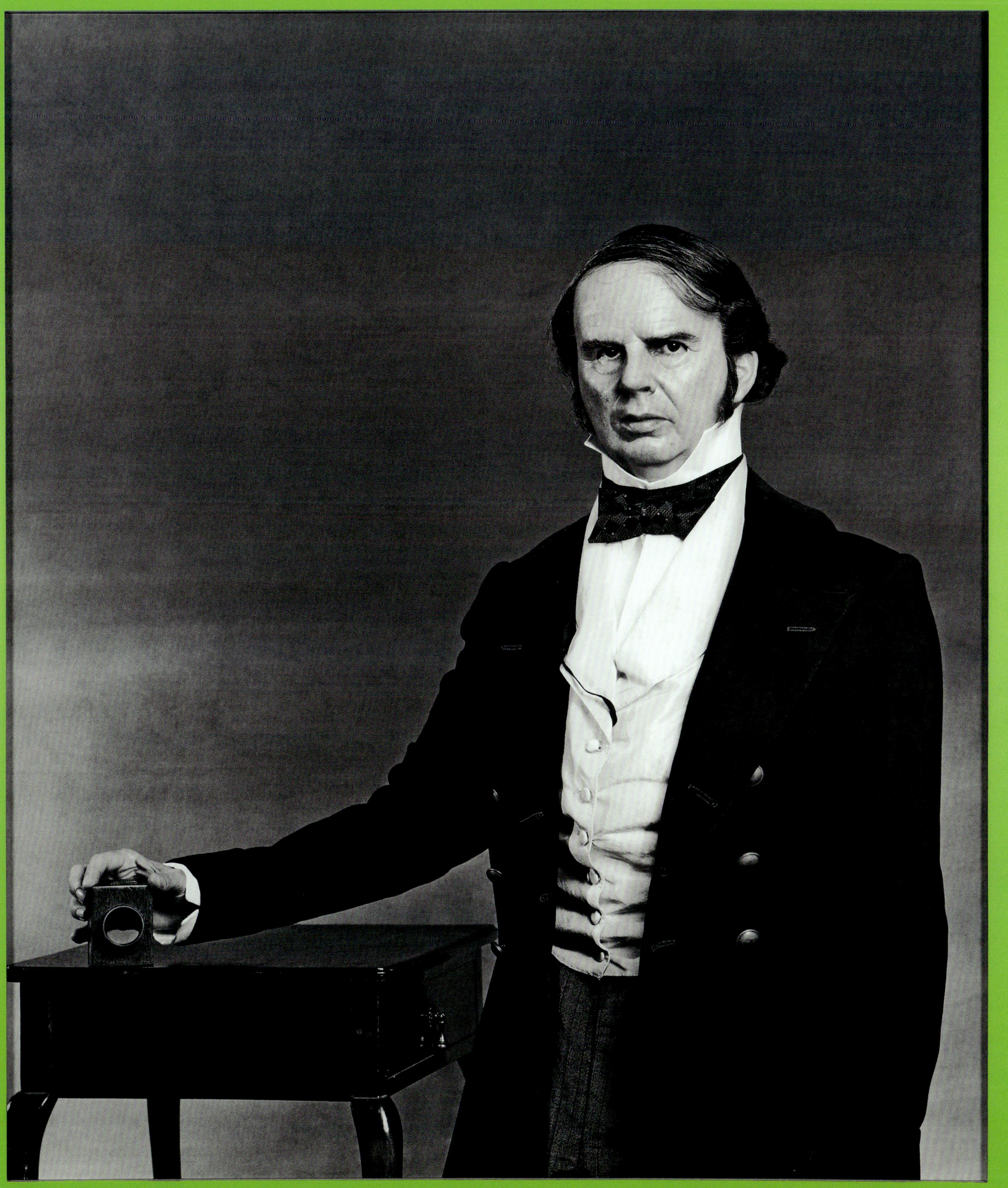

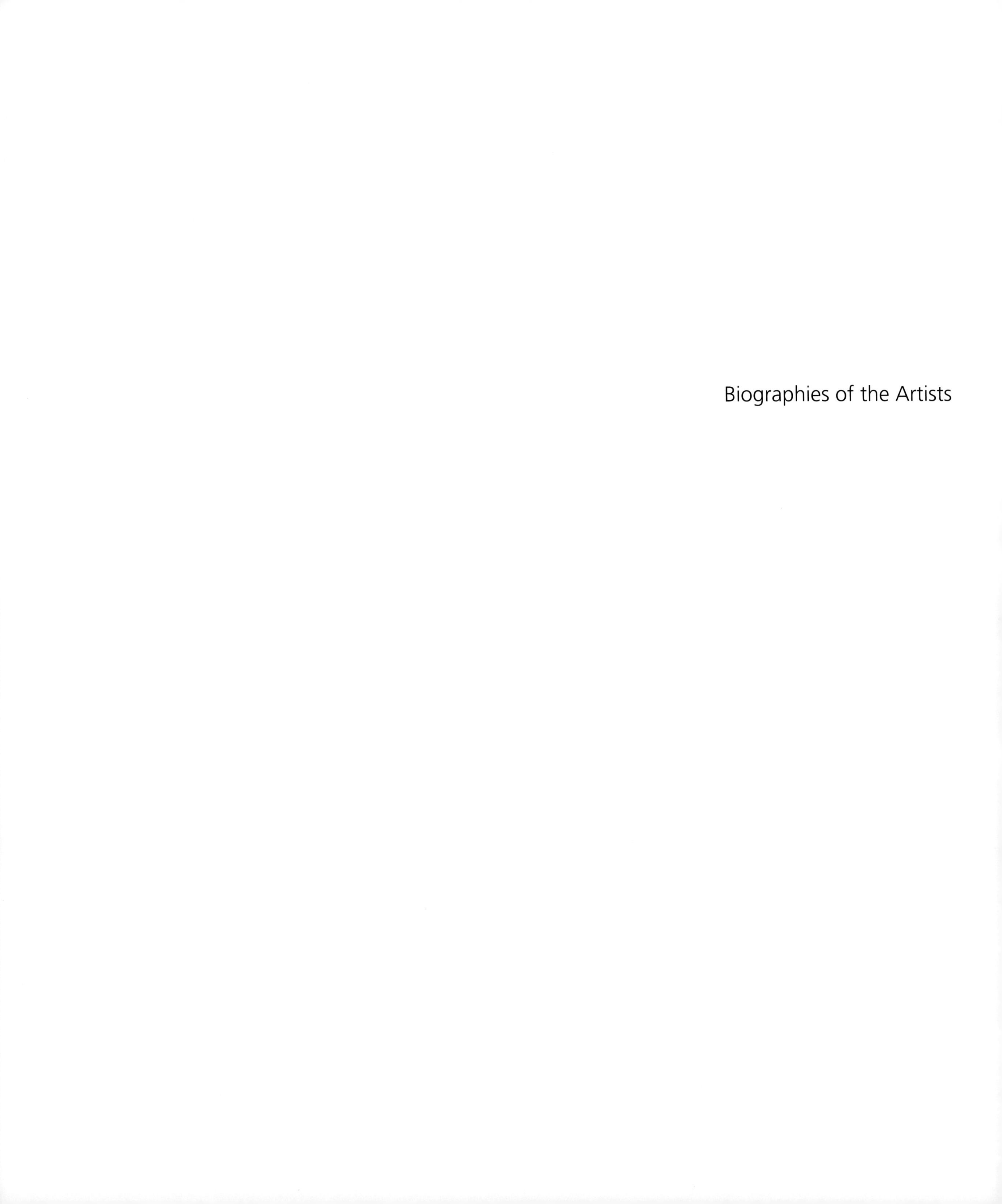

Biographies of the Artists

Morten Andenæs

Born in 1979 in Oslo
Lives and works in Oslo

Solo Exhibitions
2015
Galleri Riis, Oslo.
2014
Green Apples / Blue Sky, Paris Photo, in collaboration with Galleri MELK and Fotogalleriet, Oslo.
The Stain, The Act, The Mask and The Fact, Galleri MELK, Oslo, with Ivan Galuzin.
2013
Enclosed Circuit X, Galleri Riis, Stockholm.
Enclosed Circuit, Galleri Riis, Oslo.
2012
Plumbing, Peter Lav Gallery, Copenhagen.
2011
Observance, Galleri Riis, Oslo.
2009
Mutual Exclusion, Galleri MELK, Oslo.
Concessions, Galleri BOA, Oslo.
2007
Greyscale, Fotogalleriet, Oslo, with Ola Rindal.

Selected Group Exhibitions
2014
Preview, Galleri Riis, Oslo.
2013
1986–2013, Vestfossen Kunstlaboratorium, Vestfossen, Norway.
2012
Längtans blomma är störst på håll, Galleri Riis, Oslo.
Galleri Gann, Sandnes, Norway.
2011
Vårutstillingen, Fotogalleriet, Oslo.
Høstutstillingen, Statens Kunstutstiling, Oslo.
2010
Høstutstillingen, Statens Kunstutstiling, Oslo.
2009
Latte in Watte, Galleri Riis, Oslo.
2008
Østlandsutstillingen, Oslo and Lübeck, Germany.

Public Collections
Astrup Fearnley Museum of Modern Art, Oslo.
Kistefos-Museet, Jevnaker.
KORO (Public Art Norway) for the Ministry of Defence, Akershus Fortress, Oslo.
Stavanger Art Museum.
Statoil Art Collection.
Norsk Hydro.
The Freedom of Expression Foundation, Litteraturhuset, Oslo.

Johann Arens

Born in 1981 in Aachen, Germany
Lives and works in Amsterdam

Solo Exhibitions
2013
Internet Centre & Habesha Grocery,
Basement Projects at Paradise Row,
London.
2012
Effect Rating, De Service Garage,
Amsterdam.
Apple and Pear, ASC Gallery, London.
2011
Deceptive Eye, The Institute of
Continuation, Stockholm, with Alex
Reynolds.

Selected Group Exhibitions
2015
Pillar Huggers, Or Gallery, Berlin.
2014
RijksakademieOPEN, Amsterdam.
Emotional Resources, Northern Gallery
for Contemporary Art, Sunderland, UK.
Corso Aperto, Fondazione A. Ratti,
Como, Italy.
TTTT, Jerwood Space, London.
Chronovisor, South Kiosk, London.
Detours, Enclave, London.
Hard Copy, Fondazione Pastificio
Cerere, Rome.
2013
Friday 13th, British School at Rome,
Rome.
Home Theater, Baró Galeria, São Paulo,
Brazil.
Institute for Mathematical Sciences, Flat
Time House, London.
2012
Members Show, Outpost, Norwich, UK.
Young London 2012, V22, London.
A useful-looking useless object, Sierra
Metro, Edinburgh, UK.
I'll explain you everythiinnngggg,
Chert, Berlin.
2011
The Object as Image, Verein für Raum
und Form (Ve.sch), Vienna.
Drop after Drop, Galeria AS, Krakow,
Poland.
*Stressing spiritual needs even when
selling ice-cream*, DNA Gallery, Berlin.
2010
New Contemporaries, A Foundation,
Liverpool and ICA, London.

Uncertain Ratio, Imperial College,
London.
Of many, one, Scaramouche Gallery,
New York.
To look is to labour, Laden für Nichts,
Leipzig, Germany.
The Dictionary of Received Ideas,
Q, London.
No Soul For Sale, Tate Modern,
London.
2009
FRàGIL, Carré Bonnat, Bayonne, France.
Samenhang, MAP Gallery, Leeds, UK.
2008
Fragile, LOOP Video Art Fair,
Espai Ubú, Barcelona.
Kunstvlaai Art Pie International,
Westergasfabriek, Amsterdam.
A Pact with Joy, Rialto Santambrogio,
Rome.
2006
Catalyst, Brakke Grond, Amsterdam.
Summer Filmprogram, Huis Marseille,
Amsterdam.
2005
Cinema Bricolage, Westergasfabriek,
Amsterdam.
Overschrilderen, STUK, Leuven,
Belgium.

**Selected Screenings and
Presentations**
2014
Looking, Mediated, LUX Touring
Programme, Talbot Rice Gallery,
Edinburgh, UK.
Looking, Mediated, LUX Touring
Programme, Arnolfini, Bristol.
Film Open, The Tetley, Leeds, UK.
Kunstfilmtage, Düsseldorf, Germany.
Looking, Mediated, LUX Touring
Programme, Open School East,
London.
ENTER Media Art Festival, Siauliai,
Vilnius, Lithuania.
Film Open, Rhubaba, Edinburgh, UK.
Film Open, S1 Artspace, Sheffield, UK.
2013
Film Open, Outpost, Norwich, UK.
2012
Institute for Mathematical Sciences,
Guest Projects, London.
2011
Cinemache Video Art Festival, Agency,
Scarborough, UK.

*One Minute Cinema: The World
of Witte de With*, DZR, Rotterdam,
The Netherlands.
VIDEOTATIONAL 1, Minken und Palme,
Berlin.
Chain Letter, Samsøn Gallery, Boston,
Mass.
Kinomaton Film Abend, ACUD Kino,
Berlin.
2009
*5th International Amsterdam Film
Festival*, Amsterdam.
2007
Lost and Found, The Waag,
Amsterdam.
Media Art Friesland, Friesland,
The Netherlands.
2006
Nederlands Film Festival, Utrecht,
The Netherlands.
2005
*9. International Short Filmfestival
Winterthur*, Winterthur, Switzerland.
Dutch Open Festival, De Balie,
Amsterdam.

Public Commissions
2014
100 Arches, Arnolfini with Art and the
Public Realm, Bristol, UK.
This chair is a replica (Please sit down),
Letchworth Garden City Heritage
Foundation, Letchworth, UK.
2012
Facility, JVA Projects, Jerwood Space,
London.

Jonny Briggs

Born in 1985 in Berkshire, UK
Lives and works in London

Selected Solo Exhibitions
2015
Ncontemporary at mc2gallery, Milan.
Comfortable in My Skin, Marie-Laure
Fleisch, Rome.
2014
Monstrare, Julie Meneret
Contemporary Art, New York.
2013
Ancestral Home, Simon Oldfield
Gallery, London.
2012
Mitosis, White Project, Paris.
Familiar/Familial, FaMa Gallery, Verona,
Italy.

Selected Group Exhibitions
2015
DEAD, Saatchi Gallery, London.
The London Intensive, Camden Arts
Centre, London.
Soil Culture travelling show, including
Eden Project, Cornwall, Peninsula Arts,
Plymouth, Hauser & Wirth Somerset,
Bruton, UK (Catlin Prize World Tour).
START, Saatchi Gallery, London.
Photobook Melbourne, Melbourne.
Photo 50, London Art Fair, London.
Florilegia, Grimaldi Gavin, Mayfair,
London.
A Spectre From the Land of If no. 3,
Stilll Gallery, Antwerp, Belgium.
2014
Foam Talent, East Wing Gallery,
Dubai, UAE.
Foam Talent, Atelier néerlandais, Paris.
Ermanno Tedeschi, Tel Aviv.
2013
Art Miami, The Catlin Prize, Miami, FL.
Family Politics, Jerwood Space,
London.
The Future Can Wait, Victoria House,
London.
Ceri Hand Gallery Summer Fête,
Ceri Hand Gallery, London.
Reality Check, High House, Oxford, UK.
2012
Fresh Faced and Wild Eyed, The
Photographers' Gallery, London.
This Is London, Shizaru Gallery, London.
Courtship of the Peoples, Simon
Oldfield Gallery, London.

Out of Focus: Photography, Saatchi
Gallery, London.
The Catlin Prize, London.
The Catlin Guide, London Art Fair,
London.
2011
Prix Leica, MARTa Herford, Herford,
Germany.
The Way We Live Now, Design
Museum, London.
New Sensations, Victoria House,
London.
Paraty em Foco, International
Photography Festival, Paraty, Brazil.
The Divided Self, Cob Gallery, London.
The Royal We, Guts for Garters,
London.
2010
176 / Zabludowicz Collection,
Chalk Farm, London.
Top Ten London Photographers,
www.spoonfed.com.
Moscow Young Artist Biennale,
Moscow.
Park Night, Pumphouse Gallery,
Battersea Park, London.
Surreal Nightmares, Shunt, London
Bridge, London.
Album, Wolstenholme Projects,
Liverpool Biennial, Liverpool, UK.
Mini Exhibition, Rydges Hotel, South
Kensington, London.
2009
Art Below Zero, Westbourne Studios,
Notting Hill, London.
RCA Secret, Gulbenkian Gallery, Royal
College of Art, London.
2008
The New Sensations, Saatchi Gallery /
Channel 4, London.
Siteshow, Belgravia, London.
The Shape of Things to Come,
Battersea Park Events Arena, London.
2007
Xhibit, The Arts Gallery, London.
2006
This Way Up, Temporary Contemporary,
Deptford, London.

Willie Doherty

Born in 1959 in Derry, North Ireland
Lives and works in Derry

Solo Exhibitions
2014
Remains, Kerlin Gallery, Dublin.
Unseen, De Pont, Tilburg,
The Netherlands.
2013
Unseen, City Factory Gallery, Derry.
Secretion, Neue Galerie,
Museumslandschaft Hessen, Kassel,
Germany.
Secretion, The Annex, IMMA,
Dublin.
Without Trace, Galerie Peter Kilchmann,
Zurich.
2012
Secretion, Statens Museum for Kunst,
Copenhagen.
Lapse, Kerlin Gallery, Dublin.
Towner Art Gallery, Eastbourne, UK.
Matts Gallery, London.
One Place Twice, Photo/Text/85/92,
Alexander and Bonin, New York.
Wolverhampton Art Gallery,
Wolverhampton, UK.
2011–12
Willie Doherty: Traces, Speed Art
Museum, Louisville, KY.
2011
Disturbance, in conjunction with *Dublin
Contemporary 2011*, Dublin City Gallery
The Hugh Lane, Dublin.
The Visitor, Dublin City Gallery The
Hugh Lane, Dublin.
2010
Unfinished, Galería Moisés Pérez
de Albéniz, Pamplona, Spain.
Lack, Alexander and Bonin, New York.
Visions, Ulster Museum, Botanic
Gardens, Belfast.
2009
Three Potential Endings, Dark Light X,
Dublin.
Willie Doherty: Buried, Prefix Institute
of Contemporary Art, Toronto.
Wille Doherty: Buried, Fruitmarket
Gallery, Edinburgh.
Willie Doherty: Buried, Glynn Vivian
Art Gallery, Swansea, Wales.
Requisite Distance, Dallas Museum
of Art, Dallas, TX.
Three Potential Endings, Galerie Peter
Kilchmann, Zurich.

2008
The Visitor, Douglas Hyde Gallery, Dublin.
Venice at Farmleigh, Farmleigh Gallery,
Dublin, with Gerard Byrne.
Ghost Story, Prince Charles Cinema,
London.
*Replays: Selected video works
1994–2007*, Matt's Gallery, London.
2007
Apparatus & Closure, Void, Derry.
North Ireland Pavilion, 52nd Venice
Biennale.
Kunstverein, Hamburg, Germany.
Alexander and Bonin, New York.
2006
Empty, Kerlin Gallery, Dublin and Galerie
Peter Kilchmann, Zurich.
Out of Position, Laboratorio Arte
Alameda, Mexico City.
2005
Apparatus, Galerie Nordenhake, Berlin.
Apparatus, Galería Pepe Cobo, Madrid.
Willie Doherty: Non-Specific Threat,
Muzej savremene umetnosti, Belgrade,
Serbia.
2004
Willie Doherty: Non-Specific Threat,
Alexander and Bonin, New York.
Willie Doherty: Non-Specific Threat,
Galerie Peter Kilchmann, Zurich.
2003
De Appel, Amsterdam.
2002
Willie Doherty: False Memory, Irish
Museum of Modern Art, Dublin.
Unknown Male Subject, Kerlin Gallery,
Dublin.
Willie Doherty: Retraces, Matt's
Gallery, London.
2001
*Willie Doherty: How It Was / Double
Take*, Ormeau Baths Gallery, Belfast.
Extracts from a File, Alexander and
Bonin, New York.
2000
Extracts from a File, Gesellschaft für
Aktuelle Kunst, Bremen, Germany.
Extracts from a File, Galerie Peter
Kilchmann, Zurich.
Extracts from a file, DAAD Galerie, Berlin.
Extracts from a File, Kerlin Gallery, Dublin.
1999
Dark Stains, Koldo Mitxelena
Kulturunea, Donostia–San Sebastián,
Spain.

*Willie Doherty: New Photographs and
Video*, Alexander and Bonin, New York.
Same Old Story, Firstsite, Colchester, UK.
True Nature, The Renaissance Society,
Chicago, IL.
Somewhere Else, Museum of Modern
Art, Oxford, UK.
1998
Somewhere Else, Tate Gallery, Liverpool,
UK.
Galleria Emi Fontana, Milan.
1997
Willie Doherty: Same Old Story, Matt's
Gallery, London, travelling to Orchard
Gallery, Derry, Berwick Gymnasium,
Berwick-upon-Tweed, UK, Le Magasin,
Grenoble, France.
Galerie Peter Kilchmann, Zurich.
Kerlin Gallery, Dublin.
Blackspot, Firstsite, Colchester, UK.
1996
*Willie Doherty: The Only Good One
is a Dead One*, Edmonton Art Gallery,
Edmonton, Canada; Mendel Art Gallery,
Saskatoon, Canada; Art Gallery of
Windsor, Windsor, UK; Art Gallery
of Ontario, Toronto; Fundaçáo Calouste
Gulbenkian, Lisbon.
Alexander and Bonin, New York.
Musée d'art moderne de la ville
de Paris, Paris.
*In the Dark: Projected Works by Willie
Doherty*, Kunsthalle, Bern; Kunstverein,
Munich.
1995
Willie Doherty, Kerlin Gallery, Dublin.
Galerie Jennifer Flay, Paris.
Galerie Peter Kilchmann, Zurich.
1994
At the End of the Day, British School
in Rome, Rome.
1993
The Only Good One is a Dead One,
Arnolfini, Bristol and Grey Art Gallery,
New York.
30 January 1972, Douglas Hyde Gallery,
Dublin.
They're all the Same, Centre for Con-
temporary Art, Ujazdowski Castle, Warsaw.
The Only Good One is a Dead One,
Matt's Gallery, London.
Galerie Jennifer Flay, Paris.
1992
Galerie Peter Kilchmann, Zurich.
Oliver Dowling Gallery, Dublin.

1991
Kunst Europa, Six Irishmen, Kunstverein, Schwetzingen, Germany.
Tom Cugliani Gallery, New York.
Galerie Giovanna Minelli, Paris.
Unknown Depths, John Hansard Gallery, Southampton, UK; Angel Row Gallery, Nottingham, UK; ICA, London; Ffotogallery, Cardiff, UK; Third Eye Centre, Glasgow; Orchard Gallery, Derry.
1990
Same Difference, Matt's Gallery, London.
Imagined Truths, Oliver Dowling Gallery, Dublin.
1988
Colourworks, Oliver Dowling Gallery, Dublin.
Two Photoworks, Third Eye Center, Glasgow.
1987
The Town of Derry, Photoworks, Art & Research Exchange, Belfast.
Photoworks, Oliver Dowling Gallery, Dublin.
1986
Stone Upon Stone, Redemption!, Derry.
1982
Siren. An Installation, Art & Research Exchange, Belfast.
Collages, Orchard Gallery, Derry.
1980
Orchard Gallery, Derry.

Selected Group Exhibitions
2013
Catalyst: Contemporary Art and War, The Imperial War Museum North, Manchester, UK.
Golden Years: Oleg Klimov, Olga Chernysheva, Sarkis & Willie Doherty: Huis Marseille Collection, Huis Marseille Museum voor fotografie, Amsterdam.
Northern Ireland: 30 Years of Photography, Belfast Exposed in collaboration with The Mac, Belfast.
Keywords, INIVA Institute of International Visual Arts, London.
Concrete: Photography and Architecture, Fotomuseum Winterthur, Winterthur, Switzerland.
Changing States: Contemporary Irish Art and Francis Bacon's Studio, Bozar Centre for Fine Arts, Brussels.
Looking at the View, Tate Britain, London.

2012
dOCUMENTA 13, Kassel.
OC Collection, Orange County Museum of Art, Orange, CA.
Stimuli: Prints & Multiples, Alexander and Bonin, New York.
2011
ANGRY: Jong en Radicaal, Nederlands Fotomuseum, Rotterdam, The Netherlands.
2010
Manifesta 8, Murcia, Spain.
Kilkenny Arts Festival, Rothe House, Kilkenny, Ireland.
Summer 2010, Kerlin Gallery, Dublin.
Willie Doherty, Victor Grippo and Sylvia Plimack Mangold, Alexander and Bonin, New York.
Hugh Lane Centenary Print Exhibition, Wexford Arts Centre, Wexford, Ireland.
2009
Terror and the Sublime: Art in an Age of Anxiety, Crawford Art Gallery, Cork, Ireland.
Exploring a New Donation, Irish Museum of Modern Art, Dublin.
ev+a: Reading the City, Limerick City Gallery of Art, Limerick, Ireland.
2008
Fifty Percent Solitude, Kerlin Gallery, Dublin.
Peripheral Vision and Collective Body, Museoin, Bolzano, Italy.
The Morning After. Videoarbeiten der Sammlung Goetz, Weserburg Museum für moderne Kunst, Bremen, Germany.
On The Margins, Mildred Lane Kemper Art Museum, St. Louis, MO.
2007
Gehen Bleiben, Kunstmuseum, Bonn.
3rd Auckland Triennial, Auckland, New Zealand.
2006
Re: Location, Alexander and Bonin, New York.
Reprocessing Reality, PS1 Center for Contemporary Art, Long Island, New York.
2005
La actualidad revisada, Banque Neuflize, Paris.
L'esperienza dell'arte, Padiglione italiano, 51st Venice Biennale, Venice.

The Shadow, Vestsjællands Kunstmuseum, Sorø, Denmark.
Slideshow, Baltimore Museum of Art, Baltimore, MD; Contemporary Arts Center, Cincinnati, OH; Brooklyn Museum of Art, New York.
2004
Faces in the Crowd: The Modern Figure and Avant-Garde Realism, Whitechapel Gallery, London; Castello di Rivoli Museo d'Arte Contemporanea, Rivoli, Turin, Italy.
Dwellan, Charlottenborg, Copenhagen.
Glocal: apuntes para videorepresentaciones de lo global y lo local, Galería Moisés Pérez de Albéniz, Pamplona, Spain.
3. Berlin Biennale für zeitgenössische Kunst, Berlin.
2003
Turner Prize 2003, Tate Britain, London.
8th International Istanbul Biennial, Istanbul, Turkey.
2002
Willie Doherty, Paul Étienne Lincoln, Rita McBride, Alexander and Bonin, New York.
RE-RUN, XXV Bienal de São Paulo, Brazil.
2001
Double Vision, Galerie für Zeitgenössische Kunst, Leipzig, Germany.
The Inner State (The image of man in the video art of the 1990s), Kunstmuseum Liechtenstein, Vaduz, Liechtenstein.
Trauma, Dundee Contemporary Arts, Hayward Gallery, London; Firstsite, Colchester, UK; Museum of Modern Art, Oxford; Museum of Modern Art, Nottingham, UK.
The Uncertain (Eija-Liisa Ahtila, Willie Doherty, Guillermo Kuitca, Taro Sinoda), Galería Pepe Cobo, Seville, Spain.
Bloody Sunday (Willie Doherty, Locky Morris, Philip Napier), Orchard Gallery, Derry.
Gisela Bullacher /Willie Doherty, Produzentengalerie, Hamburg, Germany.
2000
Blackspot: New Acquisitions, Vancouver Art Gallery, Vancouver, Canada.
Hitchcock and Art: Fatal Coincidences, Musée des Beaux-Arts de Montréal, Montreal.
Shifting Ground; Selected Works of Irish Art 1950–2000, Irish Museum of Modern Art, Dublin.

1999
Irish Art Now: From the Poetic to the Political, McMullen Museum of Art, Boston College, Boston, Mass.; Art Gallery of Newfoundland and Labrador, Chicago Cultural Center, Chicago, IL.
1998
Wounds: between democracy and redemption in contemporary art, Moderna Museet, Stockholm.
Art from the UK (Part II), Sammlung Goetz, Munich.
Real/Life: New British Art, Tochigi Prefectural Museum of Fine Arts; Fukuoka City Art Museum; Hiroshima City Museum of Contemporary Art; Tokyo Museum of Contemporary Art; Ashiya City Museum of Art and History, Japan.
1997
PS1 Opening Project, Long Island, New York.
Re/View: Photographs from the Collection, Dallas Museum of Art, Dallas, TX.
Surroundings, Tel Aviv Museum of Art, Tel Aviv.
1996
Face à l'Histoire 1933-1996, Centre Georges Pompidou, Paris.
ID, Stedelijk Van Abbemuseum, Eindhoven, Germany; Nouveau Musée/Institut, Villeurbanne, France.
NowHere, Louisiana Museum of Modern Art, Humlebæk, Denmark.
The 10th Biennale of Sydney, Sydney.
1995
Willie Doherty/Andreas Gursky, Moderna Museet, Stockholm.
1994
Turner Prize 1994, Willie Doherty, Peter Doig, Antony Gormley, and Shirazeh Houshiary, Tate Gallery, London (*The Only Good one is a Dead One*).
Cocido y Crudo, Museo Nacional Centro de Arte Reina Sofía, Madrid.
1993
Critical Landscapes, Tokyo Metropolitan Museum of Photography, Tokyo.
An Irish Presence, 46th Venice Biennale.
1989
InternationalE Foto-Triennale, Esslingen, Germany.
Through the Looking Glass, Barbican Arts Centre, London.

Annabel Elgar

Born in 1971 in Aldershot, UK
Lives and works in London

Selected Solo Exhibitions
2011
Metronom, Modena, Italy.
2010
The Wapping Project Bankside, London.
2008
MONA Museum Of New Art, Detroit, MI.
2007
Nepente Art Gallery, Milan.
Month of Photography, Bratislava,
Slovakia.
2006
Secrets and Mysteries, Zephyr,
Mannheim, Germany, with Anne
Kathrin Greiner.
Black Flag (2), The Wapping Project,
London.
We Were Until We Weren't, Galleri
Image, Aarhus, Denmark.
2004
Black Flag (1), The Wapping Project,
London, The Jerwood Commissions.
Upstream Gallery, Amsterdam, with
Cristian Andersen.
2000
Southampton City Art Gallery,
Southampton, UK.
South Hill Park Arts Centre, Bracknell,
UK.
1996
Islington Arts Factory, London.
Zone Gallery, Newcastle upon Tyne, UK.

Selected Group Exhibitions
2015
Nominees' Exhibition – Prix Elysée,
Musée de l'Elysée, Lausanne,
Switzerland.
2014
Belfast Photo Festival, Belfast; travellled
to Sirius Arts Centre, Cobh, Ireland.
In Between, Metronom, Modena, Italy.
2013
*Sitting with the Qualities of a
Mountain*, Blyth Gallery, Imperial
College, London.
Spectacle, Ormeau Baths Gallery,
Belfast.
Creekside Open 2013, APT Gallery,
London.
The Wapping Project Bankside,
London.

2012
First come first served, The Lion & Lamb
Gallery, London.
wunderCAMERA, Metronom,
Modena, Italy.
Edition IV, The Wapping Project
Bankside, London.
The Party Show, Viktor Wynd Fine Art,
London.
2011
The Wapping Project Bankside, London.
Photomedia Open Salon 2011, Charlie
Dutton Gallery, London.
Please drive slowly through our village,
Fold Gallery, London.
2010
Beasts Royal, Viktor Wynd Fine Art,
London.
Photography 1948–2010: Women,
The Wapping Project Bankside, London.
*Exquisite Trove. The House of Fairy
Tales*, travelling to Millennium Gallery,
Sheffield, Newlyn Gallery, Penzance
and Salisbury Arts Centre, Salisbury,
UK.
2009
Horn of Plenty, Viktor Wynd Fine Art,
London.
*Exquisite Trove. The House of Fairy
Tales*, New Art Gallery Walsall,
Walsall, UK.
Theatres of the Real, FotoMuseum,
Antwerp.
Creekside Open 2009, APT Gallery,
London.
The Fairy Tale Art Collection, The East
Room, London.
No End in Sight, Vegas Gallery,
London.
2008
Error One, Extra City, Antwerp.
*Singapore International Photography
Festival*, Singapore.
Refuge, The Wapping Project, London,
with Elina Brotherus and Ailbhe ni
Bhriain.
No End in Sight, Galerie Polaris, Paris.
*In Our World: New Photography in
Britain*, Galleria Civica di Modena,
Modena, Italy.
2007
ArtSway Open 07, Sway, UK.
The Joy, Nettie Horn Gallery, London.
Creekside Open, APT Gallery,
London.

The Power of Language, Academy
of Arts, Berlin.
*Off Programme, Month of
Photography*, Krakow, Poland.
Lodz Art Centre, Lodz, Poland.
2006
Here and Now, Jersey Galleries,
Osterley Park, London.
Plug, County Hall Gallery, London.
2005
Narratives of the Presumed Invisible,
Kunsthalle, Lophem, Belgium, with
Anthony Goicolea and Kristof
Vrancken.
The Madness of Paradise, Anne Gary
Pannell Art Gallery, Sweet Briar
College, Sweet Briar, VA, with Gregory
Crewdson and Justine Kurland.
Fashion, Film and Fiction, The Wapping
Project, London.
Locus Loppem, Kunsthalle, Lophem,
Belgium.
2004
Adolescenz, Fotogalerie Wien, Vienna.
2003
Upstream Gallery, Amsterdam.
Twenty White Chairs, The Wapping
Project, London and The Jerwood
Space, London.
Urban Raw, Millais Gallery,
Southampton, UK.
2002
Inside Space, London.
2001
14 x 14, Mafuji Gallery, London.
Miniature Madness, Winkley Street
Studios, London.
2000
Assembly, Whitechapel, London.
1997
Cambridge Darkroom Gallery,
Cambridge, UK.
1995
The Fabergé Photography Awards,
Victoria & Albert Museum, London.

Hallgerður Hallgrímsdóttir

Born in 1984 in Reykjavík
Lives and works in Reykjavík

Solo Exhibitions
2014
Fog Patches, Listasafn ASÍ,
Reykjavík.
2012
Landscape, Reykjavík Museum
of Photography, Reykjavík.

Selected Group Exhibitions
2015
Rökkur, Musée de l'Elysée, Lausanne,
Switzerland, part of "La Nuit des
Images".
ÍSÓ, Ísafjörður, Iceland, organized
by The Icelandic Contemporary
Photography Association.
Verksummerki, Reykjavík Museum
of Photography, Reykjavík.
Young Icelandic Photography,
part of the Warsaw Festival
of Art Photography, Warsaw.
2014
Landsköp, Norðurljósahátíð,
Stykkishólmur, Iceland.
*Betur sjá augu… or From a Different
Angle…*, National Museum of Iceland,
Reykjavík.
2013
*Samtímalandslagið or The
Contemporary Landscape*, Reykjavík
Museum of Photography, Reykjavík.
New Nordic Photography, Hasselblad
Center, Gothenburg.
European Borderlines: Visual Narratives,
Nordic House, Reykjavík.
2012
Fresh Faced + Wild Eyed,
The Photographers' Gallery,
London.
European Borderlines: Visual Narratives,
Bursa Foto Fest, Bursa, Turkey.
European Borderlines: Visual Narratives,
Encontros da Imagem, Braga,
Portugal.
Manifesto11: a comedy of errors,
Lighthouse, Glasgow, part of the
Glasgow International Festival.
2011
Glasgow School of Art Degree Show,
Glasgow.
*Will Nothing Be Understood By the
Totems of Today?*, Studio 41, Glasgow.

2010
Maelström, WASPS Gallery, Glasgow.
2005
Please YoursELF, an artistic approach
to tourism in Iceland shown in
Hafnarhúsið, Reykjavík Art Museum,
Reykjavík.

Ilkka Halso

Born in 1965 in Orimattila, Finland
Lives and works in Orimattila

Solo Exhibitions
2010
Wagner + Partner, Berlin.
Orimattila Art Museum, Orimattila,
Finland.
2009
Synart Art Gallery, Frankfurt
am Main.
Galerie Christian Roellin, St. Gallen,
Switzerland.
2008
Photology, Milan.
Maerzgalerie, Leipzig, Germany.
2007
Galerie PF, Poznan, Poland.
2006
Kuopio Museum, Kuopio, Finland.
2005
Galerie Anhava, Helsinki.
Galerie Frank Elbaz, Paris.
Synart Art Gallery, Frankfurt am Main.
2004
Quicksilver Galerie für
Gegenwartskunst, Berlin.
Rubicon Gallery, Dublin.
2003
Galleri Magnus Åklundh, Malmö,
Sweden.
2002
Institut Finlandais, Paris.
Häme-Gallery, Lahti, Finland.
2001
Photography Center, Mikkeli, Finland.
Lusto The Finnish Forest Museum,
Punkaharju, Finland.
2000
F48 Fotografiskt galleri, Stockholm.
Restoration, Gallery Hippolyte, Helsinki.
1998
Excavations – Kaivauksia, Cable Factory,
Helsinki.
1997
Anatomisch Cabinet, museological
installation at Esplanade stage,
Helsinki.
1994
Cultural Landscape, Helsinki City Art
Museum, Kluuvi Gallery, Orimattila Art
Museum, Orimattila, Finland.
1991
Evolution, Gallery Hippolyte,
Helsinki.

Selected Group Exhibitions
2014
Helsinki Photography Biennial,
organised by the Union of Artist
Photographers, The Finnish Museum
of Photography, Helsinki.
2013
DistURBANces / LandEscape, MNHA
Musée national d'histoire et d'art,
Luxembourg.
Afterlives of Gardens, Kumu Art
Museum, Tallinn, Estonia.
Extra Ordinary, Canal Erica-Ter Apel,
countryside of Drenthe, The
Netherlands, curated by Noorderlicht.
2012
Bildspuren – unruhige Gegenwarten,
Darmstädter Tage der Fotografie,
Darmstadt, Germany.
distURBANces, MUSA Museum
Startgalerie Artothek, Vienna.
Sense of Place, BOZAR, Brussels.
Arctic Hysteria, Rosphoto, St.
Petersburg, Russia.
Ekolandia, Lahti Art Museum, Lahti,
Finland.
*Aris Kalaizis and Ilkka Halso: Parallel
Worlds*, Kunstverein, Schwäbisch Hall,
Germany.
2011
SLOW, Kunsthalle Helsinki.
*Aris Kalaizis und Ilkka Halso:
Parallelwelten II*, Maerzgalerie, Berlin.
Architecture of Fear, Z33 – House for
Contemporary Art, Hasselt, Belgium.
Forest, Serlachius-museo Gösta,
Mänttä, Finland.
Spatial Places: The Poetic of Place,
Kuparipaja, Fiskars, Finland.
2010
*Aris Kalaizis und Ilkka Halso:
Parallelwelten II*, Maerzgalerie, Leipzig,
Germany.
Daegu Photo Biennale, Daegu, South
Korea.
Arctic Hysteria, Kuntsi Museum of
Modern Art, Vaasa, Finland.
Arctic Hysteria, DA2 Domus Artium,
Salamanca, Spain.
BREDAPHOTO, International Photo
Festival 2010, The Netherlands.
Bumpy ride, Fotografia Festival,
MACRO Future, Rome, curated by
Paul Wombell.
Zur Nachahmung Empfohlen! –

Examples to Follow, Uferhallen, Berlin
and several locations during 2010–13.
*Close to Nature. Zeitgenössische
Finnische Kunst*, Neuer Kunstverein
Aschaffenburg e.V.im KunsLANDing,
Aschaffenburg, Germany.
Climate Capsules, Museum für Kunst
und Gewerbe, Hamburg, Germany.
*Helsinki10. Contemporary Photography
and Video from The Helsinki School in
the Statoil Art Collection*, Rogaland
Museum of Fine Arts, Stavanger,
Norway.
2009
Arctic Hysteria, Ludwig Múzeum,
Budapest.
Maerzflimmern, Maerzgalerie, Berlin.
Arctic Hysteria, Kunsthalle, Helsinki.
*Ulsan International Photography
Festival*, Ulsan, South Korea.
Nature en Kit, MUDAC Musée de
design et d'arts appliqués
contemporains, Lausanne, Switzerland.
The Best of Photography – g27, Galerie
Christian Roellin, Zurich.
Manipulating Reality, CCCS Centro di
Cultura Contemporanea Strozzina,
Palazzo Strozzi, Florence.
2008
Arctic Hysteria, MoMA PS1, New York.
*Nordic Moods – Landscape
Photography in Our Time*,
ARKEN, Museum for moderne Kunst,
Ishoj, Denmark.
Maan Asema / La position de la Terre,
CRAC Alsace Centre Rhénan d'Art
Contemporain, Altkirch, France.
De natura…, Centre photographique
d'Île-de-France, Pontault-Combault,
France.
2007
Photo Finnish – The Helsinki School,
Stenersen Museum, Oslo.
*Contact 2007– Toronto Photography
Festival, The Constructed Image*,
MOCCA, Museum of Contemporary
Canadian Art, Toronto.
Into the Landscape, Preus Museum,
Horten, Norway.
Finn Art, Eskilstuna Konstmuseum,
Eskilstuna, Sweden.
Mapping the Unknown, Overbeck-
Gesellschaft, Lubeck, Germany.
Case Studies, Copper Smithy, Fiskars
Village, Fiskars, Finland.

C International Photo Magazine, Phillips de Pury & Company, New York.
Collection-Selection, Galerie Christian Roellin, St. Gallen, Switzerland.
Garten Eden, Kunsthalle Emden, Emden, Germany.

2006
Talvimaa-Winterland, 5th Finnish Photography Triennale, Salo Art Museum, Salo, Finland.
The Helsinki School. Finnish Photography from the 21st Century, Hôtel de ville de Bruxelles, Brussels.
More than this. On sustainability in contemporary art, Jyväskylä Art Museum, Jyväskylä, Finland.
Landscape, Kiasma Museum of Contemporary Art, Helsinki.
6th Shanghai Biennale, Shanghai Art Museum, Shanghai, China.
Green Art, Salo Art Museum, Salo, Finland.
Presence, Wäinö Aaltonen Museum, Turku, Finland.
Nature Attitudes, A21, Thyssen-Bornemisza Art Contemporary, Vienna.
The Faraway Nearby, White Box, New York.

2005
Waking Up, Cortex Athletico Galerie, Bordeaux, France.
Fractures of Life, Kiasma Museum of Contemporary Art, Helsinki.
The Helsinki School, Galleria Photology, Milan.
Personligt. Fotografier från The Helsinki School, Kulturhuset, Stockholm.
The Helsinki School, Kunstlerhaus Bethanien, Berlin.

2004
Galería Salvador Díaz, Madrid.
Finnsche Fotografie, Roellin I Duerr Galerie, St. Gallen, Switzerland.
30 by TaiK – The Helsinki School, The Finnish Museum of Photography, Helsinki.
Fata morgana, le Crédac: centre d'art contemporain d'Ivry, Ivry-sur-Seine, France.
MOMENTUM. Nordic Festival of Contemporary Art, Moss, Norway.
Chassez le naturel…, 4° Biennale de Liège, Liège, Belgium.
Platsens Natur, Gävle konstcentrum, Gävle, Sweden.

2003
SUOMI, Galerie Frank Elbaz, Paris.
The Cube, installation, Lepaa, Finland.
3th Ars Baltica Triennial, Stadtgalerie Kiel, Kiel, Germany; travelling to Bergen, Vilnius, Riga, Tallinn, Pori, Malmö in 2003–05.
New Realities, Hasselblad Center, Gothenburg.

2002
On the Edge of the Unknown, Kultur-Räume im Norden, Kultur abteilung Beyer, Leverkusen, Germany.
XXVII Bienal de Pontevedra, Pontevedra, Spain.
VII Mänttä Art Weeks. Summer Exhibition, Mänttä, Finland.
Photography and Video, Sara Hildén Art Museum, Tampere, Finland.

2001
NORDIC, The leisure club Mogadishni, Copenhagen.
FINLANDIA!, Fotografisk Center, Copenhagen.
Finnish Photography, Galleri Christian Dam, Oslo.

2000
Söderhamn Fotobiennale, Söderhamns Museum, Söderhamn, Sweden.

1999
Invisible Light, The Finnish Museum of Photography, Helsinki.

1998
Me Myself and I, Gallery TaiK, Helsinki.

1997
Diverse Memories, The Manchester Museum, Manchester, UK.
Northern Reflections, Gray's Gallery, Robert Gordon University, Aberdeen, Scotland.

1995
The Script, The 2nd Triennale of Finnish Photography, Kunsthalle, Helsinki.
The 100th exhibition of Finnish Artists, Kunsthalle, Helsinki.

Sarah Jones

Born in 1959 in London
Lives and works in London

Solo Exhibitions
2015
Double Take: Photography and the Garden, Hestercombe Gallery, Somerset.
2014
Maureen Paley, London.
Anton Kern Gallery, New York.
2013
Minneapolis Institute of Arts, Minneapolis, MN.
2008
Maureen Paley, London.
2007
Sarah Jones: Photographs, National Media Museum, Bradford.
2006
Anton Kern Gallery, New York.
2002
Maureen Paley Interim Art, London.
Anton Kern Gallery, New York.
2000
Le Consortium, Dijon, France (as part of *I Love Dijon*).
Huis Marseille Foundation for Photography, Amsterdam.
1999
Museum Folkwang, Essen, Germany.
Anton Kern Gallery, New York.
Centre for Photography, Universidad de Salamanca, Salamanca, Spain.
Museo Nacional Centro de Arte Reina Sofía, Madrid.
Maureen Paley Interim Art, London.
Jerwood Space, London.
1998
Galerie Anne de Villepoix, Paris.
L'Ecole supérieure des Beaux-Arts, Tours, France.
Sites, Sabine Knust Galerie Maximilian Verlag, Munich.
1997
Le Consortium, Dijon, France.
Maureen Paley Interim Art, London.
1995
Consulting Room, Galerie du Dourven, Trédrez-Locquémeau, France (Office départemental de développement culturel, mission arts plastiques).
Consulting Room (Couch), Camerawork Gallery, London.

1993
Hales Gallery, London.
1988
Watershed Arts Centre, Bristol, UK.
1987
F. Stop Gallery, Bath, UK.

Selected Group Exhibitions
2014
The Marseillaise(s) / fifteen years of collecting, Huis Marseille, Amsterdam.
Nouvelle génération, FRAC Nord-Pas de Calais, Dunkerque, France.
Your Tongue in My Mouth, Stanley Picker Gallery, London.
2013
Collective Apparitions, Contemporary Art Space, La Rochelle, France.
Le meilleur profil, Centre de photographie de Lectoure, Lectoure, France.
The First 15, Photography from the Meredith S. Moody Residency at Yaddo, The Frances Young Tang Teaching Museum and Art Gallery at Skidmore College, New York.
Seduced by Art: Photography Past and Present, National Gallery, London, travelling to CaixaForum Barcelona and CaixaForum Madrid.
2012
Family Matters: The Family in British Art, Art Gallery, Millennium Galleries, Sheffield, UK, Laing Art Gallery, Newcastle, UK and Tate Britain, London.
Der Mensch und Seine Objekte, Museum Folkwang, Essen, Germany.
Observers: Photographers of the British Scene from 1930s to Now, Galeria de Arte do Sesi, Avenida Paulista, São Paulo, Brazil.
Focal Points: Art and Photography, Manchester Art Gallery, Manchester, UK.
Melancholia, Villa Klinger, Leipzig, Germany.
2011
Nothing In the World But Youth, Turner Contemporary, Margate, UK.
Family Matters: The Family in British Art, Norwich Castle Museum, Norwich, UK.
Signs of a Struggle: Photography in the Wake of Postmodernism, Victoria and

Albert Museum, London.
A Sense of Perspective, Tate Liverpool, Liverpool, UK.
Herein! Interieurs in der DZ Bank Kunstsammlung, DZ Bank, Frankfurt am Main.
Heroines, Museo Thyssen-Bornemisza & Fundación Caja, Madrid.
Stripped (Tate Visual Dialogues), Nottingham Castle Museum, Nottingham, UK.
Dutch Still Life, Peabody Essex Museum, Salem, Mass.
Peeping Tom, Kunsthal KAdE, Amersfoort, The Netherlands.
Streetlife & Homestories Fotografien aus der Sammlung Goetz, Museum Villa Stuck, Munich.
Femme Objet / Femme Sujet, Abbaye St André – Centre d'art contemporain, Meymac, France.
2010
Peeping Tom, Vegas Gallery, London, curated by Keith Coventry.
The Barts Hospital Commission / Vital Arts, London.
Photograph(e)s, Musée Nicéphore Niepce – Musée de la Photographie, Chalon-sur-Saône, France.
2009
The Casini Cruise, Ardi Poels Projects, Maastricht, The Netherlands.
Flower Power, Villa Giulia, CRAA Centro Ricerca Arte Attuale, Verbania, Italy.
Passing Thoughts and Making Plans, Jerwood Space, London.
2008
Friends and Family, Anton Kern Gallery, New York.
Interior / Exterior: Living in Art, Kunstmuseum Wolfsburg, Wolfsburg, Germany.
Intim/Ita, Museum Kampa, Prague.
Within: New Photographic Portraits, Bloomberg Space, London.
Street & Studio: An Urban History of Photography, Tate Modern, London and Museum Folkwang, Essen, Germany.
The Society of London Ladies, dispari&dispari project, Reggio Emilia, Italy.
2007
Garden Eden, The Garden in Art Since

1900, Kunsthalle in Emden, Emden, Germany.
7th Internationale Foto Triennale Esslingen, Galerien der Stadt Esslingen, Esslingen am Neckar, Germany.
Something that I'll Never Really See, Contemporary Photography from the V&A, Sainsbury Centre for Visual Arts, Norwich; Nottingham Castle, Nottingham, UK.
Northern Lights: Reflecting with Images, Galleria Civica di Modena, Modena, Italy.
Beautiful People (et la blessure secrète), CRAC Alsace Centre Rhénan d'Art Contemporain d'Alsace, Altkirch, France.

2006
Implosion, Anton Kern Gallery, New York.
XX – Encontros de Fotografia, Centro de Artes Visuais, Coimbra, Portugal.
La Collection photographique du Frac des Pays de la Loire, Galerie Le Lieu, Lorient, France.
Portrait – 1960 to today, by Die Photographische / SK Stiftung Kultur, Cologne, to coincide with the 40th anniversary of Art Cologne.
Simon & Sarah, Platform, London.

2005
Pour de Vrai, Musée des Beux-Arts, Nancy, France.
Motor Blues, Museum der bildenden Kunste, Leipzig, Germany.
Attentes, Casino Luxembourg, Forum d'art contemporain, Luxembourg.
New Photography, Norton Museum of Art, Palm Beach, FL.
The Wonderful Fund Collection, Le Musée de Marrakech, Marrakech, Morocco; travelling to Pallant House Gallery, Chichester, UK; and others.

2004
Stranger Than Fiction, Abersytwyth Arts Centre, Aberystwyth, UK.
Take Five! Huis Marseille Turns Five, Huis Marseille, Amsterdam.
Art of the Garden, Tate Britain, London and Manchester Art Gallery, Manchester, UK (2005).
Biennale, MoNA Museum of New Art, Pontiac, MI.
Just Love Me, Fries Museum, Leeuwarden, The Netherlands.

2003
A Bigger Splash. British Art from Tate 1960–2003, Pavihão Lucas Nogueira Garcez – Oca, Parque Ibirapuera and Instituto Tomie Ohtake, São Paulo, Brazil.
Double Exposure, ING-bank, Courtai, Belgium.
Virtual Eye, Norwich Castle Museum, Norwich, UK.
Girls' Night Out, Orange County Museum of Art, Newport Beach, CA; travelling to Addison Gallery of American Art, Andover, Mass.; Contemporary Art Museum, St. Louis, MO (2005); Blaffer Gallery, University of Houston, Houston, TX (2006).
Painting Pictures, Kunstmuseum, Wolfsburg, Germany.
Photography, Eleni Koroneou Gallery, Athens, Greece.
Child In Time: Views of contemporary artists on youth and adolescence, Gemeentemuseum Helmond, The Netherlands.

2002
Die Wohltat der Kunst: Post/Feministische Positionen der 90er Jahre aus der Sammlung Goetz, Sammlung Goetz, Munich and Staatliche Kunsthalle, Baden-Baden, Germany.
Telling Tales: Narrative Impulses in Recent Art, Tate Liverpool, Liverpool, UK.

2001
Making Your Dreams Come True – Young British Photography, Representing Britain, Tate Britain, London.
I LOVE NY, Anton Kern Gallery, New York.
No World Without You – Reflections of Identity in New British Art, Herzliya Museum of Art, Tel Aviv.

2000
Les trahisons du modèle, Galerie Nei Liicht, Dudelange, Luxembourg.
Intersection I: intimate/anonymous, Espace d'art Contemporain HEC, Jouy-en-Josas, France.
docudrama, Bury St. Edmunds Art Gallery, Bury St. Edmunds, UK.
Pause/Pose, Galerie Anne de Villepoix, Paris.

Wooden Heart, AVCO, London.
Quotidiana, Castello di Rivoli Museo d'Arte Contemporanea, Rivoli, Turin, Italy.

1999
Another Girl Another Planet, Lawrence Rubin Greenberg Van Doren Fine Art, New York.
3rd International Tokyo Photo Biennale, Tokyo Metropolitan Museum of Photography, Tokyo.
Dreamlands, Portfolio Gallery, Edinburgh.

1998
dijon/le consortium.coll, tout contre l'art contemporain, Centre Georges Pompidou, Paris.
Sorted, Ikon Gallery, Birmingham, UK.
The new neurotic realism, Saatchi Gallery, London.
Bill Henson, Sarah Jones, Philip-Lorca DiCorcia, Galerie Gebauer, Berlin.
Jennifer Bornstein, Jenny Cage, Anna Gaskell, Dana Hoey, Sarah Jones, Valérie Jouve, Gillian Wearing, Galerie Anne de Villepoix, Paris.

1996–97
New Contemporaries, Tate Gallery, Liverpool, UK and Camden Arts Centre, London.

Selected Public Collections
Arts Council of Great Britain.
Coimbra Visual Arts Centre.
Le Consortium, Dijon.
Museum Folkwang, Essen.
FRAC Nord-Pas de Calais.
FRAC Region Poitou-Charentes.
Galerien der Stadt Esslingen.
Galleria Civica di Modena.
Goetz Collection, Germany.
Government Art Collection, UK.
Koninklijke PTT Nederland NV.
Huis Marseille, Foundation for Photography, Amsterdam.
Museum of Modern Art, San Francisco.
National Media Museum, Bradford.
Orange County Museum of Art.
Saatchi Collection, London.
Universidad de Salamanca.
Tate Gallery, London.
Victoria & Albert Museum, London.

Sanna Kannisto

Born in 1974 in Hämeenlinna, Finland
Lives and works in Helsinki

Selected Solo Exhibitions
2015
Helsinki Contemporary, Helsinki.
Galerie La Ferronnerie, Paris.
2013
FAR Fabbrica Arte Rimini, Galleria
d'arte moderna e contemporanea,
Rimini, Italy.
2012
Fieldwork, Le Château d'Eau, Toulouse,
France.
Gallery TaiK Persons, Berlin.
Metronom, Modena, Italy.
Galerie La Ferronnerie, Paris.
2011
Fieldwork, SKMU Sørlandets
Kunstmuseum, Kristiansand, Norway.
Fieldwork, Aperture Gallery, New York.
Gallery Kalhama & Piippo
Contemporary, Helsinki.
2008
Domaine de Kerguéhennec,
Contemporary Art Centre, Bignan,
France.
De natura…, Centre photographique
d'Île-de-France, Pontault-Combault,
France, with Ilkka Halso.
Galerie La Ferronnerie, Paris.
Galerie Wilma Tolksdorf, Frankfurt
am Main.
Korjaamo Culture Factory,
Gallery 1 & 2, Helsinki.
2007
Galerie Georg Kargl, Vienna.
2006
Jackson Fine Art, Atlanta, GA.
Galerie La Ferronnerie, Paris.
Yours Gallery, Warsaw.
Galerie Wilma Tolksdorf, Berlin.
Gallery F-Station at Photomonth,
Krakow, Poland.

Selected Group Exhibitions
2014
Collective Collection, 2, BBB centre
d'art, Toulouse, France.
Summer Selections, De Buck Gallery,
New York.
What's Life Anyway?, Tromsø
Kunstforening, Tromsø, Norway.
Asombrosas afinidades, Photo España
2014, Fundación Antonio Saura,
Casa Zavala, Cuenza, Spain.
*Nordic Light International Festival of
Photography*, Kristiansund, Norway.
*Photography into Art. The Hannula &
Hinkka Collection*, Aboa Vetus & Ars
Nova, Turku, Finland.
Le bestiaire des photographes, Centre
culturel Henri-Desbals, Toulouse,
France.
2013
ARTE Vidéo Night 5, Palais de Tokyo,
Paris.
Drôles d'oiseaux, Galerie La
Ferronnerie, Paris.
Vermessene Dinge / Measured Things,
Eres Stiftung, Munich.
Reality Bites, Kiasma Museum of
Contemporary Art, Helsinki.
Spécimens, Domaine de Chamarande,
Chamarande, France.
*The Near and the Distant: Photography
and Space*, Künstlerhaus Dortmund,
Dortmund, Germany.
*Photography into Art. The Hannula &
Hinkka Collection*, The Finnish Museum
of Photography, Helsinki.
2012
*State of the Art. New Contemporary
Photography*, NRW-Forum, Düsseldorf,
Germany.
International Photo Festival, Knokke-
Heist, Belgium.
*Hunters and Hunted: Insects in
contemporary art*, Museum Villa Rot,
Burgrieden, Germany.
Sammen/Together, Trondheim
Kunstmuseum, Trondheim, Norway.
Révélations, Galerie La Ferronnerie,
Paris.
Äärimmäisyyksien yhteinen tekijä,
WAM, Turku, Finland.
Finders Keepers, Mänttä Art Festival,
Mänttä, Finland.
*Regards photographiques finlandais sur
la nature*, Abbaye de Jumièges,
Jumièges, France.
2011
*A Female View. Part 2: aus der Helsinki
School*, Foto Raum, Vienna.
Für Hund und Katz ist auch noch Platz,
Art Foyer DZ Bank, Frankfurt am Main.
Beautiful Vagabonds, Yancey
Richardson Gallery, New York.
The Romantic Construct, Prague
Biennale, Prague.
Essays on Geopoetics, 8th Mercosul
Biennial, Porto Alegre, Brazil.
2010
Strange Travelers, Tanya Bonakdar
Gallery, New York.
*elles@centrepompidou, women artists
in the collections of the Centre
Pompidou*, Centre Georges Pompidou,
Paris.
Wald, Städtische Galerie Waldkraiburg,
Waldkraiburg, Germany.
Repeat All, Centro Cultural Chacao,
Caracas, Venezuela.
Speed, Ulrich Museum of Art,
Wichita, KS.
2009
The Tree, Fuglsang Art Museum, Island
of Lolland, Denmark.
*Variations on Transcending the
Finiteness of Human Vision*, Riga Art
Space, Riga, Latvia.
FotoRio Short List: The Dream Machine,
Museu de Arte Contemporânea
de Niterói, Rio de Janeiro, Brazil.
Repeat All, MIS Museu da Imagem
e do Som, São Paulo, Brazil.
Arctic Hysteria Onscreen, Ludwig
Museum of Contemporary Art, Budapest.
Descubrimientos, PhotoEspaña, Madrid.
Får ej övertäckas, Eskilstuna Art
Museum, Eskilstuna, Sweden.
Nature en Kit, MUDAC Musée de
design et d'arts appliqués
contemporains, Lausanne, Switzerland.
Struggle for Life, Eres Stiftung, Munich.
2008
Other florae, Galeria Nara Roesler,
São Paulo, Brazil.
*Video Short List: Machines à rêver /
Dream machine*, Passage de Retz, Paris.
REAL, Städel Museum, Frankfurt am
Main.
Observing beast, time, evolution,
Kunstverein Hildesheim, Hildesheim,
Germany.
Arctic Hysteria Onscreen, MoMA
Museum of Modern Art, New York.
Cinéma et vidéos d'artistes, Maison
Européenne de la Photographie, Paris.
*Five variations on the finiteness of
human vision*, Artget Gallery, Cultural
Centre of Belgrade, Belgrade, Serbia.
Tapis, coussins et videos, 36ème
Festival international du film de La
Rochelle, La Rochelle, France.

2007
Research and Invention,
Fotomuseum Winterthur, Winterthur,
Switzerland.
Bird Watching in Haarlem, De Vishal
exposition space, Haarlem, The
Netherlands.
*Garden Eden –The Garden in Art since
1900*, Kunsthalle Emden, Emden,
Germany.
Self-timer, MNAC National Museum of
Contemporary Art, Bucharest, Romania.
Age of the Animal, Ateneum Art
Museum, Helsinki.
Grey Matters: Photography is Thinking,
The Finnish Museum of Photography,
Helsinki.
Repeat All, Centro Cultural Matucana
100, Santiago de Chile.
Photo Finnish – The Helsinki School,
Stenersen Art Museum, Oslo.
Repeat All, La Casa de la Cultura,
Buenos Aires.

2006
Self-timer, Nikolaj Contemporary,
Copenhagen.
Art, Life & Confusion, The Belgrade
Biennial, Belgrade, Serbia.
Streams of Story, Glasgow Festival of
Contemporary Visual Art, Tramway,
Glasgow.
The Faraway Nearby, White Box,
New York.
Focus Finland, KBB, Kültur Büro
Barcelona, Barcelona.
Self-timer/ Selbstauslöser, Kunsthalle
Fridericianum, Kassel, Germany.
Presence, Wäinö Aaltonen Art
Museum, Turku, Finland.
Vad är fotografi? The Helsinki School,
Borås Museum of Modern Art, Borås,
Sweden.

Public Collections
Centre Pompidou – Musée national
d'art moderne, Paris.
Fotomuseum Winterthur.
MEP Maison européenne de la
photographie, Paris.
Kiasma Museum of Contemporary Art,
Helsinki.
The Finnish Museum of Photography,
Helsinki.
Helsinki City Art Museum.
Le Fonds national d'art contemporain
(FNAC), The State Art Collection,
France.
Fonds régional d'art contemporain,
FRAC Haute-Normandie.
Fonds régional d'art contemporain,
FRAC Bretagne.
Statoil Art Collection, Norway.
State Art Collection, Finland.
Vihuri Foundation, Rovaniemi Art
Museum.
Salo Art Museum.
SKMU Sørlandets Kunstmuseum.
Le Château d'Eau, Toulouse.
Domaine départemental de
Chamarande.
Artothèque, Bibliothèque d'Auxerre.

Sandra Kantanen

Born in 1974 in Helsinki
Lives and works in Hangö, Finland

Solo Exhibitions
2013
Stockholms sjukhem, Stockholm,
commissioned artwork.
2012
Purdy Hicks Gallery, London.
2011
Korjaamo Galleria, Helsinki.
2010
Pobeda Gallery, Moscow.
2009
Gallery Hippolyte, Helsinki.
2008
Shadow Images, Gallery TaiK Persons,
Berlin.
2005
Seydler AG Bank Frankfurt, Frankfurt am
Main.
Landscape and Variations, Galerie
Anhava, Helsinki.
Galleri Brandstrup, Oslo.
Seydler AG Bank Frankfurt,
Frankfurt am Main.
2003
Black Landscape, Galerie Anhava,
Helsinki.

Selected Group Exhibitions
2013
*Blutenzauber. Fotografien und
Installationen internationaler Kunstler*,
Museum Bad Arolsen, Bad Arolsen,
Germany.
*Vesiputoussateenkaari ja muita
tapahtumia luonnossa*, EMMA Espoo
Museum of Modern Art, Tapiola, Espoo,
Finland.
Sensibility, Korjaamo Galleria,
Helsinki.
Summer Exhibition, Purdy Hicks
Gallery, London.
2012
7. Aalto–Taiteen Wihuri, Kunsthalle,
Helsinki.
Female View – Part 2, Fotoraum, Vienna.
2011
Flowers / Time, Death And Beauty,
FO.KU.S. Foto Kunst Stadtforum,
Innsbruck, Austria.
BFAMI Auction, Phillips de Pury, London.
Christophe Guye Galerie, Zurich.
Purdy Hicks Gallery, London.

Pyhäniemi Manor, Hollola, Finland.
Nature Forte, opening exhibition,
Rovaniemi Art Museum at Korundi,
Rovaniemi, Finland.
2010
Highlighted, Nieuw Dakota, Amsterdam.
Ikkuna portfolio, Gallery Hippolyte,
Helsinki.
Echoes of Light, Photographic Centre
Nykyaika, Tampere, Finland.
2009
Internal and External Landscapes,
Shiseido Gallery, Tokyo.
2008
Simple Life, Fiskars, Finland.
*Incertitudes de la vision / Reflections
of Reality*, Tour & Taxis, Brussels.
100% Finlande, Bibliothèque Mériadec,
Salle d'exposition, Bordeaux, France.
Views on Finnish Photography,
Nordic_Artworks, London.
Det blommar!, Galleri Elverket Pro
Artibus, Eknäs, Finland.
2007
TAJU – Idän taju, Hyvinkää Art Museum,
Hyvinkää, Finland.
Purdy Hicks Gallery, London.
Stenersen Museum, Oslo.
2006
Flower as Picture, Galerie Anhava,
Helsinki.
Naturally!, Mogadishni Gallery,
Copenhagen.
Joutsenen jäljillä, Lasipalatsi Gallery /
LUME Center, Helsinki.
The Helsinki School, Brussels.
The Helsinki School, Borås konsthall,
Borås, Sweden.
2005
Helsinki School, Kulturhuset, Stockholm.
2004
Galerie Roellin/Duerr, St. Gallen,
Switzerland.
CAFA Gallery, Beijing.
30 by TaiK, The Finnish Museum
of Photography, Helsinki.
The Helsinki School, Brandts
Klaedefabrik, Odense, Denmark.
Fotofinlandia, The Finnish Museum
of Photography, Helsinki and Oulu City
Art Museum, Oulu, Finland.
2003
*HANKI–03 Union of Artist
Photographers Annual Exhibition*,
Helsinki.

Landscape Now, City Art Museum,
Mikkeli, Finland.
2002
*Kultur-Räume Norden: An der Schwelle
des Unbekannten*, Kulturabteilung
Bayer, Leverkusen, Germany.
Masters of Art, The Finnish Museum
of Photography, Helsinki.
2001
CAFA Department of Photography,
Beijing.
Bordets Lust och Lov, Millesgården,
Stockholm.
Galleri Brandstrup, Oslo.
2000
Having a Ball, video installation, Pro-
founders Gallery, Helsinki.
(SIC), CuLTUREN, Västerås, Sweden.
Takaikkuna, photo.doc, Kiasma Museum
of Contemporary Art, Helsinki.

Public Collections
J. Paul Getty Museum, Los Angeles.
Stockholms sjukhem, Stockholm.
Kiasma Museum of Contemporary Art,
Helsinki.
Pro Artibus Foundation, Finland.
Helsinki City Art Museum.
Tampere Art Museum.
Olorvisual Collection, Barcelona.
EMMA Espoo Museum of Modern Art.
Saastamoinen Foundation, Finland.
SOK collections, Helsinki.
Wihuri Foundation, Rovaniemi.
State Art Collection, Finland.
Parliament of Finland.
Oulu City Hospital.

Astrid Kruse Jensen

Born in 1975 in Aarhus, Denmark
Lives and works in Copenhagen

Solo Exhibitions
2015
Esbjerg Kunstmuseum, Esbjerg,
Denmark.
2014
Within the Landscape, Johannes Larsen
Museet, Kerteminde, Denmark.
Within the Landscape, Sven-Harrys
Kunstmuseum, Stockholm.
2013
La Ville Culture, Ganshoren, Belgium.
La Vénerie, Brussels.
Château de Bourglinster, Luxembourg.
2012
Disappearing into the Past, Martin
Asbæk Gallery, Copenhagen;
Fotoforum, Stadtmuseum Schleswig,
Schleswig, Germany; Rønnebæksholm,
Næstved, Denmark; Museet for
Fotokunst, Odense, Denmark.
2011
On the other side of twilight, Stedelijk
Museum, Hertogenbosh, The
Netherlands, with Elle Kooi.
Enchanted Spaces, Ruchika's Art
Gallery, Goa, India.
Parallel Realities, Backslash Gallery,
Paris.
Disappearing into the Past, Brundlund
Slot, Aabenraa, Denmark.
2010
Between the Real and the Imaginary,
Maison du Danemark, Paris; Galerie
Mikael Andersen, Berlin.
The Construction of Memories, Galerie
Mikael Andersen, Copenhagen.
Enchanted Spaces, Ganges Art Gallery,
Kolkata, India.
2009
Between the Real and the Imaginary,
Artothèque de Caen, Caen, France.
Hidden Places / Enchanted Spaces,
The Viewing Room, Mumbai.
2008
Between the Real and the Imaginary,
Vestsjællands Art Museum, Sorø,
Denmark.
Indefinite Spaces, Galerie Mikael
Andersen, Berlin.
2007
Konrad-Adenauer-Stiftung,
Berlin.

2006
Hypernatural, Centrum Kultury Zamek,
Poznan, Poland; Galleri Hornbaek,
Hornbaek, Denmark; Kaunas Photo
Days, Kaunas, Lithuania.
Parallel Landscapes, La Galería,
Barcelona; Galerie Mikael Andersen,
Copenhagen.
Power of Place, Harbourfront Centre,
Toronto.
2005
Allusions of Home, Women's Festival,
Ljubljana, Slovenia.
Hypernatural, Galleri Image, Aarhus,
Denmark.
2004
Imaginary Realities, Philips
Contemporary Art Gallery, Manchester,
UK; Galleri Skuggi, Reykjavík.

Selected Group Exhibitions
2015
*Nolde, Eckersberg og Clausen –
alt du skal vide om sønderjysk kunst*,
Kunstmuseet Brundlund Slot,
Aabenraa, Denmark.
100 år med Grønningen, Den
Frie Udstillingsbygning &
Museumsbygningen, Copenhagen.
2014
Summer in the City, Martin Asbæk
Gallery, Copenhagen.
*Et Brask Spark. Selected Works from
Brask Collection*, Munkeruphus,
Dronningmølle, Denmark.
Visages, Centre de la Vieille Charité,
Marseille, France.
Drømme, KUNSTEN Museum of
Moderns Art, Aalborg, Denmark.
Just Add Water, CCA, Andratx
Mallorca, Spain.
*Viewfinders: Contemporary Baltic
and Nordic Photography*, Riga, Latvia.
Contemporary Art from Denmark,
The European Central Bank, Frankfurt
am Main.
2013
*Couleurs danoises. Interpretations
de la lumière par deux artistes danoise,
contemporains et feminins*, Den Danske
Ambassade, det danske kulturinstitut,
Luxembourg and Brussels.
Summer in the City, Martin Asbæk
Gallery, Copenhagen.
State of the Art, Slottet, Copenhagen

Photo Festival, Copenhagen.
Espace Delvaux, Cultural Centrum
of Watermal-Boisfort, Brussels.
Directors Choice 7-9-13, ARoS, Aarhus,
Denmark.
SUBLIMATE SUBLIME SUBLIMINA,
Underdog Gallery and Lloyd Club,
London.
*View on a country: Denmark at La Villa
Centre culturel de Ganshoren*,
Ganshoren, Belgium.
VIDEO, Martin Asbæk Gallery,
Copenhagen.
Zeigen, Nikolaj Kunsthal, Copenhagen.
2012
Sådan set, Rønnebæksholm, Næstved,
Denmark.
A Journey through a Nordic Fairytale,
Guided by Invoices, New York.
Grønningen, Docken, Copenhagen.
Summer in the City, Martin Asbæk
Gallery, Copenhagen.
Family and Friends, Backslash Gallery,
Paris.
2011
Backslash presents, Backslash Gallery,
Paris.
Places / Steder, HEART, Herning,
Denmark; Rosphoto, St. Petersburg,
Russia; Sophienhom, Lyngby, Denmark.
*Body of Memory: A Tribute to Louise
Bourgeois*, Galerie Mikael Andersen,
Copenhagen.
Dolls House, Galleri Christoffer
Egelund, Copenhagen.
New Danish Photography, Fotografisk
Center, Copenhagen.
2010
Fokus, Janusbygningen, Tistrup,
Denmark.
Grænselandsudstillingen, Aabenraa,
Denmark.
Grønningen, Docken, Copenhagen.
Places / Steder, Brandts Klædefabrik,
Odense, Denmark.
2009
The Christmas Photo Album, Ost
Gallery, Moscow.
Altid som aldrig før, Skagens Museum,
Skagen, Denmark.
Nytt nordisk fotografi, Skånes
Kunstforening, Malmö, Sweden.
Das Unheimliche, Modulorhaus, Berlin.
Human.Nature.Machine, WAS,
Copenhagen.

The buzz of urban surroundings, Gallery Poulsen, Copenhagen.
Danish Art, Museum der Stadt Bad Berleburg, Bad Berleburg, Germany.
Photography is Dead, Three White Walls Gallery, Birmingham, UK.
Bova Images Festival, Bova, Italy.
The Party, Beaver Gallery, Copenhagen.
Søen, Vestsjællands Kunstmuseum, Sorø, Denmark.
Højen, Oddsherreds Kunstmuseum, Asnæs, Denmark.
Real / Fiction, Nick Clifford Contemporary, Daugaard, Denmark.
Kontrapunkt, Esbjerg Kunstmuseum, Esbjerg, Denmark.
2008
Real.ly?, Peter Lav Photo Gallery, Copenhagen.
Solidaritetsudstillingen, Galleri Signe vad, Copenhagen.
Grænselands Exhibition, Aabenraa, Denmark.
Parallel Landscapes, Gallery Myymälä 2, Helsinki.
Evergreens, Rumkammerat, Copenhagen.
Guest at Grønningen, Bornholm Art Museum, Bornholm, Denmark.
Disturbance, Johannesburg Art Gallery, Johannesburg, South Africa.
Grænseland, Sydslesvigs danske Kunstforening, Flenburg, Germany.
Inside Out, Galerie Mikael Andersen, Berlin.
2007
Aspects of Danish Photography, Nordic Embassies, Berlin.
New Adventures, dARTex, The Danish Cultural Institute, Beijing; Shangcheng Gallery, Shanghai; Lai Shaoqi Gallery, Hefei; Modern Art Gallery, Chongqing; Yang Guang Gallery, Fuzhou; Forte Gallery, Chongqing; Jin Yi Xuan Gallery, Shenzhen, China.
Philips Contemporary Art Gallery, Manchester, UK.
The Year's Best Photography Books, PhotoEspaña, Madrid.
Kunstforeningen Pakhuset, Nykøbing Sjælland, Denmark.
One Shot Each, Museet for Fotokunst, Brandts Klædefabrik, Odense, Denmark.

Achtung! Kunst!, The National Museum for Photography, Copenhagen.
Salon 1, Lauritz Kunsthal, Copenhagen.
This way 07, Museet for Fotokunst, Branst Klædefabrik, Odense, Denmark.
Accessories, Galerie Mikael Andersen, Copenhagen.
Lianzhou International Photo Festival 2007, Lianzhou, China.
2006
Naturally, Mogadishni, Copenhagen.
A Day in Denmark, Fotografisk Center, Copenhagen.
Phantasm, Market Gallery, Glasgow.
Palle Fogtdal Photography Prize, Fotografisk Center, Copenhagen.
I skumringen, LARMgalleri, Copenhagen.
Indefinite Spaces, Charlottenborg Udstillingsbygning, Copenhagen.
New Adventures, Gallery Sejul, Seoul, South Korea.
10th Anniversary Exhibition, Philips Contemporary Art Gallery, Manchester, UK.
The Gift, Beaver Project, Copenhagen.
2005
Young Danish Photography, Fotografisk Center, Copenhagen.
The Collection for Contemporary Art, AROS Aarhus Kunstmuseum, Aarhus, Denmark.
Imaginary Realities, Galerie Mikael Andersen, Copenhagen.
Membershow, Transmission Gallery, Glasgow.
Photographers:network, Thomas Kellner Art Galerie, Siegen, Germany.
Vital Signs, George Eastman House, Rochester, NY.
Noorderlicht Photo Festival, Groningen, The Netherlands.
Light, Philips Contemporary Art Gallery, Manchester, UK.
Singular Photographs, Galleri Hornbæk, Hornbæk, Denmark.
2004
Photography, Hafnarborg, Hafnarfjördur, Iceland.
Kvinder stiller skarpt, Dannerhuset, Copenhagen.
Membershow, Transmission Gallery, Glasgow.
Outlook & Insight, Museet for

Fotokunst, Brandts Klædefabrik, Odense, Denmark.
Don't mention it, The National Museum of Photography, Copenhagen.
Easter Exhibition, Aarhus Kunstbygning, Aarhus, Denmark.
Spring Exhibition, Charlottenborg, Copenhagen.
2003
Allusions of Home, part of the *Odense Foto Triennale 2003*, Faaborg Museum, Faaborg, Denmark.
Philips Contemporary Art Gallery, Manchester, UK.
Real Photography, Manege – Museum for Contemporary Art, St. Petersburg, Russia.
Membershow, Transmission Gallery, Glasgow.
The Danish Cultural Institute, St. Petersburg, Russia.
The Artists Summer Exhibition, Janusbygningen, Tistrup, Denmark.
Easter Exhibition, Aarhus Kunstbygning, Aarhus, Denmark.
2002
The John Kobal Photographic Portrait Award 2002 Exhibition, National Portrait Gallery, London.
New Generation Show, Compass Gallery, Glasgow.
Membershow, Transmission Gallery, Glasgow.

Public Collections
The George Eastman House, Rochester, NY.
AROS Aarhus Kunstmuseum.
The National Museum of Photography, Copenhagen.
Museet for Fotokunst, Brandts Klædefabrik, Odense.
Artothèque de Caen.
The John Kobal Foundation, London.
Hafnarborg Institute of Culture and Fine Art, Hafnerfjördur, Iceland.
Manchester City Gallery.
Vestsjællands Art Museum, Sorø.
Statens Kunstfond, Denmark.

Lilly Lulay

Born in 1985 in Frankfurt am Main
Lives and works in Frankfurt am Main

Solo Exhibitions
2015
Reframe Memory, Athens Photofestival
2015, Athens, Greece.
2014
Indistance, Kuckei + Kuckei,
Berlin.
2013
Lichtbilder, Stiftung Opelvillen,
Russelsheim, Germany.
Morceaux Choisis, Galerie Ilka Bree,
Bordeaux, France.
2011
Mindscapes, Galerie Ilka Bree,
Bordeaux, France.

Selected Group Exhibitions
2014
Nouvelles Aquisitions 2014, Artothèque
de Pessac, Pessac, France.
FdJT, Offenbach am Main, Germany.
Even my mom can make a book #4,
Project Room, Berlin.
Les dérivés de la photographie, FRAC
Aquitaine, Artothèque de Pessac,
Pessac, France.
2013
House of Vetti, Koenig & Clinton,
New York.
All Hands Manöver, Kunstverein Speyer,
Speyer, Germany.
*Ausgezeichnet, Art Collection Deutsche
Börse*, Eschborn, Germany.
2012
Cartes Postales d'Artistes, Goethe-
Institut, Lyon, France.
Rethinking Reality, Kuckei + Kuckei,
Berlin.
Spieglein, Spieglein, in collaboration
with HfG Offenbach and Goethe
University, Frankfurt am Main.
RAY Fotografieprojekte, Rhein Main,
Frankfurt am Main.
Traces to find – Things to explore, FAK,
Münster, Germany.
Überqualifiziertes Material, Zeitraum
Exit, Mannheim, Germany.
L'espace de l'autre, Centre d'art et
photographie de Lectoure, Lectoure,
France.
on-off-on, Naspa Nassauische
Sparkasse, Wiesbaden, Germany.

2011
Déballées, Galerie Ilka Bree, Bordeaux,
France.
Nouvelles Aquisitions 2011,
Arthothèque de Pessac, Pessac, France.
Cést le bon, 18:52, Offenbach,
Germany.
2010
Tête à tête, HfG Satellit, Berlin.
COOP 1, former Diamentenbörse,
Frankfurt am Main.
Even my mom can make a book,
Manzara Perspectives, Istanbul, Turkey.
Fresco Mundo, Forgotten Bar, Berlin.

Public Collections
Art Collection DZ Privatbank, Germany.
Arthothèque de Pessac.
Arthothèque de Pau.
Arthothèque du Limousin.

Melissa Moore

Born in 1978 in Nottingham, UK
Lives and works in London

Solo Exhibitions
2015
Land Ends, Museum Theo Kerg,
Schriesheim, Germany.
Land Ends, Departure Lounge Gallery,
Luton, UK.
2014
Land Ends, Hornby Island Arts Council
Gallery, Hornby Island, British
Columbia, Canada.
2013
Land Ends, Photography Rooms,
Bagni di Lucca Art Festival, Lucca,
Italy.
2008
Plasmic, Nepente Art Gallery,
Milan.

Selected Group Exhibitions
2014
*In Between: Simone Bergantini, Michele
Buda, Martina Della Valle, Annabel
Elgar, Eeva Hannula, Sanna Kannisto,
Lisa Kereszi, Filippo Luini, Esther
Mathis, Melissa Moore, Marco
Signorini, Valentina Sommariva,
The Cool Couple*, Metronom,
Modena, Italy.
Photokina, Cologne, Germany.
Ladies Only, Contemporary Women
Photographers, Zurab Tsereteli Museum
of Modern Art, Tbilisi, Georgia.
2013
Mt. Rokko International Photo Festival,
Kobe, Japan.
Curator's Choice Award Showcase,
CENTER, Santa Fe, New Mexico.
Tarantel 1, Künstlerhaus Bethanien,
Berlin.
Portraits, Theory of Clouds Gallery,
Kobe, Japan.
*Reverie: Melissa Moore / Alberta
Pellacani*, Metronom, Modena,
Italy.
2012
*Singapore International Photography
Festival*, Singapore.
2011
Songs of the Swamp, Kunsthalle
Exnergasse WUK, Vienna.
Platinum, Piazza Solferino, Turin,
Italy.

2010
The Skinned City, Yinka Shonibare's
Project Space, London.
2009
Needle, Lens, Brush, Hornby Island
Community Hall, Hornby Island, British
Columbia, Canada.
2008
*In Our World: New Photography in
Britain*, Galleria Civica di Modena,
Modena, Italy.
Phantasma, Ballhaus Düsseldorf,
Düsseldorf, Germany.
2006
Albertine Goes South, Dorothee
Schmid, London.
2005
Slick, Agallery, London.
2004
The Summer Show, Hoopers Gallery,
London.

Barbara Probst

Born in 1964 in Munich
Lives and works in New York and Munich

Solo Exhibitions
2014
Centre PasquArt, Biel, Switzerland.
Galerie Rudolfinum, Prague.
Kuckei + Kuckei, Berlin.
2013
Murray Guy Gallery, New York.
National Museum for Photography, Copenhagen.
Galleria Monica de Cardenas, Milan.
2012
Kuckei + Kuckei, Berlin.
Wilkinson Gallery, London.
Lars Bohmann Gallery, Stockholm.
2011
Murray Guy, New York.
G Fine Arts, Washington, DC.
2010
Galleria Monica de Cardenas, Zuoz, St. Moritz, Switzerland.
Kuckei + Kuckei, Berlin.
Jessica Bradley Art-Projects, Toronto.
Lars Bohman Gallery, Stockholm.
2009
Oldenburger Kunstverein, Oldenburg, Germany.
Galeria Monica de Cardenas, Milan.
Still's Gallery, Edinburgh.
Murray Guy Gallery, New York.
2008
Domain de Kerguéhennec, Centre d'art contemporain, Bignan, France.
Madison Museum of Contemporary Art, Madison, WI.
Jessica Bradley Art-Projects, Toronto.
2007
Kuckei + Kuckei, Berlin.
Museum of Contemporary Photography, Chicago, IL.
G Fine Arts, Washington, DC.
2006
Murray Guy Gallery, New York.
2005
Kuckei + Kuckei, Berlin.
Jessica Bradley Art-Projects, Toronto, with Pascal Grandmaison.
G Fine Arts, Washington, DC.
2004
Murray Guy Gallery, New York.

2003
Sprüth Magers Projekte, Munich.
2002
Kunstverein Cuxhaven, Germany.
Galerie Otto Schweins, Cologne, Germany..
2001
Kunstverein, Schwerte, Germany.
Was Wirklich Geschah, ESCALE, Düsseldorf, Germany.
2000
stop #1, Galerie Philomene Magers, Munich.
1998
Interviews, Galerie Otto Schweins, Cologne, Germany.
1995
Der Geplante Augenblick, Galerie Otto Schweins, Cologne, Germany.
1994
In Expectation, Galerie Binder & Rid, Munich.
My Museum, Galerie Philomene Magers, Cologne, Germany.
1993
Interieur, Galerie Otto Schweins, Cologne, Germany.
1992
Vier Interieurs, Galerie FOE, Munich.
1990
Akademiegalerie, Munich.

Selected Group Exhibitions
2015
Perfect Likeness: Photography and Composition, Hammer Museum, Los Angeles, CA.
2014
Moving Parts: Time and Motion in Contemporary Art, Kemper Art Museum, Washington University, St. Louis, MO.
Eyes on the Street, Cincinnati Art Museum, Cincinnati, OH.
Reliable Tension, or: How to Win a Conversation about Jasper Johns, 32 Edgewood Avenue Gallery, Yale School of Art, New Haven, CT.
Paparazzi! Photographers, Stars and Artists, Centre Pompidou, Metz, France.
(Mis)Understanding Photography, Museum Folkwang, Essen, Germany.

2013
Per Speculum Me Video, Frankfurter Kunstverein, Frankfurt am Main.
The Other Portrait, MART Museo d'Arte Moderna e Contemporanea di Trento e Rovereto, Rovereto, Italy.
Drone, The Automated Image, Le Mois de la Photo a Montréal, Vox Contemporary Image Center, Montreal.
Women's World: Contemporary Views of Women by Women, Museum of Art Lauderdale, Fort Lauderdale, FL.
Das Fenster im Blick, Art Foyer DZ Bank, Frankfurt am Main.
2012
From the Margulies Collection, The Margulies Collection, Miami, FL.
Views and Windows, Galerie Sabine Knust, Munich.
Lost Places – Orte der Photographie, Hamburger Kunsthalle, Hamburg, Germany.
An Orchestrated Vision – The Theater of Contemporary Photography, St. Louis Art Museum, St. Louis, MO.
2011
Persona: A Body in Parts, Weatherspoon Art Museum, Greensboro, NC.
Exposed: Voyeurism, Surveillance and the Camera, Walker Arts Center, Minneapolis, MI.
Things are Queer. Highlights der Sammlung UniCredit, MARTa Herford, Herford, Germany.
2010
Exposed: Voyeurism, Surveillance and the Camera, Museum of Modern Art, San Francisco, CA.
Elles@centrepompidou, Centre Georges Pompidou, Paris.
Pictures by Women: A History of Modern Photography, Museum of Modern Art, New York.
Mixed Use, Manhattan, Museo Nacional Centro de Arte Reina Sofía, Madrid.
Exposed: Voyeurism, Surveillance and the Camera, Tate Modern, London.
To a Degree; Rational, Galleria Gentili, Prato, Italy.
Esopus 14: Projects, Esopus Space, New York.

2009
Süsser Vogel Jugend. Kindheit und Jugend in der zeitgenössischen Fotografie. Arbeiten aus den Beständen der Sammlung Moderne Kunst sowie Neuerwerbungen, Pinakothek der Moderne, Munich.
2008
Role Models, National Museum of Women's Art, Washington, DC.
A Matter of Time, Andrea Meislin Gallery, New York.
2007
Art Unlimited, Art Basel, Basel, Germany.
StereoVision, University of South Florida Contemporary Art Museum, Tampa, FL.
Urban Conditions. Reflexionen über den Raum, Rathausgalerie, Munich.
Modeling the Photographic: The Ends of Photography. A short critical history, McDonough Museum, Youngstown State University, Youngstown, OH.
Frame of Reference, Clifford Chance Projects, New York.
Tell Me a Story: Narrative Photography, Museum of Photographic Arts, San Diego, CA.
2006
Next Next Visual Art, Brooklyn Academy of Music, Brooklyn, New York.
New Photography, MoMA Museum of Modern Art, New York.
German Photography, Richard Levy Gallery, Albuquerque, NM.
2005
After the Fact, Martin-Gropius-Bau, Berlin.
This Side Toward Screen, Murray Guy Gallery, New York.
Wir arbeiten immer noch daran, nicht mehr zu arbeiten, Galerie der Künstler, Munich.
Loop, G Fine Art, Washington, DC.
Geo, Foxy Productions, New York.
2004
Camera Action, Museum of Contemporary Photography, Chicago, IL.
Der Widerstand der Fotografie, Camera Austria, Kunsthaus, Graz, Austria.
Between Spaces, Galeri Asbaek, Copenhagen.

2003
Double Exposure, Edition Schellmann, Munich.
20th Anniversary Show, Galerie Monika Sprüth, Cologne, Germany.
Between Spaces, Centro Cultural Andratx, Mallorca, Spain.
Off, Murray Guy Gallery, New York.
Shadow and Light, Galerie Sprüth Magers Lee, Salzburg, Austria.
2002
Hollywood Revisited, Kunstmuseum, Aarhus, Denmark.
QUIVID I – im öffentlichen Auftrag, Technisches Rathaus, Munich.
Heute bis Jetzt – Im Labor der Bilder, Museum Kunstpalast, Düsseldorf, Germany.
2001
Moving Pictures, Triennale der Photographie, Galerien der Stadt Esslingen, Villa Merkel, Esslingen, Germany.
Countdown, Kunstverein, Munich.
Mentalscape (eine Bibliothek), FOE 156, Munich.
2000
Transporter. A Reading Room, Bangkok.
Simili, De Chiara/Stewart Gallery, New York.
1995–97
photography after photography, Praterinsel, Munich; travelling to Kunsthalle Krems, Krems, Germany; Städt Galerie Erlangen, Erlangen, Germany; Brandenburgische Kunstsammlungen, Cottbus, Germany; Museet for Fotokunst, Odense, Denmark; Fotomuseum Winterthur, Winterthur, Switzerland; The Finnish Museum of Photography, Helsinki; Institute of Contemporary Art, Philadelphia, PA.

Public Collections
Akron Art Museum.
Centre PasquArt, Biel.
Centre Georges Pompidou, Paris.
Centro de Artes Visuales Fundación Helga de Alvear, Cáceres.
Folkwang Museum, Essen.
Galerie fuer Zeitgenössische Kunst, Leipzig.
Johnson Museum of Art, Cornell University, Ithaca, New York.

Kolumba, Kunstmuseum des Erzbistums Köln.
Lenbachhaus, Munich.
Los Angeles County Museum of Art.
The Margulies Collection at the Warehouse, Miami.
Musée d'Art Contemporain de Montréal.
Museo Cantonale d'Arte, Lugano.
Museum of Contemporary Art, Denver.
Museum of Contemporary Photography, Chicago.
Museum of Fine Arts, Houston.
MoMA Museum of Modern Art, New York.
National Gallery of Canada, Ottawa.
Nelson-Atkins Museum, Kansas City.
Pinakothek der Moderne, Munich.
San Francisco Museum of Modern Art.
Shpilman Institute for Photography, Tel Aviv.
The Art Gallery, University of Maryland, College Park.
Whitney Museum of American Art, New York.

Olivier Richon

Born in 1956 in Lausanne, Switzerland
Lives and works in London

Solo Exhibitions
2014
Punks, IBID Projects, London.
2013
Acedia, IBID Projects, London.
2009
Anima(l), IBID Projects, London.
2008
Anima(l), Bendana / Pinel Art
Contemporain, Paris.
Real Allegories, Bildkultur, Stuttgart,
Germany.
2006
The Spirit is a Bone, IBID Projects,
London.
Nepente Art Gallery, Milan.
2004
*Trilogia. Disegni di Mimmo Paladino,
fotografie di Olivier Richon, grafiche e
multipli di Richard Artschwager*,
Galleria Civica di Modena, Modena,
Italy.
2000
Allegories (animals looking sideways),
Galerie de l'Aquarium, Valenciennes,
France.
1998
A Touch of Realism, Dryphoto – Arte
Contemporanea, Prato, Italy.
1997
A Touch of Realism, Marlène Eleini,
London.
1996
The Hunt, Galerie Françoise Knabe,
Frankfurt am Main.
1995
After DL, Galerie Yvonamor Palix, Paris.
FStop Gallery, Bath and Zone Gallery,
Newcastle, UK.
Portfolio Gallery, Edinburgh and
Montage Gallery, Derby, Ireland.
1994
After DL, Forum Stadtpark, Graz,
Austria.
1993
After DL, Jack Shainman Gallery,
New York.
L'Académie, Galerie de l'Aquarium,
Valenciennes, France.
1992
Et in Arcadia Ego, Galerie des
Beaux-Arts, Nantes, France.

University of Essex Gallery,
Colchester, UK.
Galerie Samia Saouma, Paris.
1991
Imitatio Sapiens, Espace d'art
contemporain, Lausanne, Switzerland.
1990
A Devouring Eye, Jack Shainman
Gallery, New York and Galerie Samia
Saouma, Paris.
Lawrence Olivier, Philadelphia, PA.
1989
Imprese, Jack Shainman Gallery,
New York.
Galerie Samia Saouma, Paris.
1987
Iconologia, Galerie Samia Saouma,
Paris.
1986
The Academy, Galerie Samia Saouma,
Paris.
1985
The Grand Tour, Cash/Newhouse,
New York.
1984
The Grand Tour, Institute of
Contemporary Arts, London.
1982
Orientation, Institute of Contemporary
Arts, London.

Selected Group Exhibitions
2015
Anima Mundi, Max Lust Gallery,
Vienna.
We Could be Heroes, The
Photographers' Gallery, London.
2014
Waren und Wissen, Weltkulturen
Museum, Frankfurt am Main.
2012
Another London, Tate Britain,
London.
2011
Session_18_Flat Works, presented by
Am Nuden Da, Outpost Summer Fayre,
Norwich, UK.
*Signs of a Struggle, Photography in the
Wake of Postmodernism*, Victoria &
Albert Museum, London.
2010
Le Bestiaire imaginaire, Palais Lumière,
Évian, France.
Teaching Photography, Museum
Folkwang, Essen, Germany.

2008
Exhibition Road, Handel Street Projects,
London.
2007
Generations, Galerie les Filles du
Calvaire, Brussels.
2006
Zoo, la centrale électrique – centre
d'art contemporain, Brussels.
2005
Das Fotografierte Tier, Museum
Folkwang, Essen, Germany.
2004
The Goat, Medievalmodern, London,
with Mark Fairnington.
2002
*Sans commune mesure – image et texte
dans l'art actuel*, Musée d'art moderne,
Lille Métropole, Lille, France.
Seeing Things, Canon Gallery, Victoria
& Albert Museum, London.
Love, Labour and Loss, Tullic House and
Art Gallery, Carlisle, UK.
Cinema India, Contemporary Space,
Victoria & Albert Museum, London.
2001
L'oeuvre démultipliée, Musée d'art
moderne, Lille Métropole, Lille, France.
M Family, Migros Museum, Zurich.
Players, Insidespace at Selfridges,
London.
2000
Eat. Fuck. Die, Platform, London.
1999
Un jardin d'hiver, Institut d'art
contemporain, collection FRAC en
Rhône Alpes, France.
1998
Gesichter und Dinge, Neue Gesellschaft
für Bildende Kunst, Berlin.
What is a Photograph, Five Years,
London.
*Chemical Traces. Photography and
Conceptual Art 1968–1998*, Ferens Art
Gallery, Hull, UK.
Hygiène, Galerie Yvonamor Palix, Paris.
*The Promise of Photography – The DG
Bank Collection*, Hara Museum of
Contemporary Art, Tokyo.
1997
*History, The Mag Collection. Image
based art in Britain in the late 20th
century*, Ferens Art Gallery, Hull, UK.
*Virtue and Vice. Derivations of Allegory
in Contemporary Photography*, Site

Gallery, Sheffield, UK; Portalen Koge
Bugt Kulturhus, Bugt, Germany; Zone
Gallery, Newcastle, UK.
Curiosity Room, Jack Shainman Gallery,
New York.
1996
Foto Text, Text Foto, Museion, Bolzano,
Italy; Kunstverein, Frankfurt am Main.
Jocaste en Arcadie, Château des
Adhémars, Montélimar, France.
1995
L'immagine riflessa (Collection Lac,
Geneva), Centro per l'Arte
Contemporanea, Museo Luigi Pecci,
Prato, Italy.
Der Ton des Raums, Galerie Angelo
Falzone, Mannheim, Germany.
Espace d'art contemporain, Lausanne,
Switzerland.
Printemps de Cahors, Galerie Yvonamor
Palix, Paris.
Image and Text in Recent Photography,
Academie Voor Schone Kunsten, Sint
Niklaas, Belgium.
1994
Revisions, Veruela Monastery, Vera
Moncayo, Spain.
1993
Leopold Godowsky Awards,
Photographic Resource Centre,
Boston, Mass.
Aus Der Romandie, Fotomuseum
Winterthur, Winterthur, Switzerland.
Diskurse der Bilder, Kunsthistorisches
Museum, Vienna.
1992
The Fortune Teller, Rochdale Art
Gallery, Rochdale, UK.
Helvetia Condensed, Forum für
zeitgenössische Fotografie,
Künstlerwerkstatt, Munich.
Glass Piece & In Arcadia, Brewery Art
Centre, Kendal, UK.
1991
*Autrement dit, les artistes utilisent la
photographie*, Ancienne caserne de la
Planche, Fribourg, Switzerland.
1990
Wichtige Bilder, Museum für
Gestaltung, Zurich.
Images in Transition, *Photographic
Representation in the 80s*, National
Museum of Modern Art, Kyoto
and Tokyo.

1989
Other than Itself, The Showroom,
London; Camerawork, London;
Cambridge Darkroom, Cambridge, UK;
Ikon Gallery, Birmingham, UK.
PhotoTriennale, Esslingen, Germany.
European Avant Garde, Albright-Knox
Art Gallery, Buffalo, NY.
1988
*The Analytical Theatre, New Art from
Britain,* University Art Museum,
California State University and Institute
of Contemporary Arts, Philadelphia, PA.
*Presi X Incantamento, la nuova
fotografia internazionale*, PAC
Padiglione di Arte Contemporanea,
Milan.
1987
*The Analytical Theatre, New Art from
Britain*, Akron Art Museum, Akron, OH
and Alberta College of Art Gallery,
Calgary, Canada.
Mysterious Coincidences, The
Photographers' Gallery, London.
1985
*Re-visions, fringe interference in British
photography*, Cambridge Darkroom
and Hansard Gallery, Southampton, UK.
Multiple Images, The Photographers'
Gallery, London.
1978
Punks and Teds, The Photographers'
Gallery, London.

Tom Sandberg

Born in 1953 in Narvik, Norway
Died in 2014 in Oslo

Selected Solo Exhibitions
2015
Diptyc, Kunstnernes Hus, Oslo.
2014
Photographs, OSL Contemporary, Oslo
(opened three weeks after the artist's
death).
2011
Uten tittel, 2004–2010, Rom for Kunst,
Oslo Central Station, Oslo.
Tom Sandberg – Nyere Arbeider,
Lillehammer Art Museum, Lillehammer,
Norway.
2009
Galleri Trafo, Asker, Norway.
2010
Nils Stærk, Copenhagen.
MGM, Oslo.
2007
Kivik Art, Pavilion with Snøhetta
Architects, Kivik Art Center,
Simrishamn, Sweden.
Künstlerhouse Bethanien, Berlin.
MoMA PS1, New York.
Nils Stærk, Copenhagen.
Galleri Riis, Oslo.
2006
Galerie Anhava, Helsinki.
2005
The Festival of North Norway, Harstad,
Norway.
2004
Galleri Riis, Oslo.
2003
Galleri Nordenhake, Stockholm.
2002
Nils Stærk, Copenhagen.
2001
Galleri Riis, Oslo.
2000
*Tom Sandberg. Fotografi. Arbeider fra
de siste 20 årene*, The Astrup Fearnley
Museum of Modern Art, Oslo.
1998
Galleri Sølvberget, Stavanger, Norway.
Gothaer Kunstforum, Cologne,
Germany, with Per Inge Bjørlo.
Galleri Riis, Oslo.
1997
The Astrup Fearnley Museum of
Modern Art, Oslo, with Per Inge
Bjørlo.

1995
Galleri Riis, Oslo.
1994
Galleri Sølvberget, Stavanger,
Norway.
1993
Fotogalleriet, Oslo.
1989
Galleri Riis, Oslo.
1987
Bergen Kunstforening, Bergen
Kunsthall, Bergen, Norway.
1986
Galeri Image, Aarhus, Denmark.
1985
Henie Onstad Art Centre, Høvikodden,
Norway.
1984
Galerie du Musée de la Photographie,
Charleroi, Belgium.
Galerie Junod, Lausanne, Switzerland.
1980
Fotogalleriet, Oslo.
1979
Centre Georges Pompidou, Paris.
Galleri Annen Etasje, Haugesund,
Norway.

Selected Group Exhibitions
2012
*I wish this was a song. Music in
Contemporary Art*, National Museum
of Contemporary Art, Oslo.
2009
Works on paper, Nils Stærk,
Copenhagen.
2008
Tom Sandberg/Stefano Casciani,
Galleria Artra, Milan.
2007
People take pictures of each other,
Lamontagne Gallery, Boston, Mass.
2004
Nordic Images, Galería Elba Benitez,
Madrid.
2003
Ronce noire, Galerie Catherine Bastide,
Brussels.
2002
Ronce noire, Galerie Praz-Delavallade,
Paris.
2001
*Å bygge en samling – samlingens
vekst*, Museum of Contemporary Art,
Oslo.

1999
Rolf Hoff's Art Collection, Bergen
Kunsthall, Bergen, Norway.
1998
Norske profiler, Museum Folkwang,
Essen, Germany and Kunsthalle
Rostock, Rostock, Germany.
Fönster mot Gården, Liljevalchs
Konsthall, Stockholm.
1994
Norfotart, Centre for Contemporary
Art, Ujazdowski Castle, Warsaw.
1993
Posisjoner I, Fotogalleriet, Oslo.
Verden Er, Lillehammer Art Museum,
Lillehammer, Norway; travelling to
Hasselbladsenteret, Gothenburg and
Museet for Fotokunst, Odense,
Denmark.
1991
Splint, Kunstnernes Hus, Oslo, with Fin
Serck-Hanssen.
1987
*Simulo. Norwegian Contemporary
Photography*, Oslo; travelling through
Norway.
Ten Norwegian Photographers, Norge
'87, Gothenburg; travelling to Austin,
TX.
1986
Skandinavisk Fotografi, Kunstmuseum,
Düsseldorf, Germany.
1985
Dialogue on Contemporary Art,
Museu Calouste Gulbenkian, Lisbon.
1984
Eksponert, Fotogalleriet/UKS, Oslo.
Zeitgenössische Europäische Fotografie,
Schaffhausen, Switzerland.
La Photographie créative, Pavillon des
Arts, Paris.
Deuxième Triennale de Photographie,
Galerie du Musée de la Photographie,
Charleoi, Belgium.
1982
Nio norske fotografer, Camera
Obscura, Stockholm.
The Frozen Image, Scandinavia Today,
Walker Art Center, Minneapolis, MN;
travelling to International Center of
Photography, New York; Fredrick S.
Wright Gallery, University of California,
Los Angeles, CA; Portland Art Museum,
Portland, OR; The Museum of
Contemporary Art, Chicago, IL;

Tacoma Art Museum, Tacoma, WA;
Kjarvalsstadir, Reykjavík; Taidehalli,
Helsinki; Fotografiska Museet, Moderna
Museet, Stockholm; Henie-Onstad
Kunstsenter, Høvikodden, Norway.
1981
Norsk Samtidsfotografi, Robert Meyer
Samlinger, Reykjavík.
1979
Fotografi her og nå, Henie-Onstad Art
Centre, Høvikodden, Norway.
Sandberg/Parslow, Ibsenmuseet, Skien,
Norway.
1978
Tusen och en Bild, Fotografiska Museet,
Stockholm.
Statens Kunstutsilling, Kunstnernes
Hus, Oslo.
1977
Sandberg/Parslow, Henie-Onstad Art
Centre, Høvikodden, Norway.

Public Collections
Bibliothèque nationale, Paris.
Bærum Kommunale Kunstsamlinger,
Sandvika.
Fotografiska Museet / Moderna
Museet, Stockholm.
Galerie du Musée de la Photographie,
Charleroi.
Henie-Onstad Kunstsenter, Høvikodden.
Magasin 3, Stockholm Konsthall.
Det Kgl. Bibliotek, Copenhagen.
Ministry of Culture, Paris.
The National Museum of Contemporary
Art, Oslo.
Museum für Kunst und Gewerbe,
Hamburg.
The Norwegian Art Council, Oslo.
Norsk Museum for Fotografi, Preus
Fotomuseum, Horten.
Rasmus Meyer Collections, Bergen
Kunstmuseum.
The Astrup Fearnley Museum of
Modern Art, Oslo.

Trine Søndergaard

Born in 1972 in Copenhagen
Lives and works in Copenhagen

Solo Exhibitions
2015
Martin Asbæk Gallery, Copenhagen.
2013
Stasis, Ffotogallery, Cardiff, Wales, UK.
Monochrome Portraits, Hagedorn
Foundation Gallery, Atlanta, GA.
Bruce Silverstein Gallery, New York,
with Nicolai Howalt.
Birds, Trees and Hunting Scenes,
Kunsthal Nord, Aalborg, Denmark, with
Nicolai Howalt.
2012
Still, Martin Asbæk Gallery,
Copenhagen.
Strude, Museum Kunst der Westküste,
Föhr, Germany.
How to Hunt, Maison du Danemark,
Paris, with Nicolai Howalt.
2011
Memento, Bildkultur, Stuttgart,
Germany.
Strude, Kunstmuseet i Tønder, Tønder,
Denmark.
*Blyge blikk, Adolph Tidemand & Trine
Søndergaard*, Nationalmuseet, Oslo.
The Volta Show, New York, solo
presentation by Martin Asbæk Gallery.
How to Hunt, Galleri Format, Malmö,
Sweden, with Nicolai Howalt.
2010
Monochrome Portraits, City Art
Museum, Ljubljana, Slovenia.
Strude II: Trine Søndergaard, Galleri
Kant, Fanø, Denmark.
Bruce Silverstein Gallery, New York.
Monochrome Portraits, Nessim Gallery,
Budapest.
Strude, Ny Carlsberg Glyptotek,
Copenhagen.
How to Hunt, ARoS Aarhus
Kunstmuseum, Aarhus, Denmark, with
Nicolai Howalt.
2009
Mono, Galleri Image, Aarhus,
Denmark.
Monochrome Portraits, Martin Asbæk
Gallery, Copenhagen.
Tree Zone, Volta, New York, with
Nicolai Howalt.
2008
Galleri Kant, Sønderho, Denmark.

2007
How to Hunt, Fotografins Hus,
Stockholm, with Nicolai Howalt.
Hunting Grounds, Le Mois de la Photo
à Montréal, Parisian Laundry, Montreal,
Canada, with Nicolai Howalt.
How to Hunt, Bruce Silverstein Gallery,
New York, with Nicolai Howalt.
2006
Statement, Paris Photo, Paris, with
Nicolai Howalt.
How to Hunt, Galerie Poller, Frankfurt
am Main, with Nicolai Howalt.
How to Hunt, Faaborg Museum of Fine
Art, Faaborg, Denmark, with Nicolai
Howalt.
2005
How to Hunt, Martin Asbæk Projects,
Copenhagen, with Nicolai Howalt.
2003
Now That You Are Mine,
Filosofgangen, Odense, Denmark.
Versus, Thorvaldsens Museum,
Copenhagen.
2001
Now That You Are Mine, Nederlands
Foto Instituut, Rotterdam, The
Netherlands.
2000
Now That You Are Mine, IFSAK,
Istanbul, Turkey.
1998
Neighbours, International Meetings of
Photography, Plovdiv, Bulgaria.
1996
Kom de bagfra, Kanonhallen,
Copenhagen.

Selected Group Exhibitions
2015
Close To Me, CM&P Rennes Beaulieu,
Rennes, France.
100 år med Grønningen, Den Frie
Udstillingsbygning &
Museumsbygningen, Copenhagen.
*Femina ou la réappropriation des
modèles*, Pavillon Vendôme, Centre
d'art contemporain, Paris.
2014
Summer in the City, Martin Asbæk
Gallery, Copenhagen.
Kunst und Küste, Museum Kunst der
Westküste, Alkersum, Föhr, Germany.
Bikuben, Utah Museum of
Contemporary Art, Salt Lake City, UT.

Still Life, Charlotte Fogh Gallery,
Aarhus, Denmark.
Contemporary Art from Denmark,
European Central Bank, Frankfurt am
Main.
OMHANDLING!, Meatpacking District,
Copenhagen.
Still Life, Charlotte Fogh Gallery,
Copenhagen, with Nicolai Howalt.
2013
Everyone Carries a Room Inside,
Museum on the Seam, Jerusalem.
Nyförvärv, Göteborgs Konstmuseum,
Gothenburg.
Nordic Art Station, Eskilstuna, Sweden.
Summer in the City, Martin Asbæk
Gallery, Copenhagen.
State of the Art, Copenhagen Photo
Festival, Copenhagen.
From Ingegerd to Estelle, Sigtuna
Museum, Sigtuna, Sweden.
Still Life/Work Life, The Hasselblad
Foundation, Gothenburg.
Das Nahe und die Ferne, Künslterhaus
Dortmund, Dortmund, Germany.
Cool Nordic, The Kennedy Center,
Washington, DC.
Tunnel Vision, Portalen, Greve,
Denmark.
New Nordic, Louisiana Museum of
Modern Art, Humlebæk, Denmark.
Flora Danica, Natural History Museum
of Denmark, Copenhagen, with Nicolai
Howalt.
2012
Grønningen, Copenhagen.
*A Journey through a Nordic Fairytale:
Danish Contemporary Art*, Guided by
Invoices, New York.
2011
*L'énigme du portrait. Œuvres de la
Collection Neuflize Vie*, MAC Musée
d'Art Contemporain, Marseille, France.
Kiyosato Museum of Photographic Arts,
Kiyosato, Japan.
Danmark Under Forvandling, Gl.
Holtegaard, Holte, Denmark.
Steder, Danmark Under Forvandling,
HEART Herning Museum of Art,
Herning, Denmark.
2010
Grønningen, Copenhagen.
Danmark Under Forvandling, Museet
for Fotokunst, Brandts, Odense,
Denmark.

Kunstforeningen af 14 august, Danish Museum of Art & Design, Copenhagen.
Summer in the City, Martin Asbæk Gallery, Copenhagen.
Sguardi e voci giovani sull'Europa, Real Academia de España en Roma, Rome.
X-Tra Light, Galleri KANT, Esbjerg, Denmark.
I Love You, ARoS Aarhus Kunstmuseum, Aarhus, Denmark.
This Way 10, Museet for Fotokunst, Brandts, Odense, Denmark.
2009
Altid som aldrig før, Skagen Art Museum, Skagen, Denmark.
D-Stop, O'born Contemporary, Toronto.
2008
Present Perfect Portraits, Martin Asbæk Projects, Copenhagen.
2007
Reality Crossings, Fotofestival Mannheim – Ludwigshafen – Heidelberg, Wilhelm-Hack-Museum, Ludwigshafen, Germany.
2006
I Skumringen, Galleri Larm, Copenhagen.
Scandinavian Photography, Houston, TX.
New Photography, Scandinavia House, New York.
Closed Eyes, Museet for Fotokunst, Brandts, Odense, Denmark.
The Open Book, The National Museum of Photography, Copenhagen.
2005
Scandinavian Photography, Faulconer Gallery, Grinnell, IA.
Emergencias, MUSAC Museo de Arte Contemporáneo de Castilla y León, León, Spain.
Young Portfolio Acquisition 2004, Kiyosato Museum of Photographic Arts, Kiyosato, Japan.
2004
Body, Galleri GimEis, Copenhagen.
Pro, Charlottenborg, Copenhagen.
Kvinder stiller skarpt, Dannerhuset, Copenhagen.
2003
Fra objektiv til objekt, Den Frie Udstillingsbygning, Copenhagen.
Making Eyes, Fotografisk Center, Copenhagen.
www.woman2003.dk, billboard exhibition, Copenhagen and Malmø, Sweden.
2002
Never Ending Story, billboard exhibition, Copenhagen.
2001
Faces and Figures, Scandinavia House, New York.
Repor På En Slat Yta, Hasselblad Center, Gothenburg.
Scrathes on a Smooth Surface, Hasselblad Center, Gothenburg.
Spejlkabinettet, Museet for Fotokunst, Brandts, Odense, Denmark.
1999
Young Danish Photography, Fotografisk Center, Copenhagen.
From The Hidden, The National Museum of Photography, Copenhagen.
Modern Times, Hasselblad Center, Gothenburg.
1998
1000 år 10, Museum of Contemporary Art, Roskilde, Denmark.

Public Collections
Collection du FMAC Clichy.
Museum on the Seam, Jerusalem.
Gothenburg Museum of Art.
Museum Kunst der Westküste, Alkersum.
ARoS Aarhus Art Museum.
The Lewis Glucksman Gallery, Cork.
Art Pradier Collection, Switzerland.
MuMa Musée d'art moderne André Malraux, Le Havre.
The National Museum of Art, Osloss.
Cornell Fine Arts Museum, Winter Park.
Statoil Art Collection, Norway.
Nykredit, Denmark.
Fanø Art Museum.
Skagens Art Museum.
Bornholms Art Museum.
Kunstmuseet i Tønder.
KUNSTEN – Museum of Modern Art Aalborg.
National Museum of Women in the Arts, Washington, DC.
Art Foundation Mallorca.
The Israel Museum, Jerusalem.
La Casa Encendida, Madrid.
Fondation Neuflize Vie, Paris.
The Ny Carlsberg Foundation.
The Danish Arts Foundation, Denmark.
Maison Européenne de la Photographie, Paris.
Museum of Fine Arts, Houston.
Hasselblad Foundation, Gothenburg.
Museet for Fotokunst, Brandts.
The National Museum of Photography, Copenhagen.
MUSAC Museo de Arte Contemporáneo de Castilla y León.
Kiyosato Museum of Photographic Arts.

Wolfgang Tillmans

Born in 1968 in Remscheid, Germany
Lives and works in Berlin and London

Solo Exhibitions
2015
Hasselblad Center, Gothenburg.
House of Art, Budweis, Czech
Republic.
David Zwirner, New York.
The National Museum of Modern Art,
Osaka, Japan.
Lignine Duress, Galerie Chantal
Crousel, Paris.
Book for Architects, The Metropolitan
Museum of Art, New York.
2014
Second Exhibition (collection display),
Fondation Louis Vuitton, Paris.
Fondation Beyeler (collection display),
Riehen, Switzerland.
Affinity, Wako Works of Art, Tokyo.
2013
Silver, Galerie Buchholz, Berlin.
central nervous system, Maureen Paley,
London.
Neue Welt, Rencontres d'Arles, Arles,
France.
from Neue Welt, Andrea Rosen Gallery,
New York.
*Wolfgang Tillmans. Düsseldorf Raum
2001–2007* (collection display),
Museum Kunstpalast, Düsseldorf,
Germany.
2012
Moderna Museet, Stockholm;
travelled to Kunstsammlung
Nordrhein-Westfalen, K21 Ständehaus,
Düsseldorf, Germany (2013).
Neue Welt, Kunsthalle Zürich, Zurich.
*Works from the Arts Council
Collection, Onion and Headlights*,
The Common Guild, Glasgow.
MAM Museu de Arte Moderna de
São Paulo, Brazil; travelled to Museo
de Arte del Banco de la República,
Bogotá, Columbia, MALI Museo de
Arte de Lima, Lima, Peru (2013) and
MAVI Museo de Artes Visuales,
Santiago de Chile (2013).
2011
Zachęta Ermutigung, Zachęta National
Gallery of Art, Warsaw.
Galerie Chantal Crousel, Paris.
*Out of the Boxes Part 1, Gallery 3:
Wolfgang Tillmans, curated by Beatrix*

Ruf, Andrea Rosen Gallery, New York.
*Out of the Boxes Part 2, Gallery 3:
Wolfgang Tillmans, curated by Stefan
Kalmár*, Andrea Rosen Gallery,
New York.
Regen Projects, Los Angeles, CA.
New Entrants, Staatsgalerie Stuttgart
(collection display), Stuttgart,
Germany.
Wolfgang Tillmans y Franz West,
Galería Juana de Aizpuru, Madrid.
2010
Galerie Daniel Buchholz, Berlin.
Walker Art Gallery, Liverpool, UK.
Serpentine Gallery, London.
Andrea Rosen Gallery, New York.
Panoramabar, Berlin (permanent
installation).
2009
*Ten: 1999–2009 at Sommer
Contemporary Art*, Sommer
Contemporary Art, Tel Aviv.
2008
Half Page, Regen Projects,
Los Angeles.
String, Galerie Chantal Crousel, Paris.
*Tegenwoordigheid van Geest –
Presence of Mind* (collection display)
and *Stedelijk Room* (installation for the
permament collection by Wolfgang
Tillmans), Stedelijk Museum,
Amsterdam.
Maureen Paley, London.
*Wolfgang Tillmans – Düsseldorf Raum
2001–2007*, Museum Kunstpalast,
Düsseldorf, Germany.
Lichter, Wako Works of Art, Tokyo.
2008, Galería Juana de Aizpuru,
Madrid.
Neugerriemschneider, Berlin.
Tate Britain, London (collection
display).
Lighter, Hamburger Bahnhof –
Museum für Gegenwart, Berlin.
2007
All The Time / Time, Galleria S.A.L.E.S.,
Rome.
Faltung, Camera Austria, Graz,
Austria.
Beugung, Kunstverein München,
Munich.
Still Lifes, Oroom Gallery, Seoul,
South Korea.
paper drop, Galerie Daniel Buchholz,
Cologne, Germany.

Bali, Kestner-Gesellschaft, Hanover,
Germany.
Bibliographie, Buchhandlung Walther
König, Cologne, Germany.
Atair, Andrea Rosen Gallery, New York.
Richard Branson, White Cubicle
Gallery, George & Dragon, London.
2006
Sprengel Installation (+4), Sprengel
Museum, Hanover, Germany
(collection display).
Helsinki-Festival, Taidehalli, Helsinki.
München Installation, Pinakothek der
Moderne, Munich (collection display).
Freedom from the Known, MoMA PS1,
New York.
Museum of Contemporary Art,
Chicago, IL; travelled to Hammer
Museum, Los Angeles, CA; Hirshhorn
Museum and Sculpture Garden,
Washington, DC (2007) and Museo
Tamayo, Mexico City (2008).
2005
2005, Galería Juana de Aizpuru,
Madrid.
Markt, Galerie Meerrettich, Berlin.
Truth Study Center, Maureen Paley,
London.
Press to Exit Project Space, Skopje,
Macedonia.
2004
Regen Projects, Los Angeles, CA.
Freischwimmer, Tokyo Opera City Art
Gallery, Tokyo.
New Photographs, Wako Works of Art,
Tokyo.
Freischwimmer, Neugerriemschneider,
Berlin.
2003
Andrea Rosen Gallery, New York.
Frans Hals Museum, Haarlem,
The Netherlands.
Galerie Daniel Buchholz, Cologne,
Germany.
*if one thing matters, everything
matters*, Tate Britain, London.
View From Above, Louisiana Museum
of Modern Art, Humlebæk, Denmark.
2002
Wolfgang Tillmans – Still Life, The
Fogg Art Gallery, Busch Reisinger
Museum, Harvard, Cambridge, MA.
Sommer Contemporary Art, Tel Aviv.
Lights (Body), Andrea Rosen Gallery,
New York.

Partnerschaften, nGbK neue
Gesellschaft für bildende Kunst,
Berlin, with Jochen Klein.
Maureen Paley Interim Art, London.
Lights (Body), Galleria S.A.L.E.S.,
Rome.
Regen Projects, Los Angeles, CA.
Vue d'en Haut, Palais de Tokyo, Paris.
Veduta dall'alto, Castello di Rivoli
Museo d'Arte Contemporanea, Rivoli,
Turin, Italy.
2001
*AC: Isa Genzken / Wolfgang Tillmans,
Science Fiction / Hier und jetzt
zufrieden sein*, Museum Ludwig,
Cologne, Germany.
Aufsicht, Deichtorhallen Hamburg,
Hamburg, Germany.
Super Collider, Galerie Daniel
Buchholz, Cologne, Germany.
Wako Works of Art, Tokyo.
Andrea Rosen Gallery, New York.
2000
Galerie Rudiger Schöttle, Munich,
with Thomas Ruff.
Galerie Meyer Kainer, Vienna,
with Jochen Klein.
Blushes, fig-1, London.
1999
Soldiers – The Nineties, arsFutura
Galerie, Zurich.
Galleria S.A.L.E.S., Rome.
Regen Projects, Los Angeles, CA.
Soldiers – The Nineties, Andrea Rosen
Gallery, New York.
*Space between Two Buildings /
Soldiers – The Nineties*, Maureen Paley
Interim Art, London.
*part I: Recent Works / part II:
Concorde*, Wako Works of Art,
Tokyo.
Soldiers – The Nineties, Neuer
Aachener Kunstverein, Aachen,
Germany.
*Eins ist sicher: Es kommt immer ganz
anders, als man denkt*, Städtische
Galerie, Remscheid, Germany.
Saros, Galerie Daniel Buchholz,
Cologne, Germany.
Neugerriemschneider, Berlin.
1998
Andrea Rosen Gallery, New York.
Fruicciones, Museo Nacional Centro de
Arte Reina Sofía, Espacio Uno, Madrid.
Café Gnosa, Hamburg, Germany.

1997
Hale-Bopp, Galerie Daniel Buchholz,
Art Cologne, Cologne, Germany.
I didn't inhale, Chisenhale Gallery,
London.
Galleria S.A.L.E.S., Rome.
1996
Wer Liebe wagt, lebt morgen,
Kunstmuseum Wolfsburg, Wolfsburg,
Germany.
Andrea Rosen Gallery, New York.
Galleri Nicolai Wallner, Copenhagen.
arsFutura Galerie, Zurich.
Kunstverein Elsterpark, Leipzig,
Germany.
Faltenwürfe, Galerie Daniel Buchholz,
Cologne, Germany.
1995
Neugerriemschneider, Berlin.
Kunsthalle Zürich, Zurich.
Stills Gallery, Edinburgh, UK.
Portikus, Frankfurt am Main.
Regen Projects, Los Angeles, CA.
Interim Art, London.
1994
Galerie Thaddaeus Ropac, Paris.
Galerie Daniel Buchholz, Cologne,
Germany.
Andrea Rosen Gallery, New York.
1993
Interim Art, London.
arsFutura Galerie, Zurich.
L.A. Galerie, Frankfurt am Main.
Galerie Daniel Buchholz – Buchholz
& Buchholz, Cologne, Germany.
1992
Diptychen, 1990–1992, PPS. Galerie
F. C. Gundlach, Hamburg, Germany.
1991
Grauwert Galerie, Hamburg, Germany.
1989
Café Gnosa, Hamburg, Germany.
1988
Approaches, Fabrik – Foto – Forum,
Stadtbucherei Remscheid, Hamburg,
Germany.
Blutsturz, Front, Hamburg, Germany.
Approaches, Café Gnosa, Hamburg,
Germany.

Selected Group Exhibitions
2015
The Persistence of Objects, Lismore
Castle Arts, Lismore, Ireland.
The Day Will Come When Man Falls,

Triennale der Photographie, Hamburg,
Germany.
What We Call Love, Irish Museum of
Modern Art, Dublin.
Ident-alter-ity: Organizing Body,
5th Biennale of Contemporary Art
of Thessaloniki, State Museum
of Contemporary Art, Thessaloniki,
Greece.
Simple Forms: Contemplating Beauty,
Mori Art Museum, Tokyo.
*Zabludowicz Collection: 20 Years of
Collecting: Between Discovery and
Invention*, Zabludowicz Collection,
London.
*Open Rhapsody: A journey into
photography and video collections*,
Beirut Exhibition Center, Beirut,
Lebanon.
Partial Presence, Zabludowicz
Collection, London.
The Gesamtsexwerk (presented by M/L
artspace), The Spectrum, New York.
The Noing Uv It, Bergen Kunsthall,
Bergen, Norway.
Zoom in on Architecture,
Architekturmuseum der TU München,
Pinakothek der Moderne, Munich.
*Pretty Raw: After and Around Helen
Frankenthaler*, Rose Art Museum,
Waltham, Mass.
flats, Team Gallery, New York.
2014
Dancing Light / Let it move you, Huis
Marseille Museum voor fotografie,
Amsterdam.
They used to call it the moon, BALTIC
Centre for Contemporary Art,
Gateshead, UK.
*Lumières: carte blanche à Christian
Lacroix*, Musée Cognacq-Jay, Paris.
Simple Shapes, Centre Pompidou,
Metz, France.
*Unstable Places: New in Contemporary
Art*, The Israel Museum, Jerusalem.
In Dialogue: Wolfgang Tillmans,
Philadelphia Museum of Art,
Philadelphia, PA.
*Une histoire, art, architecture et
design, des années 80 à aujourd'hui*,
Musée national d'art moderne, Centre
Pompidou, Paris (collection display).
*Manifesta 10 – European Biennial of
Contemporary Art*, St. Petersburg,
Russia.

In NO time, The Modern Institute,
Glasgow.
Colour on Paper, Galeria Leme,
São Paulo, Brazil.
*(Mis)Understanding Photography.
Werke und Manifeste*, Museum
Folkwang, Essen, Germany.
*Space Interventions – Gordon Matta
Clark and beyond*, Salon Dahlmann,
Berlin.
*A Private View präsentiert: Die ROCCA
Stiftung*, Autocenter, Berlin.
Dark Waters, Galerie Chantal Crousel,
Paris.
Summer Exhibition 2014, Royal
Academy of Arts, London.
KAOS – Visions of KAOS, The Flying
Dutchman and Mori + Stein Gallery,
London.
Fundamentals, La Biennale di Venezia –
14th International Architecture
Exhibition, Venice.
*8. Berlin Biennale für zeitgenössische
Kunst*, Berlin.
I'm Isa Genzken, The Only Female Fool,
Kunsthalle Wien, Vienna.
1984–1999. La Décennie, Centre
Pompidou, Metz, France.
Abandon the Parents, Statens Museum
for Kunst, Copenhagen.
Intimität – Intimacy, Galerie der Stadt
Remscheid, Remscheid, Germany.
The Disappearence of the Fireflies
(collection display), The Collection
Lambert at Prison Sainte-Anne,
Avignon, France.
*Somewhat Abstract – Selections
from the Arts Council Collection*,
Nottingham Contemporary,
Nottingham, UK.
Brush Fires in the Social Landscape,
Aperture Foundation David
Wojnarowicz, London.
Booster – Kunst Sound Maschine,
MARTa Herford, Herford, Germany.
Love Aids Riot Sex 2, nGbK – neue
Gesellschaft für bildende Kunst, Berlin.
The Body Issue, Hannah Hoffman
Gallery, Los Angeles, CA.
2013
*Macho Man. Tell It To My Heart,
Collected by Julie Ault*, Museum für
Gegenwartskunst, Basel; travelled to
Culturgest, Lisbon and Artists Space,
New York.

Ausweitung der Kampfzone. Die Sammlung 1968–2000, Neue Nationalgalerie, Berlin.
Weltreise. Kunst aus Deutschland unterwegs. Werke aus dem Kunstbestand des ifa 1949 – heute, ZKM – Zentrum für Kunst und Medientechnologie Karlsruhe, Germany; travelled to Moscow Museum of Modern Art, Moscow (2014).
Foto Europa. 1840 to Present, Detroit Institute of Arts, Detroit, MI.
Heimat – no place like home – Fotografien aus der DZ BANK-Kunstsammlung, Kunsthalle HGN, Duderstadt, Germany.
Aquatopia. The Imaginary of the Ocean Deep, Nottingham Contemporary, Nottingham, UK; travelled to Tate St Ives, Saint Ives, UK.
Xerography, First Site, London.
Der Schein. Glanz, Glamour, Illusion, Kestnergesellschaft, Hanover, Germany.
Dear Portrait, MOSTYN, Llandudno, Wales.
When Now is Minimal. Die unbekannte Seite der Sammlung Goetz, Neues Museum Nürnberg, Nuremberg, Germany; travelled to Museion, Bolzano, Italy.
Think First, Shoot Later: Photography from the MCA Collection, Museum of Contemporary Art, Chicago, IL (collection display).
LAT. 41° 7' N., LONG. 72° 19' W, Martos Gallery, New York.
Vue d'en Haut, Centre Pompidou, Metz, France.
Sin motivo aparente, CA2M Centro de arte Dos de Mayo, Madrid.
Kunst nach 1945, Städtische Galerie im Lenbachhaus und Kunstbau München, Munich (collection display).
Tate Britain, London (collection display).
Abstrakt, Sammlung Haubrok, Berlin.
Paint it Black, FRAC Île-de-France, Paris.
NYC 1993: Experimental Jet Set, Trash and No Star, New Museum, New York.
La Sentinelle, CAPC Musée d'art contemporain de Bordeaux, Bordeaux, France.

Looking at the View, Tate Britain, Millbank Project, London (collection display).
Cranford Collection – Out of the House, Fundación Banco Santander, Madrid.
The Gallery of Modern Art, Glasgow (collection display).

2012

Slg. Wilhelm Otto Nachf. Werkräume von Kai Althoff bis Thomas Zipp, Leopold-Hoesch-Museum, Duren, Germany.
A Bigger Splash: Painting After Performance, Tate Modern, London.
Color, Upon Paper Space, Berlin.
Private / Corporate VII, Daimler Contemporary, Berlin.
Durchsucht, fixiert, geordnet – Zeitgenössische Fotografie in der Sammlung Rheingold, Museum für Gegenwartskunst, Siegen, Germany.
Juwelen im Rheingold, Sammlung Rheingold, Kunsthalle Düsseldorf, Düsseldorf, Germany.
Inaugural Exhibition in new Hollywood space, Regen Projects, Los Angeles, CA.
Regarding Warhol: Sixty Artists, Fifty Years, The Metropolitan Museum of Art, New York; travelled to The Andy Warhol Museum, Pittsburgh, PA (2013).
Bernadette Corporation – 2000 Wasted Years, Artists Space, New York.
Verlangsamte Performance, Van Horn, Düsseldorf, Germany.
Intérieur jour, Galerie Chantal Crousel, Paris.
The Feverish Library (organized in cooperation with Matthew Higgs), Petzel Gallery, New York; travelled to Capitain / Petzel, Berlin (2013).
Figure and Form in Contemporary Photography, LACMA Los Angeles County Museum of Art, Los Angeles, CA.
Wir sind die anderen, DZ Bank Kunstsammlung, Frankfurt am Main.
Treffpunkt: Berlin, ARKEN Museum for Moderne Kunst, Skovvej, Denmark.
Abstraction and Motion, Centro Andaluz de Arte Contemporáneo, Seville, Spain.
Paper, Musée d'art moderne et d'art

contemporain, Nice, France.
Zauberspiegel: Die Sammlung nach 1945, Kunsthalle Bremen, Bremen, Germany.
Superbody, Galerie Chantal Crousel, Paris.
Reflecting Fashion – Kunst und Mode seit der Moderne, mumok - Museum moderner Kunst Stiftung Ludwig Wien, Vienna.
Duplicate it! (event June 14), Stedelijk Museum, Amsterdam.
Malerei in Fotografie. Strategien der Aneignung, Städel Museum, Frankfurt am Main.
Boy: A Contemporary Portrait, Leo Xu Projects, Shanghai, China.
Fotografie Total. Werke aus der Sammlung, MMK Museum für Moderne Kunst, Frankfurt am Main.
Pink Caviar, Louisiana Museum of Modern Art, Humlebæk, Denmark.
Powerflower – Blutenzauber in der zeitgenössischen Kunst, Galerie ABTART, Stuttgart, Germany.
Dark Sky, Adam Art Gallery, Wellington, New Zealand.
Klang & Stille, Sammlung Goetz im Haus der Kunst, Munich.
Contemporary Collection Display: The Space Between, Tate Britain, London.
The Sports Show, Minneapolis Institute of Arts, Minneapolis, MN.
30 Kunstler / 30 Räume, Institut für moderne Kunst Nürnberg, Kunsthalle Nürnberg, Neues Museum in Nürnberg and Kunstverein Nürnberg, Nuremberg, Germany.
German Photography 1960–2012: A Survey, Ben Brown Fine Arts, Hong Kong.
Relocated, Galerie Neu & MD 72, Berlin.
Measuring the Universe: from the transit of Venus to the edge of the cosmos, Royal Observatory Greenwich, London.
Gegenwartskunst (1945–heute) im Städel Museum, Städel Museum, Frankfurt am Main.
Circus Wols – Eine Hommage, Stiftung Neues Museum Weserburg, Bremen, Germany.
Inside a book a house of gold. Artists' editions with parkett, UCCA Ullens

Center for Contemporary Art, Beijing.
Print / Out (organized by Christophe Cherix, Ellen Gallagher and Sarah Suzuki), MoMA Museum of Modern Art, New York.
Living with Video, The Pavilion Downtown, Dubai, UAE.
Lost & Found: Anonymous Photography in Reflection, Ambach & Rice, Los Angeles, CA.
Boros Collection #2, Sammlung Boros, Berlin (collection display).
Stedelijk Room, Stedelijk Museum, Amsterdam (collection display).
Freischwimmer: The World of Contemporary Photography, The National Museum of Art, Osaka, Japan.

2011

Danser sa vie, Musée national d'art moderne, Centre Pompidou, Paris.
Cultured nature, Stedelijk Museum, Amsterdam.
Photography Calling! Fotografie und Gegenwart, Sprengel Museum, Hanover, Germany.
25 Jahre! Samlung Henri Nannen, Kunsthalle Emden, Emden, Germany.
Fame, DZ Bank Kunstsammlung, Frankfurt am Main.
Meer Licht (More Light), Museum de Fundatie, Zwolle, The Netherlands.
Lichtempfindlich – Zeitgenössische Fotografie aus der Sammlung Schaufler, SCHAUWERK Sindelfingen, Sindelfingen, Germany.
Precarious Worlds. Contemporary Art from Germany, Mildred Lane Kemper Art Museum, St. Louis, MO.
Quodlibet III – Alphabets and Instruments, Galerie Daniel Buchholz, Berlin.
Objectiv, Sammlung Haubrok – Haubrokshows, Berlin.
Jean Genet. Act 1 & Act 2, Nottingham Contemporary, Nottingham, UK.
Loud Flash: British Punk on Paper, Honor Fraser Gallery, Los Angeles, CA.
It's Great To Be In New Jersey, Honor Fraser Gallery, Los Angeles, CA.
Distant Star – an exhibition organized around the writings of Roberto Bolaño, Regen Projects, Los Angeles, CA; traveling to Kurimanzotto, Mexico City.

Syntax: Text and Symbols for a New Generation, Tampa Museum of Art, Tampa, FL.
Number Five: Cities of Gold and Mirrors, Julia Stoschek Foundation, Düsseldorf, Germany.
Falling Up: The Gravity of Art, The Courtauld Gallery, London.
MMK 1991–2011: 20 Jahre Gegenwart, MMK Museum für Moderne Kunst, Frankfurt am Main.
Absentee Landlord, Walker Art Center, Minneapolis, MN.
Streetlife and Homestories, Museum Villa Stuck / Sammlung Goetz, Munich.
Gallery Selection – Slominski, Tillmans, Visch, Hayakawa, Hirokawa, Wako Works of Art, Tokyo.
Die Deutsche Show, Divus Prager Kabarett, Prague.
Sin realidad no hay utopia, Centro Andaluz de Arte Contemporáneo, Seville, Spain.
Collections contemporaines du Centre Pompidou des années 1960 à nos jours, Musée national d'art moderne, Centre Pompidou, Paris (collection display).
The Art of Pop Video, Museum für Angewandte Kunst, Cologne, Germany.
The First Last Decade, Ellipse Foundation Contemporary Art Collection, Cascais, Portugal.
Glimmer, Jumex Collection, Mexico City.
After the Gold Rush: Contemporary Photography from the Collection (organized by Douglas Eklund), The Metropolitan Museum of Art, New York.
Von Engeln und Bengeln – 400 Jahre Kinder im Portrait, Kunsthalle Krems, Krems, Austria.
Black Swan: The Exhibition, Regen Projects, Los Angeles, CA.
Portraits, Gerhardsen Gerner, Berlin.
The Gong Show, Galerie Micky Schubert, Berlin.
New Space, New Works, Wako Works of Art, Tokyo.
Nature morte vivante, Galerie Chantal Crousel, Paris.
Dreamscapes, Pulitzer Foundation for the Arts, St. Louis, MO.

Playground and Field of Disaster, Pavillon des Images, Montpellier, France.
Anti-Photography, Focal Point and The Beecroft Art Gallery, Southend-on-Sea, UK.
Eating Art, Fundació "la Caixa" Catalunya, Barcelona.
Past Present Future #2, Contemporary Art Centre Winzavod, Moscow.

2010
20 Jahre Texte zur Kunst: Mit Deiner Kunst, Editionen 1990–2010, Sammlung Haubrok, Berlin.
Pleated Blinds, Petach Tivka Museum of Art, Petach Tivka, Israel.
BigMinis: Fetishes of Crisis, CAPC Musée d'art contemporain de Bordeaux, Bordeaux, France.
The British Art Show 7. The Days of the Comet, Hayward Gallery, London; travelled to Nottingham, Glasgow and Plymouth, UK.
Lust und Laster, Kunstmuseum Bern and Zentrum Paul Klee, Bern, Switzerland.
Wolfgang Tillmans, Isa Genzken, abc – art berlin contemporary, Berlin.
The Last Newspaper, New Museum, New York.
The Private Museum, Galleria d'Arte Moderna, Bergamo, Italy.
Not in Fashion, MMK Museum für Moderne Kunst, Frankfurt am Main.
Portraits de collectionneurs. Collection Jocelyne & Fabrice Petignat, Muro, Geneva.
Male, Maureen Paley, London.
Internationale Kunst aus der Sammlung Reininghaus, Köln, Sammlung Falckenberg, Deichtorhallen Hamburg, Hamburg, Germany.
Held up by Columns, Renwick Gallery, New York.
I am a cliché, Les Rencontres d'Arles 2010, The International photography Festival, Arles, France.
Just a Matter of Time, Galerie Iris Kadel, Karlsruhe, Germany.
Zu Tisch. Meisterwerke aus der Sammlung Ludwig von der Antike bis Picasso, von Durer bis Demand, Ludwiggalerie Schloss Oberhausen, Oberhausen, Germany.
The Ground Around: idylls, earthworks

& thunderbolts, Vilma Gold, London.
At Home/Not At Home: Works from the Collection of Martin and Rebecca Eisenberg, Center for Curatorial Studies at Bard College, Annandale-on-Hudson, NY.
Nothing is in the place, Photomonth, Krakow, Poland.
Weltsichten. Landschaft in der Kunst vom 17. bis zum 21. Jahrhundert, Kunstsammlungen der Ruhr-Universität Bochum; travelled to Kunsthalle zu Kiel (2011), Museum Wiesbaden (2011), Kunstsammlungen Chemnitz (2011/12), Kunstmuseum Dieselkraftwerk Cottbus (2012), Germany, Bonnefantenmuseum Maastricht, The Netherlands (2014, *Weltsichten – The landscape represented in six centuries of art*).
Julia Stoschek Collection – I want to see you, Deichtorhallen Hamburg, Hamburg, Germany.
John Baldessari, Thorsten Brinkmann, Christopher Brown, Carsten Holler..., Richard Levy Gallery, Albuquerque, NM.
In Praise of Simplicity, Fondazione Stelline, Milan.
Territories of Desire, MUAC Museo Universitario Arte Contemporáneo, Mexico City.
MEAN STREETS – Malas Calles, IVAM Instituto Valenciano de Arte Moderno, Valencia, Spain.
The Future Demands Your Participation: Contemporary Art from the British Council Collection, Minsheng Art Museum, Shanghai, China.
Brave New World, Musée d'Art Moderne Grand-Duc Jean, Luxembourg.
PressArt. Die Sammlung Annette und Peter Nobel, Kunstmuseum St. Gallen, Switzerland and Museum der Moderne Salzburg, Austria.
I Put a Frame on You, TÄT, Berlin.
Through the Window, Martha Parrish & James Reinish, New York.
Ordinary Madness, Carnegie Museum of Art, Pittsburgh, PA.

2009
Fax, Drawing Center, New York; travelled to Contemporary Museum,

Baltimore; Torrance Art Museum, Torrance, CA; Burnaby Art Gallery, Burnaby, Canada; Dowd Gallery, State University of New York, College at Cortland, Cortland, NY; Museo de Arte Carrillo Gil, Mexico City; Para/Site Art Space, Hong Kong.
Susser Vogel Jugend, Pinakothek der Moderne, Munich.
The reach of realism, MoCA Knight Exhibition Series, Museum of Contemporary Art, Miami, FL.
Twentysix Gasoline Stations ed altri libri d'artista – Una Collezione, Museo Regionale di Messina, Messina, Italy.
Processed: Considering Recent Photographic Practices, The Bertha And Karl Leubsdorf Art Gallery, Hunter College, New York.
Carte Blanche IX: Vor heimischer Kulisse, Galerie für Zeitgenössische Kunst, Leipzig, Germany.
Against Exclusion, The Third Moscow Biennale of Contemporary Art, Moscow.
Pete and Repeat – Works from the Zabludowicz Collection, Zabludowicz Art Projects, London.
Berlin 89 / 09 – Kunst zwischen Spurensuche und Utopie, Berlinische Galerie, Berlin.
I Love Malmö, KUMU Art Museum, Tallinn, Estonia.
Die Kunst ist super!, Hamburger Bahnhof – Museum für Gegenwart, Berlin.
Tel Aviv Time, Tel Aviv Museum, Tel Aviv.
In Bewegung / in Motion – Leichtathletik und Fotografie 1984–2009, Akademie der Kunste am Pariser Platz, Berlin.
Sehnsucht nach dem Abbild – Das Portrait im Wandel der Zeit, Kunsthalle Krems, Krems, Austria.
Sammlung Reloaded, Kunstmuseum Bonn, Bonn, Germany.
Das Porträt. Fotografie als Buhne, Kunsthalle Wien, Vienna.
Fare Mondi – Making Worlds, 53rd Venice Biennale, Venice.
Quodlibet II, Galerie Daniel Buchholz, Cologne, Germany.
En todas as partes – Everywhere. Políticas de la diversidad sexual en el

arte, CGAC Centro Galego de Arte Contemporánea, Santiago de Compostela, Spain.
60 Jahre – 60 Werke. Kunst aus der Bundesrepublik Deutschland 1949–2009, Martin-Gropius-Bau, Berlin.
Surface Tension: Contemporary Photographs from the Collection, The Metropolitan Museum of Art, New York.
Lyst – Overgaden, Institut for Samtidskunst, Copenhagen.
The Photographic Object, The Photographers' Gallery, London.
Extended – Sammlung Landesbank Baden-Wurttemberg, ZKM / Museum für Neue Kunst, Karlsruhe, Germany.
Phot(o)bjects, Presentation House Gallery, Vancouver, Canada.
Holbein bis Tillmans. Prominente Gäste aus dem Kunstmuseum Basel, Schaulager, Basel, Switzerland.
Mi Vida – From Heaven to Hell. Life Experiences in Art From MUSAC Collection, Műcsarnok, Budapest.
Incidental Affairs, Suntory Museum, Osaka, Japan.
Spazio Libro d'Artista, Palazzo Manganelli, Catania, Italy.
Bijoux de famille, Galerie Chantal Crousel, Paris.
N'importe quoi, Musée d'art contemporain de Lyon, Lyon, France.
From Here To There, The Arts Institute at Bournemouth, Bournemouth, UK.
A Twilight Art, Harris Lieberman, New York.
Photography in the Abstract, Lora Reynolds Gallery, Austin, TX.
2008
Pictures, Wako Works of Art, Tokyo.
8 1/2 x 11 / A4, James Fuentes LLC, New York.
50 moons of Saturn: T2 Torino Triennale, T–Torino Triennale, Turin, Italy.
Other People: Portraits from Grunwald and Hammer Collections, Hammer Museum, Los Angeles, CA.
When it's a Photograph, Otis College of Art and Design, Los Angeles, CA.
Noli Me Legere, Michael Lett Gallery, Auckland, New Zealand.
Peter Saville – Accessories to an artwork, Paul Stopler, London.
The Art of the Real, Vanmoerkerke Collection, Oostende, Belgium.
Untitled (Vicarious), Gagosian Gallery, New York.
Darkside. Photographic Desire and Sexuality Photographed, Fotomuseum Winterthur, Winterthur, Switzerland.
Summer Show, Wako Works of Art, Tokyo.
History Keeps Me Awake at Night: A Genealogy of David Wojnarowicz, PPOW Gallery, New York.
3 a.m. Eternal, Alexandre Pollazzon Ltd, London.
REAL – Fotografien aus der Sammlung der DZ BANK, Städel Museum, Frankfurt am Main.
Gewoon Anders! (Just Different!), Cobra Museum, Amsterdam.
Spiegel geheimer Wunsche, Hamburger Kunsthalle, Hamburg; travelled to Städtische Galerie Bietigheim-Bissingen, Germany.
Street & Studio. An Urban History of Photography, Tate Modern, London; travelled to Museum Folkwang, Essen, Germany.
Vertrautes Terrain, ZKM – Zentrum für Kunst und Medientechnologie, Karlsruhe, Germany.
Life on Mars: Carnegie International 2008, Carnegie Museum of Art, Pittsburgh, PA.
The Implications of Image – Las Implicaciones de la Imagen, MUAC Museo Universitario Arte Contemporáneo, Mexico City.
Every Body Counts, Vestfossen Kunstlaboratorium, Vestfossen, Norway.
History in the Making: A Retrospective of the Turner Prize, Mori Art Museum, Tokyo.
Courtesy Hans Kemna – Een keuze uit de fotografiecollectie van Hans Kemna, Museum de Hallen, Haarlem, The Netherlands.
Hotel Marienbad 002: Sammlung Rausch, Kunst-Werke Berlin – KW Institute for Contemporary Art, Berlin.
Konstellationen III – Neue Ankäufe und Schenkungen im Kontext der Sammlung, Städel Museum, Frankfurt am Main.
The Real World, Ludlow 38, New York.
Depreciation and Devastation, Gavin Brown's Enterprise, New York.
Der große Wurf. Faltungen in der Gegenwartskunst, Kaiser Wilhelm Museum, Museum Haus Lange, Krefeld, Germany.
The Possible Document, Herald St, London.
Yes, No & Other Options, Art Sheffield 08, Sheffield, UK.
Schöner wohnen, Neugerriemschneider, Berlin.
abstract / abstract, Museum Moderner Kunst Kärnten, Klagenfurt, Austria.
15 Years / Part III, Wako Works of Art, Tokyo, with Christopher Williams.
Body Work, Le Case d'Arte, Milan.
2007
Betrifft: Israel, Judisches Museum, Berlin.
Pop am Rhein, Stadtmuseum Köln, Cologne, Germany.
Getroffen. Otto Dix und die Kunst des Portraits, Kunstmuseum Stuttgart, Stuttgart, Germany.
Rebecca Camhi Gallery, Athens, Greece.
MODE:BILDER – Fotografien aus der Sammlung F. C. Gundlac, NRW-Forum Kultur und Wirtschaft, Düsseldorf, Germany.
PLAYBACK, Musée d'art moderne de la ville de Paris, Paris.
Stardust or the Last Frontier, Musée d'art contemporain du Val-de-Marne, France.
Weltempfänger – 10 Jahre Galerie der Gegenwart, Kunsthalle Hamburg, Hamburg, Germany.
The Turner Prize: A Retrospective. 1984–2006, Tate Britain, London.
Depth of Field: Modern Photography at the Metropolitan, The Metropolitan Museum of Art, New York.
Existencias, MUSAC Museo de Arte Contemporáneo de Castilla y León, León, Spain (collection display).
Seeing Things, Dorsky Gallery, Long Island City, NY.
Generational Issue, CGAC Centro Galego de Arte Contemporánea, Santiago de Compostela, Spain.
Franz West: Soufflé, Kunstraum Innsbruck, Innsbruck, Austria.
Viewfinder, Henry Art Gallery, University of Washington, Seattle, WA.
At Home, Yvon Lambert, New York.
Edit! Photography and Film in the Ellipse Collection, CAV Centro de Artes Visuais, Coimbra, Portugal.
The Droste Effect, Esther Schipper, Berlin.
PERSPEKTIVE 07 – Neuerwerbungen und Wunsche der Sammlung für Gegenwartskunst im Lenbachhaus, Städtische Galerie im Lenbachhaus und Kunstbau, Munich.
Numerica, Palazzo delle Papesse, Centro arte contemporanea, Siena, Italy.
The Naked Portrait, Scottish National Portrait Gallery, Edinburgh; travelled to Compton Verney, Warwickshire, UK.
Garten Eden – Der Garten in der Kunst seit 1900, Kunsthalle Emden, Emden, Germany.
What Does the Jellyfish Want, Museum Ludwig, Cologne, Germany.
No Such Thing as Society. Photography in Britain 1967–87 from the Arts Council Collection and the British Council, Hayward Touring Exhibitions, London.
Visit(e). Selection from the contemporary art collection of the Federal Republic of Germany – Werke aus der Sammlung zeitgenössischer Kunst der Bundesrepublik Deutschland, Palais des Beaux-Arts, Brussels; travelled to Kunst- und Ausstellungshalle der Bundesrepublik Deutschland, Bonn, Germany (2008).
Dateline Israel: New Photography and Video Art, The Jewish Museum, New York.
Hava Boşluğu – Air Pocket, galerist, Istanbul, Turkey.
Unter Sternen, Museum Franz Gertsch, Burgdorf, Switzerland.
Reality Bites: Making Avant-Garde Art in Post-Wall Germany, Mildred Lane Kemper Art Museum, St. Louis, MO; travelled to Opelvillen, Russelsheim, Germany.
Into Me / Out of Me, MACRO Museo d'Arte Contemporanea di Roma, Rome.
2006
Personal Affairs, Museum Morsbroich, Städtisches Museum Leverkusen Schloss Morsbroich, Leverkusen, Germany.

Peace Camp, The Brick Lane Gallery, London.
The Studio, Dublin City Gallery The Hugh Lane, Dublin.
From Fair to Fine, Stephen Daiter Gallery, Chicago, IL.
The Gold Standard, MoMA PS1, New York.
Modernity and Self, Mildred Land Kemper Art Museum, St. Louis, MO.
In the Face of History: European Photographers in the 20th Century, Barbican Art Gallery, London.
Idylle, Sammlung Falckenberg, Harburg, Germany; travelled to Domus Artium 2002, Salamanca, Spain and Národní galerie, Prague.
The Secret Public: The last days of the British underground 1978–1988, Kunstverein München, Munich; travelled to Institute of Contemporary Arts, London (2007).
The Wonderful Fund Collection, Pallant House Gallery, Chichester, UK.
Out of Place, New Art Gallery Walsall, Walsall, UK.
The Heartbeat of Fashion, Deichtorhallen Hamburg, Hamburg, Germany.
Peintres de la vie moderne, Musée national d'art moderne, Centre Pompidou, Paris.
FASTER! BIGGER! BETTER! – Signetwerke der Sammlungen, ZKM / Museum für Neue Kunst, Karlsruhe, Germany.
As if by Magic, The Bethlehem Peace Centre, Bethlehem, Palestine.
Das Achte Feld – Geschlechter, Leben und Begehren in der bildenden Kunst seit 1960, Museum Ludwig, Cologne, Germany.
Surprise Surprise, Institute of Contemporary Arts, London.
Landscapes, Wako Works of Art, Tokyo.
Toutes Composition Florales, Counter Gallery, London.
The Starry Messenger: Visions of the Universe, Compton Verney, Warwickshire, UK.
Thank You For the Music (London Beat), Sprüth Magers Lee, London.
It's Not a Photo, Chelsea Art Museum, New York.
Galerie Daniel Buchholz at Metro Pictures, Metro Pictures Gallery, New York.
Sweet Ecstasy, Galerie Nicola von Senger, Zurich.
Good Vibrations – Visual Arts and Rock Music, Palazzo delle Papesse, Centro arte contemporanea, Siena, Italy.
Abstract Art Now 1 – Floating Forms, Wilhelm Hack-Museum, Ludwigshafen, Germany.
An Ongoing Low-Grade Mystery, Paula Cooper Gallery, New York.
Y ahora sin ti…, Galería Juana de Aizpuru, Madrid.
Arquivar Tormentas, CGAC Centro Galego de Arte Contemporánea, Santiago de Compostela, Spain.
The Sublime is Now!, Museum Franz Gertsch, Burgdorf, Switzerland.
Mas de lo que los ojos pueden ver, MARCO Monterrey, Mexico.
Click Doubleclick, Haus der Kunst, Munich; travelled to Bozar Expo, Brussels.
Auto-Nom-Mobile, Kunstverein and KulturBahnhof Kassel, Kassel, Germany.
Portrait und Menschenbild, SK Stiftung Kultur, Cologne, Germany.
Frankfurter Positionen – Gut ist, was gefällt, Klasse Wolfgang Tillmans, MMK Museum für Moderne Kunst, Frankfurt am Main.
Gut ist was gefällt – Versuche uber die zeitgenössische Urteilskraft, How Queer Everything is Today, Queer Festival, Copenhagen, with Hans-Peter Feldmann, Lucien Samaha and class.
Deckchair Dreams, London's Royal Parks, London.

2005
Thank You for the Music, Sprüth Magers, Munich.
Superstars. Das Prinzip Prominenz. Von Warhol bis Madonna, Kunsthalle Wien and Kunstforum Wien, Vienna.
Zwischen Wirklichkeit und Bild: German Contemporary Photography – Positionen deutscher Fotografie der Gegenwart, National Museum of Modern Art, Tokyo; travelled to National Museum of Modern Art, Kyoto and Marugame Genichiro-Inokuma Museum of Contemporary Art, Kagawa, Japan (2006).
Goethe abwärts – deutsche Jungs etc.
The Falckenberg Collection, Meilahti Art Museum, Helsinki; travelled to Mönchehaus-Museum, Goslar, Germany (2006).
46th Oktobarski Salon, Belgrade, Serbia.
Projekt Migration – Roadmap to Europa, Kölnischer Kunstverein, Cologne, Germany.
The Wonderful Fund Collection, Le Musée de Marrakech, Marrakech, Morocco.
Welt-Bilder, Helmhaus Zürich, Zurich.
BYO. Bring Your Own, MAN Museo d'arte della Provincia di Nuoro, Nuoro, Italy.
Shadowplay – A Homage to H. C. Andersen, Kunsthallen Brandts Klaedefabrik, Odense, Denmark; travelled to Kunsthalle zu Kiel and Landesgalerie Linz, Austria.
Projekt Migration, Kölnischer Kunstverein, Cologne, Germany.
Nischen – von der Architketur und Landschaft bis zur Szene, Galerie der Stadt Tuttlingen, Tuttlingen, Germany.
Coolhunters, ZKM – Zentrum für Kunst und Medientechnologie, Karlsruhe, Germany; travelled to Kunstlerhaus Wien, Vienna and Műcsarnok, Budapest (2006).
Extreme Abstraction, Albright-Knox Gallery, Buffalo, NY.
Sammlung 2005, Kunstsammlung Nordrhein-Westfalen, K21 Ständehaus, Düsseldorf, Germany (collection display).
What I did on my Summer Vacation, Clampart, New York.
Motor Blues – Fotografien aus der Schenkung der BMW Group, Museum der Bildenden Kunste Leipzig, Germany.
Visions of the Body 2005, Seoul Museum of Art, Seoul, South Korea.
Always a Little Further, 51st Venice Biennale, Venice.
Il Teatro dell'Arte – The Theatre of Art. Masterpieces from the collection of the Ludwig Museum, Cologne, Villa Manin, Passariano, Italy.
Bidibidobidiboo, Fondazione Sandretto Re Rebaudengo, Turin.
Blumenstuck, Museum Morsbroich, Städtisches Museum Leverkusen Schloss Morsbroich, Leverkusen, Germany.
Covering the Real. Kunst- und Pressebild von Warhol bis Tillmans, Kunstmuseum Basel, Basel, Switzerland.
25 Jahre Sammlung Deutsche Bank, Deutsche Guggenheim, Berlin (collection display).
Das verlorene Paradies – Die landschaft in der zeitgenössischen Photographie, Kunst- und Kulturstiftung Opelvillen, Russelsheim, Germany.
Miradas y conceptos en la Colección Helga de Alvear, MEIAC Museo Extremeño e Iberoamericano de Arte Contemporáneo, Badajoz, Spain.
Europe in Art, National Museum of Contemporary Art, Bucharest.
In Bloom, Mark Moore Gallery, Los Angeles, CA.
Atlantic & Bukarest, Kunstmuseum Basel, Basel, Switzerland.
Telefónica's Photography Collection, MARCO Museo de Arte Contemporánea de Vigo, Vigo, Spain.
Growing Up Absurd, Herbert Read Gallery, Canterbury, UK.

2004
Jetzt und zehn Jahre davor, Kunst-Werke Berlin – KW Institute for Contemporary Art, Berlin.
15 Jahre Deichtorhallen, Deichtorhallen Hamburg, Hamburg, Germany.
Colección Taschen, Museo Nacional Centro de Arte Reina Sofía, Madrid.
Encounters in the 21st Century, 21st Century Museum of Contemporary Art, Kanazawa, Japan.
Friedrich Christian Flick Collection, Hamburger Bahnhof – Museum für Gegenwart, Berlin.
The Flower as Image, Louisiana Museum of Modern Art, Humlebæk, Denmark; travelled to Fondation Beyeler, Riehen, Switzerland.
Im Rausch der Dinge, Fotomuseum Winterthur, Winterthur, Switzerland.
Speaking with Hands – Photographs from the Buhl Collection, Guggenheim Museum, New York; travelled to Guggenheim Bilbao, Spain; Museum Folkwang, Essen and Russian Museum,

St. Petersburg (all 2006).
Relating to Photography, Fotografie Forum International, Frankfurt am Main.
Von Körpern und anderen Dingen… Fotografie des 20. Jahrhunderts, Kunstmuseum Bochum, Bochum, Germany.
Likeness: Portraits of artists by other artists, Wattis Institute for Contemporary Arts, San Francisco, CA.
Atmosphere, Museum of Contemporary Art, Chicago, IL.
Werke aus der Sammlung Boros, ZKM / Museum für Neue Kunst, Karlsruhe, Germany.
Monument to Now, The Dakis Joannou Collection, Athens, Greece.
Stephan Balkenhol – Wolfgang Tillmans, Galerie Rudiger Schöttle, Munich.
Il Nudo, Galleria d'Arte Moderna, Bologna, Italy.
Landscape 2, Tower Art Gallery, Eastbourne, UK.
Rose C'est la Vie, Tel Aviv Museum of Art, Tel Aviv.
Enthullt, Städtische Museen Heilbronn, Heilbronn, Germany.

2003
Auto-nom, NRW-Forum Kultur und Wirtschaft, Düsseldorf, Germany.
A Clear Vision – Photographische Werke aus der Sammlung F. C. Gundlach, Deichtorhallen Hamburg, Hamburg, Germany.
Looking In – Looking Out, Kunstmuseum Basel, Basel, Switzerland.
20th Anniversary Show, Sprüth Magers, Cologne, Germany.
actionbutton, Hamburger Bahnhof – Museum für Gegenwart, Berlin.
Berlin – Moskau / Moskau – Berlin. 1950–2000, Martin-Gropius-Bau, Berlin.
Warum!, Martin-Gropius-Bau, Berlin.
Öffentlich / privat, Gesellschaft für zeitgenössische Kunst, Leipzig, Germany.
Attack – Kunst und Krieg im Zeitalter der Medien, Kunsthalle Wien, Vienna.
Heiliger Sebastian, Kunsthalle Wien, Vienna.
M_ARS – Kunst und Krieg, Neue Galerie Graz, Graz, Austria.
Outlook, Cultural Olympiade, Athens, Greece.

Mixtapes, California College of Arts and Crafts, San Francisco, CA.
Montagna: arte, scienza, mito da Durer a Warhol, Museo di arte moderna e contemporanea di Trento e Rovereto, Rovereto, Italy.
Fast Forward, Sammlung Goetz, ZKM – Zentrum für Kunst und Medientechnologie, Karlsruhe, Germany.
After the Observatory, Paula Cooper Gallery, New York.
Deutsche Fotografie im 20. Jahrhundert, Deutsches Historisches Museum, Berlin.
Architektur der Obdachlosigkeit. Biss zu Gast in der Pinakothek der Moderne, Pinakothek der Moderne, Munich; travelled to Museum der Arbeit, Hamburg and Berlinische Galerie, Berlin (all 2005).
The Society for Contemporary Art Selection, The Art Institute, Chicago, IL.
Abstraction in Photography, Von Lintel Gallery, New York.
Sex, Karyn Lovegrove Gallery, Los Angeles, CA.
Anniversary Exhibition, Gavin Brown's Enterprise, New York.
Somewhere Better Than This Place: Alternative Social Experience in the Spaces of Contemporary Art, Contemporary Arts Center, Cincinnati, OH.
Painting Pictures, Kunstmuseum Wolfsburg, Wolfsburg, Germany.

2002
Sensationen des Alltags, Kunstmuseum Wolfsburg, Wolfsburg, Germany.
Moving Pictures, Solomon R. Guggenheim Museum, New York; travelled to Guggenheim Bilbao, Spain (2003).
Remix: Contemporary Art & Pop, Tate Liverpool, Liverpool, UK.
Hossa – Arte Alemàn del 2000, CCA Andratx, Mallorca.

2001
Shopping, Schirn Kunsthalle, Frankfurt am Main; travelled to Tate Liverpool, Liverpool, UK.
Transform the World 2002, Wako Works of Art, Tokyo.
Club Club Club, Le Confort Moderne, Poitiers, France.

Record Collection, VTO gallery, London; travelled to The International 3, Manchester, UK and Forde Espace d'Art Contemporain, Geneva.
Why bother? – The Burger King Exhibition, 90 Whitechapel High Street, London.
Museum unserer Wunsche, Museum Ludwig, Cologne, Germany.
Un mundo feliz / Brave new world, Galería OMR, Mexico City.
Sex – Vom Wissen und Wunschen, Hygienemuseum Dresden, Desden, Germany.
La natura della natura morta, Galleria d'Arte Moderna, Bologna, Italy.
Uniforms: Order and Disorder, Pitti Immagine, Florence; travelled to MoMA PS1, New York.
Century City: Art and Culture in the Modern Metropolis, Tate Modern, London.
Contemporary Utopia, Latvian Centre for Contemporary Art, Riga, Latvia.
Zero Gravity, Kunstverein Düsseldorf, Düsseldorf, Germany.
Neue Welt, Frankfurter Kunstverein, Frankfurt am Main.
Open City: Street Photographs since 1950, Museum of Modern Art, Oxford, UK; travelled to Hirshhorn Museum and Sculpture Garden, Washington, DC.

2000
Landscape (organized by The British Council); travelled to Weimar, Moscow, St. Petersburg, Rome, Madrid, Paris, Sofia, Rio de Janeiro, São Paulo and Curitiba, Brazil, Brussels and Ljubljana, Slovenia.
Quotidiana. The Continuity of the Everyday in 20th Century Art, Castello di Rivoli Museo d'Arte Contemporanea, Rivoli, Turin, Italy.
Photography Now, Contemporary Arts Center, New Orleans, LO.
Lost, Ikon Gallery, Birmingham, UK.
Some Parts of this World, Helsinki Photography Festival, Helsinki.
Look at Me: Fashion and Photography in Britain 1960 to the present, The British Council touring exhibition, Kunsthal, Rotterdam; travelled to Fondazione Nicola Trussardi, Milan; The Centre for Contemporary Arts, Ujazdowski Castle, Warsaw;

Maly Manezh, Moscow; State Museum of the History of St. Petersburg, St. Petersburg; Tallinna Kunstihoone Fond, Tallin; Oksnehallen, Copenhagen; Centro de Documentación y Museo Textil, Terrasa, Spain; Recinto Ciudadela, Pamplona; Palacio de Abrantes, Salamanca; House of Art, Bratislava.
Oldest Possible Memory – Collection Hauser and Wirth, Lokremise St. Gallen, St. Gallen, Switzerland.
British Art Show 5 (organized by the Hayward Gallery, London); travelled to Edinburgh, Southampton, Cardiff and Birmingham, UK.
Présumés innocents, CAPC Musée d'art contemporain de Bordeaux, Bordeaux, France.
Deep Distance. Die Entfernung der Fotografie, Kunsthalle Basel, Basel, Switzerland.
90 60 90, Museo Jacobo Borges, Caracas, Venezuela.
Dire AIDS. Art in the Age of Aids, Promotrice delle Belle Arti, Turin, Italy.
The Sea & the Sky, The Royal Hibernian Academy, Philadelphia, PA.
Complicity, Australian Centre for Photography, Sydney.
Eine Munition unter anderen, Frankfurter Kunstverein, Frankfurt am Main.
Vanishing Points, Groupe Première Heure, Saint-Cloud, France.
Protest and Survive, Whitechapel Art Gallery, London.
Apocalypse, Royal Academy of Arts, London.
AutoWerke, Deichtorhallen Hamburg, Hamburg, Germany.
Turner Prize, Tate Britain, London.

1999
Flashes – Contemporary Trends, Fondation Cartier pour l'art contemporain, Centro Cultural de Belém, Lisbon; travelled to Fundació Joan Miró, Barcelona; Centro Arte Contemporanea Palazzo delle Papesse, Siena, Italy.
… om det sublima … / … on the sublime …, Rooseum, Malmö, Sweden.
The Image of the Other, Fundació Fòrum Universal de les Cultures, Barcelona.

Vision of the Body: Fashion or Invisible Corset, National Museum of Modern Art, Kyoto; travelled to Museum of Contemporary Art, Tokyo.
Can You Hear Me?, 2nd Ars Baltica Triennial of Photographic Art, Stadtgalerie im Sophienhof, Kiel, Kunsthalle, Rostock, Germany, et al.
1998
Collection un autre regard, CAPC – Musée d'art contemporain de Bordeaux, Bordeaux, France.
Still Life: 1900–1998, Marlborough Graphics, Marlborough Gallery, New York.
From the Corner of the Eye, Stedelijk Museum, Amsterdam.
Berlin / Berlin – 1. Berlin Biennale für zeitgenössische Kunst, 1st Berlin Biennale, Berlin.
1997
Zeitgeist Becomes Form – German Fashion Photography 1945–1995, Pat Hearn Gallery and Morris Healy Gallery, New York.
Absolute Landscape – Between Illusion and Reality, Yokohama Museum of Art, Yokohama.
Positionen kunstlerischer Photographie in Deutschland von 1945–1995, Berlinische Galerie and Martin-Gropius-Bau, Berlin.
1996
Manifesta 1, Rotterdam.
By Night, Fondation Cartier pour l'art contemporain, Paris.
Traffic, CAPC – Musée d'art contemporain de Bordeaux, Bordeaux, France.
"Urgence", CAPC – Musée d'art contemporain de Bordeaux, Bordeaux, France.
Visitors' Voices: Recomposing the Collection, Walker Art Center, Minneapolis, MN.
New Photography #12, MoMA Museum of Modern Art, New York.
1995
Take Me (I'm Yours), Serpentine Gallery, London; travelled to Kunsthalle Nürnberg, Nuremberg and Castello di Rivoli Museo d'Arte Contemporanea, Rivoli, Turin, Italy.
Human Nature, New Museum of Contemporary Art, New York.

1994
Dinos and Jake Chapman, Georgina Starr, Wolfgang Tillmans, Andrea Rosen Gallery, New York.
Sonne München, Galerie Daniel Buchholz, Cologne, Germany.
Soggetto Soggetto, Castello di Rivoli Museo d'Arte Contemporanea, Rivoli, Turin, Italy.
The Winter of Love, PS1, New York.
Streetstyle, Victoria & Albert Museum, London.
1993
Fuck the System, Villa Rossi, Lucca, Italy.
Belcher, Höller, General Idea, Tillmans, Odenbach, Galerie Daniel Buchholz, Cologne, Germany.
1992
i-D Now, Pitti Imagine, Palazzo Corsini, Florence.

Selected Public Collections
21st Century of Contemporary Art, Kanazawa.
Arken Museum of Contemporary Art, Denmark.
Art Institute of Chicago.
The Arts Council Collection, London.
Carnegie Museum of Art, Pittsburgh, PA.
Castello di Rivoli Museo d'Arte Contemporanea.
Centre d'arts plastiques contemporains – (CAPC) Musée d'art contemporain, Bordeaux.
Centre national des arts plastiques, Paris.
Musée national d'art moderne, Centre Pompidou, Paris.
Centro Andaluz de Arte Contemporáneo, Seville.
Centro de Arte Dos de Mayo, Madrid.
Centro de Artes Visuales Fundación Helga de Alvear, Cáceres.
Contemporary Art Museum St. Louis, MO.
Contemporary Arts Museum Houston.
Des Moines Art Center.
Flick Collection, Zurich.
Fondation Beyeler, Riehen.
Fonds National d'Art Contemporain, Paris.
Fotomuseum Winterthur.
FRAC – Fonds régional d'art contemporain d'Île de France.
FRAC – Fonds régional d'art contemporain de Haute-Normandie, Rouen.
Galerie für Zeitgenössische Kunst (GFZK), Leipzig.
Gallery of Modern Art (GoMA), Glasgow.
Hamburger Kunsthalle.
Hammer Museum, Los Angeles.
Hirshhorn Museum and Sculpture Garden, Washington, DC.
Institute of Contemporary Art, Boston.
The Israel Museum, Jerusalem.
Kunsthalle Bielefeld.
Kunsthalle Bremen.
Kunstmuseum Bonn.
Kunstmuseum Wolfsburg.
Los Angeles County Museum of Art.
Louisiana Museum of Modern Art, Humlebæk.
MAXXI, Rome.
Metropolitan Museum, New York.
Mildred Lane Kemper Art Museum, St. Louis, MO.
MKM – Museum Kuppersmule für Moderne Kunst, Duisburg.
MMK – Museum für Moderne Kunst, Frankfurt am Main.
Moderna Museet, Stockholm.
MUDAM Luxembourg.
Musée d'art contmeporain de Montréal.
Musée des beaux-arts de Nantes.
Museo Tamayo, Mexico City.
Museum Folkwang, Essen.
Museum für Gegenwartskunst, Basel.
Museum Kulturspeicher, Wurzburg.
Museum Kunstpalast, Düsseldorf.
Museum Ludwig, Cologne.
Museum Moderner Kunst Stiftung Ludwig Wien – mumok, Vienna.
Museum of Contemporary Art, Chicago.
Museum of Contemporary Art, Los Angeles.
Museum of Modern Art, Fort Worth.
MoMA, New York.
National Gallery of Canada, Ottawa.
National Museum of Art, Osaka.
National Museum of Modern Art, Kyoto.
National Portrait Gallery, London.
Neue Nationalgalerie, Berlin.
Nomas Foundation, Rome.
Nottingham Castle Museum.
Philadelphia Museum of Art.
Pinakothek der Moderne, Munich.
Sammlung Boros, Berlin.
Sammlung Goetz, Munich.
Sammlung Haubrok, Berlin.
Sammlung Rheingold, Düsseldorf.
Sammlung zeitgenössischer Kunst der Bundesrepublik Deutschland, Bonn.
Seattle Art Museum.
Smart Museum of Art, Chicago.
Solomon R. Guggenheim Museum, New York.
Sprengel Museum, Hanover.
Staatliche Kunstsammlungen Dresden.
Staatsgalerie Stuttgart.
Städel Museum, Frankfurt am Main.
Städtische Galerie im Lenbachhaus und Kunstbau München.
Städtisches Museum Abteiberg, Mönchengladbach.
Statens Museum for Kunst, Copenhagen.
Stedelijk Museum, Amsterdam.
Tate, London.
Tokyo Metropolitan Museum of Photography, Tokyo.
Victoria & Albert Museum, London.
University of Warwick Art Collection.
Walker Art Center, Minneapolis, MN.
Walter Art Gallery, Liverpool.

Gillian Wearing

Born in 1963 in Birmingham, UK
Lives and works in London

Solo Exhibitions
2015
IVAM Instituto Valenciano de Arte
Moderno, Valencia, Spain.
2014
everyone, Regen Projects, Los Angeles,
CA.
Rose Video 05, The Rose Art Museum
of Brandeis University, Waltham, Mass.
Maureen Paley, London.
A Real Birmingham Family, Centenary
Square, Library of Birmingham,
Birmingham, UK.
We Are Here, The New Art Gallery
Walsall, Walsall, UK.
2013
Museum Brandhorst, Munich.
*PEOPLE: Selected Parkett Artists'
Editions from 1984–2013*, Parkett
Space, Zurich.
The Apartment, Vancouver, Canada.
2012
Whitechapel Gallery, London, touring
to K20, Kunstsammlung Nordrhein-
Westfalen, Düsseldorf and Pinakothek
der Moderne, Museum Brandhorst,
Munich.
A Real Birmingham Family, Central
Library, Birmingham and HomeSense,
The Fort Shopping Park, Birmingham,
UK.
2011
People, Tanya Bonakdar Gallery, New
York.
A Real Birmingham Family, Ikon Gallery,
Birmingham, UK.
2009
Confessions: Portraits, vidéos, Musée
Rodin, Paris.
2008
"Pin Ups" and "Family History", Regen
Projects, Los Angeles, CA.
2007
Family Monument, special project,
Galleria Civica di Arte Contemporanea,
Trento, Italy.
Elsewhere?, Galleria Emi Fontana,
Milan.
2006
Living Proof, ACCA, Australian Centre
for Contemporary Art, Melbourne.
Family History, in conjunction with the

Film and Video Umbrella, The Forbury
Hotel Apartments, Reading and Ikon,
Birmingham, UK.
Family History, Maureen Paley, London.
2005
Snapshot, Bloomberg Space, London.
Outreach Award, Rencontres d'Arles,
Arles, France.
2004
Frans Hals Museum, Haarlem,
The Netherlands.
Album, Regen Projects, Los Angeles,
CA.
Kiasma Museum of Contemporary Art,
Helsinki.
2003
Album, Gorney Bravin+Lee, New York.
Album, Maureen Paley Interim Art,
London.
Mass Observation, ICA Philadelphia,
PA.
Mass Observation, Musée d'art
contemporain de Montréal, Montreal,
Canada.
2002
Mass Observation, Museum of
Contemporary Art, Chicago, IL.
A Trilogy, Vancouver Art Gallery,
Vancouver, Canada.
Kunsthaus Glarus, Glarus, Switzerland.
2001
Angel Row Gallery, Nottingham, UK.
Centro Galego de Arte
Contemporánea, Santiago, Chile.
Unspoken, Kunstverein München,
Munich.
Museo do Chiado, Lisbon.
Sous Influence, Musée d'art moderne
de la ville de Paris, Paris.
Fundació "la Caixa", Madrid.
Bluecoat Gallery, Liverpool, UK.
2000
Regen Projects, Los Angeles, CA.
Serpentine Gallery, London.
Gorney Bravin+Lee, New York.
1999
A Woman Called Theresa, Ophiuchus
Collection, The Hydra Workshop,
Hydra, Greece.
Galerie Anne de Villepoix, Paris.
Drunk, De Vleeshal, Middelburg, The
Netherlands.
Maureen Paley Interim Art, London.
1998
Spacex Gallery, Exeter, UK.

Gallery Koyanagi, Tokyo.
Centre d'art contemporain, Geneva.
1997
Galerie Drantmann, Brussels.
Jay Gorney Modern Art, New York.
Wiener Secession, Vienna.
10–16, Chisenhale Gallery, London.
Kunsthaus Zürich, Zurich.
Galleria Emi Fontana, Milan.
1996
- 7, Maureen Paley Interim Art, London.
1996
Wish You Were Here (Video Evenings at
De Appel), Amsterdam.
Le Consortium, Dijon, France.
*Gillian Wearing, City Projects – Prague,
Part II*, The British Council, Prague.
Valentina Moncada Arte
Contemporanea, Rome (British
Council).
Maureen Paley Interim Art, London.
1995
Western Security, Hayward Gallery,
London.
1994
Maureen Paley Interim Art, London.
1993
City Racing, London.

Selected Group Exhibitions
2015
Fire and forget. On violence, KW
Institute for Contemporary Art, Berlin.
Eye to Eye: Looking Beyond Likeness,
Albright-Knox Art Gallery, Buffalo, NY.
*Zabludowicz Collection: 20 Years of
Collecting: Between Discovery and
Invention*, Zabludowicz Collection,
London.
Partial Presence, Zabludowicz
Collection, London.
Self, Turner Contemporary, Margate,
UK.
*Test Run. Take it Outside: performance
in public space*, Modern Art Oxford,
Oxford, UK.
2014
Body Doubles, Museum of
Contemporary Art, Chicago, IL.
The Vincent Award 2014,
Gemeentemuseum Den Haag,
The Hague.
About Town, Video Art in Southside,
Hurst Street Car Park, Birmingham, UK.
Urban Psychosis, The Holden Gallery,

Manchester Metropolitan University, Manchester, UK.
The Bigger Picture: Work from the 1990s, Tanya Bonakdar Gallery, New York.
(Mis)Understanding Photography – Works and Manifestos, Museum Folkwang, Essen, Germany.
Nouvelle Génération, FRAC Nord-Pas-de-Calais, Dunkerque, France.
A Secret Affair: Selections From The Fuhrman Family Collection, The Contemporary Austin, Austin, TX.
40 Years of Women Artists, The New Art Gallery Walsall, Walsall, UK.
Love, Wilhelm-Hack-Museum, Ludwigshafen am Rhein, Germany.
Between the Lines, Tanya Bonakdar Gallery, New York.
2013
You Are Here, Worcester Art Museum, Worcester, Mass.
93 Exhibition, CGAC Centro Galego de Arte Contemporenea, Santiago de Compostela, Spain.
Karel's Choice. Looking Back at Contemporary Art, De Hallen, Haarlem, The Netherlands.
Alien & Familiar, Galerie im Taxispalais, Innsbruck, Austria.
Assembly: A Survey of Recent Artists' Film and Video in Britain 2008–2013, Tate Britain, London.
British British Polish Polish: Art From Europe's edges in the Long '90s and Today, The Centre for Contemporary Art, Ujazdowski Castle, Warsaw.
Salon der Angst, Kunsthalle Wien, Vienna.
Requiem for a Bank, HMKV, Dortmund, Germany.
Bellwether Series, Cleveland Museum of Art, Cleveland, OH.
Someone Else, Villa Romana, Florence.
What to Think, What to Desire, What to Do, Fundació "la Caixa", Barcelona.
NYC 1993: Experimental jet set, trash and no star, New Museum, New York.
Ensemble, Backlit Gallery, Nottingham, UK.
Homelands, British Council touring exhibition, New Delhi; touring to Kolkata, Mumbai and Bangalore, India.
Lovin' it. Symbol and Contradiction, Bromer Art Collection, Kunsthaus

Kaltenherberg, Roggwil, Switzerland.
More Love: Art, Politics and Sharing Since 1990s, Ackland Art Museum at The University of North Carolina, Chapel Hill, NC; traveling to Cheekwood Museum of Art, Cheekwood, TN.
Salon der Angst, Kunsthalle Wien, Vienna.
Performing Film, Coreana Museum of Art, Seoul, South Korea.
Still, Solent Showcase Gallery at Southampton Solent University, Southampton, UK.
Fremd & Eigen, Galerie im Taxispalais, Innsbruck, Austria.
John Bock, Keren Cytter, Paul Pfeiffer, Gillian Wearing, and Akram Zaatari, Regen Projects, Los Angeles, CA.
The System of Objects, Deste Foundation, Athens, Greece.
Lost Boys: The Territories of Youth, Lewis Glucksman Gallery, Cork, Ireland.
Brilliant Disguise: Masks and Other Transformations, CAC– Contemporary Arts Center New Orleans, New Orleans, LA.
Besser scheitern. Film + Video, Hamburger Kunsthalle, Hamburg, Germany.
Wild New Territories, Simon Fraser University Art Gallery, Burnaby, Canada.
2012
Beyond the Family Album, La Caixa Collection, Barcelona.
The Long Now, The Galleries at Moore College of Art & Design, Philadelphia, PA.
About Face, Pier 24 Photography, San Francisco, CA.
Christian Jankowski, Gillian Wearing, Guy Ben-Ner, Grand Central Art Center, California State University, Fullerton, CA.
Encounter: The Royal Academy in Asia, Institute of Contemporary Arts Singapore, Singapore.
Family Matters: The Family in British Art, Millennium Galleries, Sheffield and Laing Art Gallery, Newcastle, UK.
Made In Britain: Contemporary Art from the British Council Collection 1980–2010, Benaki Museum, Athens, Greece.
9th Shanghai Biennale, Shanghai, China.

Rxy, Galleria della Molinella, Faenza, Italy.
The Story of the Government Art Collection, Whitechapel Gallery, London, travelling to the Birmingham Museum and Art Gallery and the Ulster Museum, Belfast.
Sounds Like Silence, HMKV: Hartware MedienKunstVerein, Dortmund, Germany.
2011
Hints of the Outside World, SOMA Contemporary, Waterford City, Ireland.
The Dwelling Life of Man, Fundació Foto Colectania, Barcelona.
Let the Healing Begin, IMA Institute of Modern Art at the Judith Wright Centre of Contemporary Art, Brisbane, Australia.
Made in the UK: Contemporary Art from the Richard Brown Baker Collection, Museum of Art, Rhode Island School of Design, Providence, Rhode Island.
Moving Portraits, De La Warr Pavilion, Bexhill-on-sea, East Sussex, UK.
Robert Mapplethorpe: Night Work: Curated by Scissor Sisters, Alison Jacques Gallery, London.
Role Models – Role Playing, Museum der Moderne Salzburg, Salzburg, Austria.
Vitrine, part of the White Night Arts Festival, Brighton, UK.
Why I Never Became a Dancer, Sammlung Goetz im Haus der Kunst, Munich.
Family Matters: The Family in British Art, Norwich Castle Museum & Art Gallery (travelling).
2010
Auto-Kino, Temporäre Kunsthalle Berlin.
Aware: Art Fashion Identity, GSK Contemporary, Royal Academy of Arts, London.
CUE: Artists' Videos, Vancouver Art Gallery, Vancouver, Canada.
The Future Demands Your Participation: Contemporary Art from the British Council Collection, Minsheng Art Museum, Shanghai, China.
Haunted: Contemporary Photography / Video / Performance, Solomon R. Guggenheim Museum, New York;

travelling to Guggenheim Bilbao, Spain.
Kurt, Seattle Art Museum, Seattle, WA.
La fuerza de la palabra, Guadalajara, Mexico.
Lemaître Collection, MALI Museo de Arte de Lima, Lima, Peru.
Made In Britain: Contemporary Art from the British Council Collection 1980–2010, Suzhou Museum, Suzhou, China, travelling to various venues in China.
Niet Normaal, Beurs van Berlage, Amsterdam.
The Original Copy: Photography of Sculpture, 1839 to Today, MoMA Museum of Modern Art, New York.
Party!, The New Art Gallery Walsall, Walsall, UK.
Peeping Tom, Vegas, London; travelling to Kunsthal KAdE Amersfoort, Amersfoort, The Netherlands (2011).
Skin Fruit: Dakis Joannou Collection (curated by Jeff Koons), New Museum, New York.
Weatherspoon Art Museum, University of North Carolina, Chapel Hill, NC.
Rewind: Selected Works from the MCA Collection, 1970s to 1990s, Museum of Contemporary Art, Chicago, IL.
The Talent Show, Walker Art Center, Minneapolis, MN.
Post Monument, XIV Biennale Internazionale di Scultura di Carrara, Carrara, Italy.
2009
Be sure to attend very carefully to what I have to say to you, Fri Art: Centre d'art de Fribourg | Kunsthalle Freiburg, Fribourg, Switzerland.
British Subjects: Identity & Self-Fashioning 1965–2009, Neuberger Museum of Art, Purchase, NY.
Contemporary Outlook: Seeing Songs, Museum of Fine Art, Boston, Mass.
DLA Piper Series: This is Sculpture, Tate Liverpool, Liverpool, UK.
Once upon a time… Artists & Storytelling, Somerset House, London.
The Reach of Realism, Museum of Contemporary Art, North Miami, FL.
Through the Lens: Photography from the Lowe Art Museum, University of Miami, Miami, FL.
2008
*History in the Making: A Retrospective

of the Turner Prize, Mori Art Museum, Tokyo.
Existencias, MUSAC Museo de Arte Contemporaneo de Castilla y León, León, Spain.
Irish Museum of Modern Art: Obras Fundamentales, Sala Kubo Kutxa, San Sebastián, Spain.
La Collection d'art d'agnes b, JRP Ringier, Zurich.
Martian Museum of Terrestrial Art, Barbican Art Gallery, London.
Print the Legend: Contemporary Art and the Western, The Fruitmarket Gallery, Edinburgh.
Tarantula, Fondazione Nicola Trussardi, Milan, Italy.
You are my mirror 1: Je t'aime, moi non plus, FRAC Lorraine, Metz, France.
Worlds on Video, CCCS Centro di Cultura Contemporanea Strozzina, Florence.

2007
Breaking step / Uraskoraku, Museum of Contemporary Art, Belgrade, Serbia.
Held Together with Water, MAK, Vienna.
Passion Complex, 21st Century Museum of Contemporary Art, Kanazawa, Japan.
Role Exchange, Sean Kelly Gallery, New York.
Talking Pictures: Theatricality in Contemporary Film and Video Works, K21, Düsseldorf, Germany.
The Turner Prize: A Retrospective, Tate Britain, London.
Global Feminisms: New Directions in Contemporary Art, Brooklyn Museum, New York.
Elsewhere?, Galleria Emi Fontana, Milan.

2006
Eye On Europe: Prints, Books and Multiples / 1960 to Now, MoMA Museum of Modern Art, New York.
Aftershock, Contemporary British Art 1990–2006, Guangdong Museum of Art, Guangzhou, China and Capital Museum, Beijing.
Before the Camera: Remaking Reality and the Make-believe, Norton Museum of Art, West Palm Beach, FL.
Local Stories, Modern Art Oxford, Oxford, UK.

Live Screen, Lilian Baylis Theatre at Saddler's Wells, London.
Of Mice and Men, Fourth Berlin Biennial for Contemporary Art, Berlin.
Making History – Art and Documentary in Britain from 1929 to Now, Tate Liverpool, Liverpool, UK.
Mouvement: Des deux côtés du Rhin, Museum Ludwig, Cologne, Germany.
People, Museo d'Arte Contemporanea Donnaregina, Naples, Italy.
Portrait of Artists, Luhring Augustine, New York.
Me, Myself and I, Virginia Museum of Contemporary Art, Virginia Beach, VA.
Shoot the Family, Cranbrook Art Museum, Bloomfield Hills, MI (travelling).
The Monty Hall Problem, Blum & Poe, Los Angeles, CA.
A Short History of Performance part IV, Whitechapel Art Gallery, London.
Raconte-moi / Tell me, Casino Luxembourg, Luxembourg.

2005
The Kyber Arts Center, Nova Scotia, Canada.
The Gesture. A visual library in progress, Macedonian Museum of Contemporary Art, Thessaloniki, Greece, and Quarter – Centro Produzione Arte, Florence.
New Work / New Acquisitions, MoMA Museum of Modern Art, New York.
Sculpture in the park, The DLI Museum and Durham Art Gallery, Durham, UK.
Body: New Art from the UK, Vancouver Art Gallery (2005), The Ottawa Art Gallery (2006), Oakville Galleries (2006), Edmonton Art Gallery (2006), Canada.
Irreducible: Contemporary Short Form Video, CCA Wattis Institute for Contemporary Arts, San Francisco, CA and The Bronx Museum of the Arts, New York.
25. Twenty-five years of the Deutsche Bank Collection, Deutsche Guggenheim, Berlin.
raconte-moi, Musée national des beaux-arts du Québec, Quebec City, Canada.
Family Pictures – Fotografia contemporanea e Video dalla

Collezione del Guggenheim Museum, Galleria Gottardo, Lugano, Switzerland.

2004
Faces in the crowd – Picturing modern life from Manet to today, The Whitechapel Art Gallery, London.
With All Due Intent, Manifesta 5: European Biennial of Contemporary Art, Donostia–San Sebastián, Spain.
Inaugural Show: MoMA reopening, MoMA Museum of Modern Art, New York.
Social Creatures: How Body Becomes Art, Sprengel Museum, Hannover, Germany.
ART NEWS: Contemporary Artists Working with Newspaper, Three Colts Gallery, London.
Revolving Doors, Fundación Telefónica, Madrid.
About Face, Hayward Gallery, London.
Busan Biennale 2004, Seoul, South Korea.

2003
A Bigger Splash. British Art from Tate 1960–2003, Pavihão Lucas Nogueira Garcez – Oca, Parque Ibirapuera and Instituto Tomie Ohtake, São Paulo, Brazil.
Contemporary British Art from the Paragon Collection, Hakodate Museum of Art, Hokkaido, Japan.
fast forward. Media Art Sammlung Goetz, ZKM | Museum für Neue Kunst, Karlsruhe, Germany.
Strange Days, Museum of Contemporary Art, Chicago, IL.
Synopsis III – Fiction and Reality, National Museum of Contemporary Art, Athens, Greece.
Happiness: A Survival Guide for Art & Life, Mori Art Museum, Tokyo.
Outlook, International Art Exhibition 2003, Athens.
Inaugural Exhibition, Regen Projects, Los Angeles, CA.

2002
Face Off, Kettle's Yard, Cambridge, UK (travelling).
Die Wohltat der Kunst: Post Feministische Positionen der 90er Jahre aus der Sammlung Goetz, Staatliche Kunsthalle, Baden-Baden, Germany.
Coming of Age, The New Art Gallery Walsall, Walsall, UK.

To Whom it May Concern, California College of Arts and Crafts, San Francisco, CA.
Just Love me / Die Wohltat der Kunst, Staatliche Kunsthalle, Baden-Baden, Germany; travelling to Bergen Museum of Art, Bergen, Norway (2003), Sammlung Goetz, Munich (2003) and Fries Museum, Leeuwarden, The Netherlands (2004).
I promise it's political, Museum Ludwig, Cologne, Germany.
Remix: Contemporary Art and Pop, Tate Liverpool, Liverpool, UK.
Bienal de São Paulo, Brazil.
The Video Show, Centraal Museum, Utrecht, The Netherlands.
Acquisitions 2001 – Part 1: Photographs, Video Installations, Video, National Museum of Contemporary Art, Athens, Greece.

2001
Telling Tales: Narrative Impulses in Recent Art, Tate Liverpool, Liverpool, UK.
ABBILD recent portraiture and depiction, Landesmuseum Joanneum, Graz, Austria.
No World Without You, Reflections of Identity in New British Art, Herzliya Museum of Art, Tel Aviv.
W, Centre d'Art Mobile, Besançon, France.
Birmingham, Ikon Gallery, Birmingham, UK.
Inner State of Health: The Person in the Mirror of Contemporary Art, Kunstmuseum Liechtenstein, Vaduz, Liechtenstein.
Biennale de Lyon art contemporain 2001, Lyon, France.
Milano Europa 2001, Palazzo della Triennale, Milan.
Confidence pour confidence, Casino Luxembourg, Luxembourg.
Video Evidence, Southampton City Art Gallery, Southampton, UK.
Film Festival Rotterdam, Museum Boijmans Van Beuningen, Rotterdam, The Netherlands.
Century City, Tate Modern, London.

2000
Autowerke, Deichtorhallen Hamburg, Hamburg, Germany.

Intelligence: New British Art 2000,
Tate Britain, London.
Puerile '69, The Living Art Museum,
Reykjavík.
Tate Modern Collection, Tate Modern,
London and Contemporary Art Center,
Cincinnati, OH.
Sydney Biennale, Museum of
Contemporary Art, Sydney.
docudrama, Bury St. Edmunds Art
Gallery, Bury St. Edmunds, UK.
Tate Britain Collection, Tate Gallery,
London.
Let's Entertain, Walker Art Center,
Minneapolis, MN (travelling).
Quotidiana, Castello di Rivoli Museo
d'Arte Contemporanea, Rivoli,
Turin, Italy.
Makeshift, ArtPace, San Antonio, TX.
1999
Rewind to the Future, Bonner
Kunstverein, Bonn and Neue Berliner
Kunstverein, Berlin.
*Rattling the Frame: The Photographic
Space 1974–1999*, SF Camerawork,
San Francisco, CA.
La coscienza luccicante, Palazzo delle
Esposizioni, Rome.
6th International Istanbul Biennial,
Istanbul, Turkey.
Common People, Fondazione Sandretto
Re Rebaudengo per l'Arte, Turin.
1998
In Visible Light, Moderna Museet,
Stockholm.
Fast Forward Body Check, Kunstverein,
Hamburg.
*Sensation. Young British Artists from
the Saatchi Collection,* Museum für
Gegenwart, Berlin.
Contemporary British Art, The Museum
of Contemporary Art, Seoul, South
Korea.
A Collection in the Making, The Irish
Museum of Modern Art, Dublin.
Photography as Concept, Internationale
Foto Triennale, Galerien der Stadt
Esslingen, Esslingen, Germany.
Real/Life: New British Art, Japanese
Museum Tour: Tochigi Prefectural
Museum of Fine Arts, Fukuoka City
Art Museum, Hiroshima Museum
of Contemporary Art, Tokyo Museum
of Contemporary Art.
Musée départemental d'art

contemporain de Rochechouart,
Rochechouart, France, with Valerie
Jouve and Rineke Dijkstra.
White Noise, Kunsthalle Bern, Bern,
Switzerland.
ENGLISH ROSE in Japan, The Ginza
Artspace, Tokyo, with Tracey Emin and
Georgina Starr.
1997
The Turner Prize 1997, Tate Gallery,
London.
Sensation, Saatchi Collection, Royal
Academy of Art, London.
Pictura Britannica: Art from Britain,
Museum of Contemporary Art, Sydney,
travelling to Adelaide, Australia and
Wellington, New Zealand.
*In Visible Light: Photography and
Classification in Art, Science and the
Everyday,* Museum of Modern Art,
Oxford, UK.
1996
I.D., Van Abbe Museum, Eindhoven,
The Netherlands.
Life / Live, co-curated by Laurence
Bosse & Hans-Ulrich Obrist, Musée
d'art moderne de la ville de Paris, Paris.
*NowHere (Incandescent, curator Laura
Cottingham)*, Louisiana Museum of
Modern Art, Humlebæk, Denmark.
Auto-reverse 2, Centre national d'art
contemporain Grenoble, France.
Traffic, CAPC musée d'art
contemporain de Bordeaux, Bordeaux,
France.
*Pandaemonium. London Festival
of Moving Images*, ICA, London.
1995
The British Art Show, national touring
exhibition.
X/Y, Centre Georges Pompidou, Paris.
Campo, Venice Biennale, curated by
Francesco Bonami.
Aperto '95, Nouveau Musée, Institut
d'Art Contemporain, Villeurbanne,
France.
1994
Uncertain Identity, Galerie Analix
B & L Polla, Geneva.
Domestic Violence, curated by Alison
Jacques, Gio Marconi's House,
Milan.

Selected Public Collections
Centre National des Arts Plastiques,
Paris.
Citibank, USA.
Contemporary Art Society, London.
Dakis Joannou Collection Foundation,
Athens.
Deutsche Bank, Germany.
Ellipse Foundation, Amsterdam.
FRAC, France.
Frans Hals Museum De Hallen Haarlem.
Fundació "la Caixa", Barcelona.
Fundació Telefónica, Madrid.
Hamburger Kunsthalle, Hamburg.
Irish Museum of Modern Art, Dublin.
Kunsthaus Zürich.
MUSAC, León.
MoMA Museum of Modern Art,
New York.
National Museum of Contemporary Art,
Athens.
Rose Art Museum, Waltham.
Solomon R. Guggenheim Museum,
New York.
Southampton City Council.
South London Gallery, London.
Tate Gallery, London.
The Arts Council of England, London.
The British Council, London.
The Cranford Collection, London.
The Government Art Collection,
London.
Vancouver Art Gallery.
Zabludowicz Collection, London.

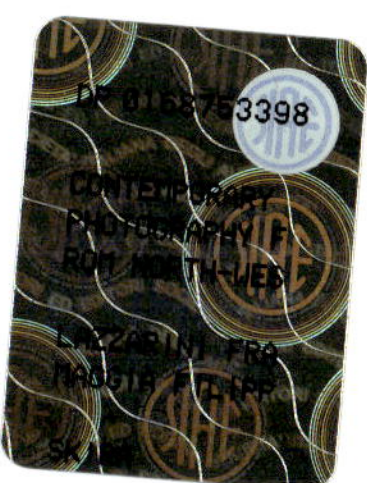